OP 75c

Caitlin

Books by Caitlin Thomas
Leftover Life to Kill
Not Quite Posthumous Letters to my Daughter

Books by George Tremlett
Seventeen Rock Music Biographies
Living Cities
Official History of the Working Men's Club and Institute Union

Caitlin

A WARRING ABSENCE

CAITLIN THOMAS
WITH
GEORGE TREMLETT

SECKER & WARBURG
LONDON

First published in England 1986 by
Martin Secker & Warburg Limited
54 Poland Street, London W1V 3DF

Copyright © 1986 by Caitlin Thomas and George Tremlett

British Library Cataloguing in Publication Data
Thomas, Caitlin
  Caitlin : a warring absence.
  1. Thomas, Dylan——Relations with women
  ——Caitlin Thomas 2. Thomas, Caitlin——
  Family 2. Poets, Welsh——20th century——
  Biography
  I. Title II. Tremlett, George
  821'.912   PR6039.H52Z/

  ISBN 0-436-51850-3

Set in Great Britain in 11 on 13 point Bembo
by Hewer Text Composition Services, Edinburgh

Printed and bound in Great Britain
by Butler & Tanner Ltd, Frome, Somerset

TO
DYLAN

Contents

Acknowledgements

The publishers wish to express their thanks to the following publishers and individuals from whose collections photographs have been reproduced:

J. M. Dent & Sons Ltd, 1; Alfred Janes, 2; Malcolm Arbuthnot, 3; Romilly John, 4; Norah Summers, 5, 6, 7, 8, 11; George Tremlett, 9, 13, 14, 15, 16, 18, 28, 29; Rollie McKenna, 10, 17, 20, 21, 22, 23, 24, 25, 27; Bill Brandt, 12; Christina Gascoigne, 19; Bill Read, courtesy of John Malcolm Brinnin, 26.

The publishers acknowledge with gratitude David Higham Associates, as Trustees for the Copyrights of Dylan Thomas, for permission to quote from *The Collected Letters of Dylan Thomas*, edited by Paul Ferris, and from *The Life of Dylan Thomas* by Constantine FitzGibbon.

Norman Cameron's poem 'The Dirty Little Accuser' is reprinted by kind permission of the Trustees for the Copyrights of Norman Cameron.

Illustrations

I make this in a warring absence when
Each ancient, stone-necked minute of love's season
Harbours my anchored tongue

> – the opening lines of
> 'Poem (for Caitlin)', written by
> Dylan Thomas shortly after
> their marriage

Preface

Soon after Dylan Thomas had been buried in Laugharne, his widow Caitlin left the town. She tried to commit suicide in London, leaping from a third-floor window in Hammersmith. For some months thereafter she was detained in a mental home in Surrey. When released, Caitlin left for the island of Elba, where she soon began to write. Furiously, day after day, she finished hundreds of pages of notes in longhand describing her emotional response to Dylan's death. These notes were eventually edited down into the manuscript of *Leftover Life to Kill*, which was published in 1957.

Even then I had long been fascinated by Dylan Thomas and his work. I had gone to school in Stratford-upon-Avon, learning language in the very room where Shakespeare was taught. My English teacher, Alan Wood, had told me several times that Dylan Thomas was the most important writer since Shakespeare. Even more to the point, he encouraged me to listen to Dylan's radio readings and to study his work. I saw Dylan Thomas reading *The Outing* on television, which was his only appearance on the small screen, and in the weeks that followed his death I read his poems and then listened to the first broadcasts of *Under Milk Wood*. Thus began a life-long interest, which has led to my settling in Laugharne with my family and, now, working on this autobiography with Caitlin.

Naturally, I read *Leftover Life to Kill* when it was first published and I found myself overwhelmed by a grief that I was too young to understand: the book was harrowing, and yet left so much unsaid that I wanted to know more. Constantine FitzGibbon's biography failed to satisfy my curiosity and so did those by Bill Read, Daniel Jones, John Ackerman, Andrew Sinclair and Paul Ferris. At one meeting of the Dylan Thomas Society in 1977 I suggested to Dylan's daughter Aeron that a definitive biography had still to be written and that her mother ought to write it: Aeron told me that Caitlin had now joined Alcoholics Anonymous in Rome, had given up drink, and was probably in a better condition to write the book than at any time since Dylan's death.

In the years that followed, Aeron and her husband Trefor became family friends; my wife Jane became Secretary of the Dylan Thomas Society, and we all worked together to raise the money for the plaque commemorating Dylan in Poets' Corner in Westminster Abbey (which we would never have been able to manage if the late Lord Harlech had not immediately offered us the services of Harlech Television to stage a special fund-raising concert, which Richard Burton compered). These events also led to the unveiling of a similar plaque at St Martin's Church in Laugharne and to the founding of the Dylan Thomas Literary Award, of which Aeron and I are both Trustees.

Out in Rome, Caitlin continued to work on her book; it proved a great disappointment, and when she came to London in 1982 I offered to work with her on a completely new book, which, I suggested, should be based on tape-recorded interviews which I would conduct, transcribe and then edit. It was my view then, and still is now, that this was the only way the book could be written because Caitlin remains much too emotionally involved to tackle the project objectively. She agreed, with a little reluctance; our respective agents were asked to draw up a collaboration agreement; we also agreed to wait a few months before starting work because Caitlin was moving to Catania in Sicily – and then she changed her mind. We wrote sad little letters assuring each other that there were no hard feelings; and that, I thought, was the end of that . . . until Caitlin wrote again towards the end of 1984, asking whether I was still interested.

We then started planning this book, exchanging letters for twelve months about the shape that the book would take while I researched every aspect of Dylan's life as I prepared myself for the taping sessions. I flew out to Catania on 31 October 1985, unaware of what was to come.

When Caitlin left Laugharne in 1953 she went first to London and then to Elba and from there to Rome, where she fell in with a crowd of artists, actors, writers and film people who used to hang around the Taverna Margutta; it was there that she met Giuseppe Fazio, an actor and assistant film director, with whom she has lived for the past thirty years. They have a son, Francesco – also known as Francis, Cico and Coco in the family – who was born when Caitlin was forty-nine. Francis is now studying architecture in Rome. All three are devoted to each other, and I have absolutely no doubt that Caitlin would have been dead at least twenty years ago but for the love and affection that she has received from Giuseppe. He has nursed her through twenty years of alcoholism, long spells in clinics, repeated depression and several attempts at suicide. I realised within a few days of my arrival that Giuseppe had literally saved her life, and that, being very wise in the raw, physical, Sicilian way, he had understood that it was the trauma of her years with Dylan that lay at the heart of her distress.

I also realised, as we sat down to record the interviews, that Caitlin had prepared herself not only to face the truth but to tell it. Within minutes of our starting work on the recordings, Caitlin said: 'I want you to understand, before we go any further, that I never had an orgasm in all my years with Dylan, and that lies at the heart of our problems . . .'

We soon settled into a daily rhythm of working. Each morning Caitlin would have a cup of strong Indian tea, do her morning exercises, get dressed, and then start recording at 10 am on the dot. At 12 noon we would break for coffee, and then start recording again at 12.30 pm, stopping for lunch at 2 pm and recording again between 3 and 5 pm. In the evenings we would meet for supper at 9 pm and run through the day's work. It was a highly disciplined routine. During my three weeks at their home in Catania I recorded fifty hours of interviews; these were transcribed into roughly 250,000 words, which I then re-arranged and edited down to this 85,000-word book. In March this year I returned to Catania and went through the manuscript with Caitlin, working to the same hours over a nine-day period, agreeing the manuscript line by line and page by page.

Our weeks together were highly traumatic. Many days she was crying, and on some days so was I. As her story unfolded, I began to realise why Caitlin had refused to co-operate with all Dylan's previous biographers – and why they had all failed to develop a rounded portrait of the man and his marriage. 'I can't help crying, but I talk best when you have got me on the raw,' said Caitlin. On another occasion, she told me: 'You must understand that our lives were raw, red, bleeding meat . . .' In some sessions, I had to keep probing away before her answers would come; in others, it would only take a word from me to prompt a stream of memories.

All the time I had this terrible awareness of pain; Caitlin was still in deep personal pain because of what had happened to her over thirty years ago. 'I feel it as sharply now as if it had all happened yesterday,' she said, as I began to understand that the pain was something far deeper than sexual jealousy: it was rooted in a feeling that Dylan had betrayed her soul. One morning, Caitlin said to me: 'There was something magic between us; I think it was an affinity of souls; I felt that right from the first moment I met him . . .' And then she went on to say: 'I am aware of Dylan every day, although I don't deliberately think about him. I can kind of feel him inside me. Inside my head. His personality, I suppose. It's very difficult to say. I suppose I might still be in love with him. Yes, I do love him, but I don't know about being *in love*. . . , I appreciate him more now than I did then.'

By the time we had finished our work together, Caitlin and I both realised that we had created a remarkable book. It is a love story but, as she says, a very sad one.

George Tremlett
Laugharne   March 1986

1

Dylan told me that he loved me the very first night we met, and although I had made love before, this was something that no other man had ever said to me. Dylan's name had first been mentioned to me by Augustus John, who said that he had met this 'bright young spark' and that I should meet him, too. We were introduced in a London pub, the Wheatsheaf, in what was then known as Fitzrovia, the area around Fitzroy Square and Charlotte Street, where the artists and writers used to gather in the Thirties in the pubs and cafés. Dylan was so busy talking that our eyes did not meet at first. I think he looked at me, but he did not look into my eyes and I cannot remember the first words that he said directly to me because he was in the middle of an endless jabber. Then, suddenly, he sort of put his head in my lap. That was the moment it started. Dylan had real charm; he could get round anybody, chiefly when he was doing this little-boy-lost act; he was so pathetic . . . and sweet.

I was sitting on a stool, and I don't know how Dylan managed to get his head on my lap; I don't know how he did it, or how he was standing, but he seemed to fold up over me, and I immediately felt a great sense of closeness that I had never felt before with anyone. He was babbling away and there were three or four other people there at the time. He was telling stories and also muttering endearments to me. He seemed very close all the time. I couldn't follow what he was saying and didn't answer him, but it all seemed very soothing and pleasant. He told me that I was beautiful, that he loved me and that he was going to marry me, and he kept on repeating these phrases as though he had at last found the girl who was right for him and we were meant for each other. I was a little overwhelmed, but I didn't want to break into what he was saying because it seemed there was nothing I could say back: I just accepted it, although I was too shy to tell him that I loved him, too.

No one had ever spoken to me like that before. In my mid-teens I had been madly in love with Caspar John; I had slept with his father Augustus and had also had an affair with a painter in Paris, but none of them had ever talked with such affection. Now here was Dylan, whom Augustus had told me was a penniless poet, pouring out these words of love in an endless, uncontrollable stream. And it all seemed so right. If some other bastard had done that, taking liberties with me, I would have shaken him off, but with Dylan there was this immediate closeness that made me realise that this was as it should be.

He was drinking beer, as he always did then, and wearing typically Dylan clothes – corduroys and a tweed jacket. He was then aged twenty-one and I was nearly eleven months older. I can clearly remember that I was wearing a white flowery dress that my sister Nicolette had lent me for the night. I felt very good in it.

I can't remember much about the other people who were there with us. There was one man whom I can recall quite clearly, though not his name, and there was a girl called Millie who had been with Dylan when he arrived. I soon sensed that she had been sleeping with him, but when she saw this closeness that just seemed to be there at once between us she was in a terrific hurry to tell me that their affair had been nothing serious. Millie gave him to me on a plate, saying that some nights when he had been in London and had had nowhere to sleep, Dylan would drop in on her; but there had been nothing much deeper than that. She seemed afraid that I would turn on her.

Dylan kept saying how much he loved me, although I said nothing much to him in return. He never stopped talking, but then he never did, and I felt so totally happy with this closeness: it was the thing that I felt more than anything else. We both knew that this was it, that it was happening to us and that we were happy. I remember being completely passive as he went on jabbering with his head across my lap. I didn't take in half of it; and though I may have looked at him I didn't register anything about him that I particularly remember. I just had a nice feeling with him being there. He was very gentle, softly spoken and a bit nervous; all that pub performance was largely a show. The drink was caused, certainly at the beginning, by timidity; that unloosed all the rest. This closeness was quite different from any feelings that I had had when making love to other men: there was no resemblance to that sort of sexual feeling; this was much more on maternal lines. I felt very protective towards Dylan. Looking back, he seemed vulnerable, although I wouldn't have thought that way then. I felt close to him in the way that I have since sometimes felt close to a child.

All this happened over fifty years ago, in April 1936, and we were both so different then, so innocent. Dylan was slim, tiny and light. I suppose he couldn't have been much more than seven stone. He was always self-conscious about his height, and sometimes claimed to be 5ft 6in tall. He would tell people that he was an inch or two taller than I was, but really he was the same sort of height, which was 5ft 2in.

We stayed drinking for a while and later moved on to another pub or drinking club, although we didn't get drunk. We later left the crowd we were with and booked into the Eiffel Tower Hotel, which was a favourite place with writers and artists because the owner, a German called Stulik, would give you a room for the night even if you didn't have any money with you. I had eaten there before with Augustus when I had been staying with him at his flat in Fitzroy Square, and I knew that his daughter Vivien would often book a room there and charge it up to his account. It was my idea that we should do the same. I was quite frank about that; it seemed a natural thing for us to do after feeling so close all evening, and Dylan was the last person to be shocked. After we had booked ourselves in, Dylan was terribly pleased. He thought it a great joke that we had brought it off because earlier Augustus had seemed to behave as though he had some kind of claim to me.

Augustus was painting my portrait at the time down at his studio in Hampshire, which wasn't far from my mother's home. He would come up to London sometimes and I would stay with him. It wasn't a real love affair because Augustus had lots of other women as well. There was nothing very deep between us, but I think Augustus was a bit struck for a while although he never asked me to live with him. Augustus would never have asked anyone to live with him permanently, I don't think, because he had too good a set-up with Dorelia McNeill.

As well as the flat in Fitzroy Square, Augustus had a rather beautiful house in Fordingbridge, where a studio had been built for him. He lived there with Dorelia and his vast family of children, and he would leave them there when he went up to London. Sometimes I travelled up with him; at other times I would meet him at the flat and then we would go for a meal at the Eiffel Tower, where Stulik always made a great fuss of him.

Stulik showed us up to our room and then left. Dylan seemed suddenly shy. He was the opposite of the macho-type, and I realised that, deep-down, Dylan was prudish, but there again, so was I. I sensed this as we went to bed together that first time. Dylan was shy about undressing, and after I had got into bed I noticed that when he stepped out of his trousers he left them literally standing up because they were so stiff. He didn't wear any underpants (he never did), and he slipped into bed like an eel. I think he was afraid of being laughed at because he was almost comic to look at. He was wearing a great long shirt down to his knees, and he came to bed in it. He would never take all his clothes off before coming to bed: he would never display his nudity deliberately. He was like that all the years that we were together, always coming to bed in those long Welsh nightshirts. I wouldn't have dreamt of laughing at him because I am sensitive to that sort of thing myself; I wouldn't have gone to bed naked either. He rushed into bed and covered himself up, without swaggering around or anything, and there was nothing very sensational about his love-making. He seemed timid, and this again emphasised his child-like quality to me. We just held each other very close, clinging to each other as we went to sleep, and we were still clinging to each other when I woke up again.

We stayed at the Eiffel Tower for five or six nights, although we only slept there. Every morning we went off to the pubs as soon as they opened at eleven o'clock, and I became more and more hungry as the week went by because I was never offered any food. We didn't appear to eat any food at all that week and by the end of it I was starving. Dylan didn't bother about food and he didn't eat when he was drinking. He didn't once ask me out for a meal and, because I was also missing the exercises I did every day as a dancer, I found the whole experience rather strange. It was the kind of world that I disapproved of and yet at the same time I was thrilled to be sharing it with him. These were the artists and writers that I admired, the people I wanted to be with. I felt I belonged with them

– people like Rayner Heppenstall, Mervyn Peake, George Barker, Roy Campbell, Norman Cameron, Louis MacNeice and Elizabeth Smart (whom we didn't know particularly well but who was in with the same crowd of people in Fitzrovia – a rich girl, thrilled to be among the poor people, which I always thought a stupid attitude because I would like to have been rich).

My mother had always told me that I would marry a duke, but here I was, falling in love with a penniless poet and spending all my days in pubs. Dylan spent every day in London going round the pubs. It was his life. He would start when they opened at eleven o'clock, always with the same routine. He would head for the nearest bar and then set up a line of light ales along the counter, which he would down one by one. If he was with a group of friends, they would all do that, each setting up their own line of drinks. They all believed that if they had hangovers from the night before this was what they had to do to clear their heads before starting all over again. Every morning Dylan went through this routine; it was his sort of recovery-drink.

As the day went on, he might move from one pub to another, telling stories, cracking jokes, playing pub games, meeting other writers and drinking endless pints of beer, while I searched my mind for something more exotic to drink. In the end I asked for a Vermouth Noilly Prat, thinking that would stump them. It did, so I got some small kind of revenge. I was always trying to out-smart them with my brilliant repartee, but I rarely got a word in edgeways. Dylan would start performing in the bars, and the others would stand back and listen. He didn't appear to monopolise the conversation deliberately but once Dylan had started he soon had an audience helpless with laughter. People loved listening to him. I never found his long, rambling shaggy-dog stories all that amusing, yet these were always the favourites, and I felt such an awful bitch standing there looking so serious when everyone else was hooting with laughter. Dylan loved telling stories that never ended: that was Dylan.

Dylan's sense of humour was a bit too whimsical for me. It wasn't Thurberish. I think Thurber's funnier. He *does* make me laugh. For me, Dylan was never a brilliant talker and only occasionally so funny that I would want to laugh, but other people always found themselves helpless and I'd hover there on the edge of a crowd, drinking a whisky and wondering how much longer it was going to go on. At the same time, Dylan had an endearing quality which you couldn't possibly deny. He was made to be loved, and everybody loved him. Yes, he *was* vulnerable and very sensitive to obvious things, like his height, his appearance and even his clothes (which was odd, because he dressed like a rag-bag). Little things would worry him, but he was never sensitive to criticism of his work. Dylan was so deeply convinced of himself and what he had got that he never cared a damn what other people thought.

During those days without food we met quite a lot of people and spent part of the time with the South African poet Roy Campbell, who was a good friend of Dylan's. Wherever we went, Dylan would tell people: 'This is the girl I am going to marry.' He wasn't very demonstrative in the pubs, seldom putting his arm around me, because to Dylan the pubs were sacred: they were like churches – places for declaiming and holding an audience. I went along with all that; it seemed all right to me, and so we spent the week, with him repeating all those endearments and telling his friends how much he loved me, and then back every night to the Eiffel Tower where we would make love and fall asleep. I don't know where on earth he got the money because drink's bloody expensive, and he always seemed to be so short, but somehow we kept it up for the week. There must have come a time when all his money ran out, but I wasn't aware of it then, although later I realised that all his life he was borrowing money for drink and bouncing cheques in pubs (although never for more than £1). So were many of his friends. His biographers seem to think that it was only Dylan who borrowed: it wasn't. When he had money he was the most generous of people and he would give it away, and when he didn't he would expect other people to be just as open-handed as he was.

By the end of that first week, I felt I really had to get back home to Ringwood. There were still some more sittings to be done for Augustus, who had not finished my portrait, and anyway I didn't enjoy all that drinking as much as Dylan did. I felt quite relieved to return to my mother's house, Blashford; I felt I couldn't go on with all that pubbing which was so much a part of Dylan's life. I thought it extraordinary that someone could go on living like that. One side of me wanted to share it with him, but there was also another side of me to whom his whole way of life seemed very wrong. I was a person who believed in hard work, determination, and all that. And yet I wanted to be with Dylan, to have all the possible experiences that I could: it seemed to me – then – an advanced thing to do.

The next episode I remember is being driven down to Laugharne by Augustus in one of his great big black cars, a six-cylinder Wolseley nicknamed 'The Bumble Bee'. Augustus was a terrifying driver. I don't think he used the gears or the clutch at all. He just went zooming along at enormous speed. He ran over one of his own sons once and killed him but as Augustus had so many it didn't seem to touch him very much. (Another son, Henry, who was going to be a priest, jumped over a cliff in Cornwall; they were a strange family, in many ways.)

Augustus had agreed to judge one of the painting sections at the National Eisteddfod, which was being held that year in Fishguard, and we had been invited to stay the weekend in Laugharne with Richard Hughes, author of *A High Wind in Jamaica*. He was then living at Castle House, a large pink-washed Georgian house adjoining the ruined castle. Augustus had been quite looking forward to it. He had been born in Tenby, and his family came from Haverfordwest, so this was a journey home. We arrived in Laugharne on the Friday night and, late on the Saturday morning, Dylan arrived. (I don't know how he had heard that we were there but it's quite possible that I may have told him, and it's equally possible that he may have heard it from Richard Hughes, whom he had already met and who had shown an interest in his work.) Anyway, Dylan turned up uninvited at lunch-time, accompanied by his great friend Fred Janes, who had borrowed his father's car and driven them both over from Swansea. Hughes welcomed them both warmly but their arrival immediately put Augustus on edge.

This was my first visit to Laugharne, although Dylan had told me all about this strange little town in West Wales during our first few days together. He had discovered it a few years earlier on a day trip with his friend Glyn Jones, and was fascinated by its people, pubs, customs and buildings. I thought it rather sweet. I was more romantic then and I thought it had a bit of me in it: the kind of wild, barren place that I rather take to. That first morning I wandered over Sir John's Hill and gazed down over the sandbanks in the estuary.

Hughes' home was pleasant and tastefully furnished, and he

showed us round the castle (a nice castle, a friendly castle, not one of those ominous grand ones), and invited us all – including Dylan and Fred – to return there in the evening for a surprise dinner, which he said he would spend the afternoon preparing. It was going to be a special treat, he said, with wines that he had been saving for such an occasion, and he was happy to stay behind working in the kitchen while we all went off to Fishguard.

Augustus seemed to like Hughes, and he and Dylan later became quite good friends, but I didn't like him at all; he was appallingly superior, trying to look the swashbuckling sailor and never quite bringing it off. He completely ignored me, which I didn't find very endearing, and his wife Frances seemed to me a rather wretched kind of woman – very much sat upon – though she obviously adored 'Diccon', as she called him. They had lots of children and believed all that baloney about children as adults which appears in his books.

My other impression about Richard Hughes, which was absolutely verified, was that he was awfully mean. It seems rather ungrateful to say this because the following year they very kindly put us up in their attic for a couple of months, and it was a very nice, large attic with two comfortable beds. No, that wasn't mean, but at the same time he was tight about little things. Their table was usually so frugal that I quite worried about their children: they were such little shrimps. When Dylan and I went to stay there, we took to pinching food from the larder. We would creep downstairs and take things like corn on the cob in tins, and sardines, which made an awful mess when we eventually got them open. (We couldn't find a tin opener anywhere so we used their silver as a substitute, which didn't do it any good.)

That first weekend Augustus kept his temper fairly well under control to begin with. He clearly thought that Dylan had an awful cheek to turn up uninvited, but as Hughes had made him welcome, and we were all guests in Hughes' house, he didn't make much of a fuss. After lunch we set off for Fishguard, with Augustus driving his car while Dylan and Fred followed on behind. The journey soon turned into a splendid pub crawl and we must have stopped for pints of beer at nearly every pub between Laugharne and Fishguard. We didn't stay very long at the Eisteddfod, and then began another pub crawl on the way back. After one stop Dylan climbed in with me in the back seat of Augustus' car and left Fred on his own. We were soon kissing and cuddling and fondling in the back, which made Augustus very angry indeed, but he didn't say much – he seldom did. Instead, he started driving faster than ever, grunting to himself over the wheel. When we arrived in St Clears, the next village to Laugharne, Augustus didn't turn off on to the side road to Laugharne but kept on driving furiously towards Carmarthen. Fred's car, meanwhile, had broken down. He later told Dylan that when his car stopped he saw our tail-lights disappearing fast over the horizon; he blew his horn and flashed his lights, but Augustus wouldn't stop.

When we reached Carmarthen, Augustus, by now more angry than ever, drove straight to the Boar's Head, where we started drinking again. Augustus still said very little and certainly didn't threaten Dylan while we were in the pub, but as we left I heard shouts and a scuffle going on somewhere behind the car as I was climbing into it, and a few moments later Augustus jumped back into the driving-seat and drove off fast, very fast. As I looked through the window there was Dylan lying on the ground, having obviously come off worse in the fight. Augustus was now in a rage, but was still saying nothing at all; the anger was all bottled up inside him. It was plain jealousy because Augustus had been sleeping with me and there was I, virtually making love to a younger man in the back of his car. I think Augustus found this an insult to his vanity, the more so because he could see that I was much too fond of Dylan.

That night Dylan had to make his own way back to Swansea. When we arrived back in Laugharne, we found Fred Janes had booked into Brown's Hotel for the night while his father's car was repaired, while at Castle House poor old Hughes was mourning the burnt remains of that special dinner which had taken him most of the day to prepare.

My last memory of that night is that I was in bed – I couldn't tell you in what room – and Augustus John was on top of me. How we got there and how it came about I can't remember, but that particular scene impressed me very much, because I wasn't at all happy lying there beneath Augustus: I can vividly remember looking at the ceiling, wondering how soon he would be finished.

I don't know where Dylan had got to by then; he was probably back in Swansea with his parents.

2

I was about eight or nine years old when my parents separated. We were never told what had caused the rift. As far as we were concerned, we just woke up one morning to find that we were a family without a man because my father, Francis Macnamara, was no longer there. I think we missed not having a man in the house, and this may have encouraged my mother's lesbianism, although I don't think that was the reason for the separation. Even now, over sixty years later, I don't really know why they parted. There was no hard drinking going on at that time. My father didn't start drinking until later and my mother only drank in a lady-like way, so it couldn't have been that. It may well have been his other women.

Francis neglected us. There was no doubt about that. He never showed us any affection at all. He never wrote to us or visited us or asked any of us out to dinner as we grew older; he just wasn't made that way. I didn't feel that I needed any affection from him because I disliked him so much. I grew up used to the idea that my father had been married to my mother and had then been married to other women and had lived with other women as well. That didn't bother me at all. I thought it was the Bohemian way of life, and everything in that life had a kind of glamour attached. But I never thought of my father as a glamorous figure, although a lot of people did. I thought he was a bastard because of all the horrible things he had done, such an egotist, leaving my poor mother to look after us all with very little money. That was one of the reasons why we never went to proper schools; she couldn't afford it.

For a long time I pondered about who was most at fault, but

eventually I was fully convinced that he was. He *was* the fault. Of course, I didn't think then about my mother's lesbianism because I didn't know about it at that stage; in any case, I think it came afterwards. It may have been a family failing (if you can call it a failing) because all of her sisters, or most of them, certainly, had lady friends; it seemed to follow a kind of pattern. We thought we were so *avant garde* that we must take it all in our stride; we would have been ashamed to be ashamed, although now that I am older I can see that I never really accepted this. Then, I thought the more scandalous a thing was the more admirable it was; that courage was needed to behave that way, and so on. I don't think it now. I don't blame my mother; she was a beautiful woman, one of those perfect ladies who did all the things that perfect ladies are supposed to do.

It was very mean of my father to have made four children – my brother John, sisters Nicolette and Brigid, and me – and then gone off and left them. He was probably always unfaithful. Francis was a great exhibitionist and show-off who loved throwing his weight around; the type of man that I detest. He was never a happy man, but much loved and admired by other Irish people, who thought him such a charmer. I could never understand what they saw in him. Talk chiefly, I would imagine. He had all sorts of nonsensical theories about how he was going to change the world and the whole economic system; he had got it all worked out and would talk to people at great length about it, often shouting with great authority, with the result that all his friends expected him to produce one great work of political philosophy. He thought he would as well, but this great book never materialised. Francis did publish one volume of poems called *Marionettes* in 1913, but they were very bad. I cannot remember a single poem he wrote, or even a line.

Francis's father, my grandfather, had been the High Sheriff of County Clare. The family had been there for many generations, but then came 'The Troubles'. My grandfather was a Protestant in a largely Catholic county, and although I never knew precisely what had happened I could see that the front of the family home at Ennistymon was pitted with bullet holes. The only other thing I can remember hearing about my grandfather was that he broke his neck on the Giant Racer at Wembley, which seemed rather a flamboyant way to go and became a sort of family joke. Francis inherited the family mansion and the whole village of Ennistymon together with a fair amount of green pasture land and a beautiful wooded glen with a river and waterfalls, and then never did a day's paid work throughout his life. He went to Oxford and studied Law, but dropped it, and all he ever did after that was talk about his great theories. Not having had to work was his chief trouble, I think. It would have been nice to have had a father to respect and depend on, bringing in the weekly money and so forth, but as it was he got through the whole estate. Later in his life Francis tried to retrieve the situation by converting the family home into the Falls Hotel, but that was another mistake. The lay-out was all wrong and the venture failed because he was always handing out free drinks, putting on a big act and talking his head off. He should never have gone into that business. He built up a beautiful cellar of fine wines, and then started selling them off for less than he had paid for them, or even giving them away – just playing the host. When I was staying there in my mid-teens I used to work behind the bar, mixing drinks, to help him, and I could see then that he had absolutely no idea how to run a hotel. The bar never seemed to shut.

At that time I had gone back to Dublin and then to Ennistymon with a very romantic vision of Ireland: it wasn't primarily to see my father – I had a huge prejudice against him. But I was completely bowled over by Ireland – the atmosphere and the magic. At first, my sister Brigid and I stayed in the basement flat of my father's house in Dublin. By then he had married his third wife, Iris O'Callaghan, who was a school friend of our eldest sister Nicolette. There was a big gulf between us. I didn't like Iris O'Callaghan at all. She was an alcoholic, and after my father died she was found dead in their flat: she had been dead for a week.

Francis was quite a well-known man-about-Dublin. He used to go down to the Abbey Theatre and took me to see *Juno and the Paycock*: he knew Sean O'Casey, Liam O'Flaherty, Synge, Cyril Cusack, Micheál Mac Liammóir, and many other Irish writers and actors. James Mason was at the Abbey Theatre then, and he became the lover of Iris O'Callaghan. My father must have introduced them because I can't think how they would have met otherwise. I remember meeting James Mason, but we were not included in their affairs. They invited him to dinner one night; then when Francis went away Iris had an affair with him. Mason was a very handsome young man in those days, much too handsome for her, I thought: I rather fancied him myself, in a very distant way.

My father was known then as a fairly wild man; although he hadn't started drinking until he was forty he was by now a heavy drinker, hanging around in the pubs with the writers and actors; he seemed to know them all. W. B. Yeats himself was living right opposite our flat in Dublin. Yeats used to have these very tasteful *soirées*; people would go on their knees to him, as though he were a sacred object. I went once and found it all appallingly pretentious. Yeats was very sloppy, sitting there with a soft face reading his poems with that special lilt of his. It all seemed nonsense to me and I really despised him because he was so pleased with himself. Yeats had been so over-praised that he now thought himself God's gift to everyone. He took no notice of me and that annoyed me, too. The room was full of poetry-worshippers and there was a sacred hush for the great man. I didn't think he was great at all, although he was one of the poets that Dylan admired most.

I suppose Francis could have been called a womaniser, although I don't think he was what I would call a real womaniser. He did have three wives, affairs with other women and an illegitimate daughter by a woman who worked as a nurse in a mental home, but he didn't seem able to treat his women very well. I think this was because he was too selfish; he wanted to be worshipped as a marvellous man, and although many people did think highly of him he never fulfilled their expectations. We girls looked upon him with a disparaging eye. It seemed to us that he talked so much nonsense and with such bombast. In the end I found him intolerable. My own worst faults come from him. Whenever I do something wrong or awful, I still say to myself, '*That* comes straight from Francis . . .'

After those few months in Dublin, I went out west to Ennistymon and camped out in one of the top rooms of the old house. Those were carefree days. In the evenings I rushed around the countryside with the Irish boys, dancing to folk music until nearly dawn. I adored dancing, in the small cottages at Doolin, to the sets and jigs with crowds gathering in the cottage doorways. It was the only time I ever heard any words of disapproval from Francis: he was always talking about free love, but when he heard about the Irish boys he said, 'Aren't you overdoing it a bit? People tell me you are going around with a lot of boys, night after night, coming back very late, sometimes not at all.' That was the only occasion I ever remember him giving me advice, and it was much too mild to be called that.

When I first realised that Francis was making love to other women, some of them not much older than myself, I was very shocked. Iris O'Callaghan was only four or five years older than I was, and when we were staying at Ennistymon he used to take her with us on this Galway hooker which he had had converted into a sailing boat. It only took an afternoon to sail to the Arran Isles, depending on the wind, and we could drop anchor and spend the night, visiting the cottage inns. He was well known there, too, because the Irish like that kind of play-acting. There was no door between the cabin he used to share with Iris and the area where we were sleeping and we could hear all their love-making. What really disgusted me was that Francis kept shouting while he was on top of her. I thought it was too ludicrous. He seemed to make love quite impersonally; it couldn't have mattered less who was beneath him because he would even break into a sea shanty, and then right at the crucial moment as he was coming to his climax he would shout, 'Ship ahoy!' I didn't find it funny at all: I thought he was just a dirty old man. To me, Francis seemed like a pale imitation of Augustus John, because that was the kind of thing Augustus did, only he did it better and more convincingly, with Society women and grand ladies.

The last time I can remember seeing my father was when he came down to Blashford to ask my mother to have him back; it must have been when I was in my late teens. I was glad she didn't go back to him. As usual, I didn't know anything about it at the time and it was Brigid who told me afterwards. Brigid always knew everything. She was that kind of warm person. Everybody confided in her whereas I was considered hard and capricious and malicious, which I was, to a certain extent, but very vulnerable.

My father never met Dylan, but I heard that he thoroughly disliked Dylan's poetry, while thinking that *Portrait of the Artist as a Young Dog* contained some of the best short stories in the English language. That was typical of Francis: his opinions were always extreme. I think he was probably envious because he had always wanted to achieve recognition as a writer himself. After I had met Dylan, I don't think I ever saw my father again. I only heard that Francis had died at Dalkey a long time afterwards. My sister Brigid went over to nurse him and help him: again, that was typical of her – she is much less prejudiced than I am. I was much more arrogant, and expected a great deal of myself – I think I got that arrogance from my father, and an aggression, too. He was always fighting; physically fighting. It was Nicolette who told me that he had died, and that his last words were 'Weighed and found wanting', which I thought strangely apt. I had a very good girl friend in Doolin, Kitty O'Brien, who became a barmaid in London, and when she heard about my father dying she was in floods of tears. This made me feel quite guilty because I couldn't have squeezed a drop out myself.

For quite a long time in my life I could never make up my mind whom I loved most – Francis or my mother. Then I decided that I hated Francis, and yet it was only after my mother died that I realised what a marvellous woman she was. I wish I had made a few more attempts to get closer to her because I think now that she must have been waiting for us to do it. We never did because we were very shy and had never been taught to show affection. She probably missed that.

My mother was a Majolier. They were very respectable people, quietly religious Quakers from Nîmes in France, the nearest large town to Congéniès, the village where my grandmother had her house and where we used to stay as children. I don't remember Grandfather Majolier very well; he was a landowner and known as a fairly strict Quaker. After he died my mother's sister discovered that for many years Grandfather Majolier had maintained a separate home in London for his mistress, who had at one time been the family's governess, and that they had had four children. This came as quite a shock to the family, and tended to confirm my theory that all men are swine. I grew up in a world where no one was ever faithful. Then I married Dylan and the same thing happened again, which enraged me because I didn't expect it to happen to us.

Grandmother Majolier was always very formal; she changed for dinner; she had silver and fine china, and a marvellous cook, Madame Bonicelle, but when we were children she never seemed to have much money. She was very beautiful – charming and gay. All her daughters thought she was an awful demon when she came to stay, but I was full of admiration for her. I didn't see that side of her character and was rather shocked when my mother and her sisters talked so nastily about her. She was one of twenty-one children; she had seven children and my mother had four, so there were always aunts and uncles, cousins and relatives all around us. Then at Blashford we grew up with all the John children as well after

Augustus had moved to Fryern Court. Augustus had had so many children by Dorelia and Ida Nettleship (quite apart from all the illegitimate ones) that there were children all around us.

We learned French from French governesses, and also when we went to stay with Grandmother Majolier. At one time Brigid and I were sent to the village school at Congéniès. We were quite horrified: if some wretched girl couldn't remember her recitations the teacher would give her enormous slaps across the face, so hard that she would nearly fall backwards over her bench. We were terrified that this was going to happen to us, and thought it very cruel because we had never seen anything like it before.

My mother was the eldest of the Majolier children and she had been brought up to be a lady. She was elegant, she always wore the right clothes, and she carried them off well because she had an aristocratic face and a fine figure. Socially, she was welcoming, amiable and knew all the right things to say, but she wasn't entirely kind. She would sometimes make shrewd and acid remarks about people she disliked. She was a snob, too: she would talk about 'these common people' and treat the maid very badly. We couldn't believe it because we had such a nice little girl, but my mother treated her like a slut. (We always had a maid during my childhood, as did the Majoliers and the Macnamaras, so later on – after I'd married Dylan and we'd had children – I always tried to get some help in the home. My mother provided me with a nurse when Llewelyn was born. Later, at South Leigh, and in Laugharne, I always had someone to help, even when I had very little money. I think life is too squalid if you have to do all the dirty work; you can't enjoy your babies unless you have someone to help you with part of it.)

My mother treated us exactly like rich children, which was a big mistake on her part. We should have had someone like Dylan's mother, Granny Thomas, teaching us how to cook and make cakes and the rest of it. I have always felt frustrated because we didn't do more with our childhood. We didn't have a very close contact with my mother; she kept herself at a distance, often staying in her own sitting room with all her books around her. It took me a long time to work out that she was highly intelligent because I had somehow developed the idea that beautiful women were only decorative. Then I discovered that she was reading difficult writers, like Proust, and that her library, which was extensive, was an extremely good one, containing all the classics, which she must have collected after her separation from Francis.

I think she may have come close to marrying again because she was very attractive and a lot of men were after her, but any thoughts of that must have ended when she moved to Blashford because she was so out of the world there, and she had also started a relationship with a rich woman friend, the odious Norah Summers. There's not much doubt that they were lesbians; Norah Summers dressed the part and acted the part as well, and even if she hadn't been so attached to my mother I am sure that I would have recognised what she was.

Norah lived with her husband in the same part of Hampshire. He was an insignificant-looking man, in steel. Norah was a painter. We children looked upon her as an absolute monster who had taken our mother from us. Norah was the father-figure of our girlhood, and an evil one; we were all influenced by her; she was a very strong character. She used to hand my mother all her cast-off clothes, expensively tailored tweed suits which my mother had to pay for: my mother liked those sorts of clothes. But Norah wasn't a naturally generous woman: she wasn't nice to us children and I suppose she may have been as jealous of us as we were of her. One thing that upset us was that my mother bought in all sorts of special food for her, like cream crackers, while we were always left with bread and jam, and whenever we wanted to speak to her, my mother was on the phone to Norah Summers. God knows what they talked about, but that was all part of the relationship. Sometimes in the afternoons they would disappear into my mother's bedroom and lock the door behind them, so it was pretty obvious what was going on.

If it hadn't been for Norah Summers, I think we would have appreciated my mother more. She knitted us beautiful sweaters, and sewed and made up cotton sacks for us (which we hated because they didn't go in and out in the right places), but she had no real skills and never had to go out to work. She was very fond of her garden, though. Whenever anyone came to see us, the first thing she said was, 'Shall I show you round the garden?' She smiled often, totally unlike me. I don't think she was like any of us, really, but less like me than my sisters.

She was the most uncommunicative person on any kind of delicate matter; she considered her relationship with Francis a

17

delicate matter and so she never talked about it. We had no idea how they had met or why they had parted. Afterwards, when we saw that he had had two other wives and various other women, we guessed that this was part of the trouble, but she never confided in us, nor talked to us in the way that a mother should. She never told us about menstruation and we were all horrified when blood started pouring out without any apparent reason: we all thought we were going to die. In fact, she didn't even teach us elementary cleanliness. She put out our clothes for us to change twice weekly, but she didn't make sure that we washed properly. When we had a bath we were allowed about three inches of water and the three of us would get in together and there would be a lot of screaming and giggling with very little soap used: she just left us to it. She herself was extremely clean and particular, but she didn't explain anything to us.

I got very depressed at Blashford. I was dying to do more, and I had too much time on my hands while I was there. I think that adults under-estimate children's feelings; children get depressed and bored when they have nothing to do; they have to be occupied, and above all they have to be taught things. There were lots of books, but we weren't taught how to use them. I never learned how to cook or mend a pair of socks, although eventually, years later, I managed to learn enough to darn Dylan's socks, always with different colours – bright colours, like red wool with black socks – so that people could see how hard-worked I was and what trouble I had taken.

Often I would say to my mother, 'What can I do now?' and she would reply, 'Go and weed the path,' or something equally inspiring. This would make me furious because I always felt that I was on a much higher level than that, and I have come to the conclusion that half the time at Ringwood I was bored to death. The only thing that saved us was the John family; they were our only strong social contact, and when they came down to live at Fryern Court we virtually moved in; their lives seemed so exciting compared to ours, and after that we were always out birds'-nesting or riding. It was a tremendous thrill if we found a nest, even a simple thrush or a blackbird, and if we found something rare like a tree creeper's nest (which I did once) we would be quite beyond ourselves. Once, Nicolette found a curlew's nest, which was just a couple of eggs on the ground with a few wisps of straw, which was hardly a nest at all. We all had collections of eggs and did egg-blowing all over the house, making a horrible mess because sometimes one couldn't be sure whether they were addled or not, and sometimes there'd be baby birds inside which couldn't be blown out. We never took all the eggs from a nest like some of the boys did; if there were a lot of eggs in a nest, we might take two but usually we just took one. The local children sometimes took all the eggs and the nest as well, which was a terrible thing to do.

Much of our life then was based on horses. We used to spend our days riding through the New Forest, which was a marvellous place to ride. There was a riding school where we could hire ponies, and there we met an extraordinary woman, Ethna Smith. She was living in a little corrugated iron shed right up in the forest. She had one racehorse and two other ponies – really nice horses. But she was a tough teacher, quite brutal. She would put us on her best horse, Brandy, then crack the crop; the horse would leap in the air, and we'd nearly fall over the back. We were very adventurous, galloping across fields and leaping over hedges. I was the one who would tackle anything. We also went hunting, not dressed in hunting clothes, needless to say – we were the stragglers behind in wellington boots and old trousers – but once I had the honour of being blooded and collecting the brush. I took the brush home, had it tanned, put it in a frame and kept it hanging on the wall for years; I was very proud of it. We also went to lots of shows and gymkhanas, sometimes travelling forty miles to compete. I always went in for the jumping, which could be quite terrifying; but in the end I collected a lot of trophies for those competitions – bending races and musical chairs and, quite unfairly, one handsome jumping cup, which was almost entirely due to the horse. I won it the day Ethna Smith let me ride Brandy in one of the main events, a silly thing for me to attempt because I had never ridden him in anything like that before. I was frightened from the start and kept losing the stirrups, flopping about in the saddle, thinking that I was going to fall, while Brandy just sailed over the jumps without brushing the top bars. But I suffered so much that day that there wasn't much satisfaction in it.

Looking back now, I suppose that it was quite a classy childhood, although we never thought of it as that. I've learned since that this is how young ladies are supposed to be brought up in the country, but we always thought ourselves rather hard-up and hard-done-by. We never went to hunt balls because we never had the right clothes, and anyway my mother didn't encourage that kind of thing. We all found life difficult when we first married because my mother taught us nothing, no manners, no domestic arts: she used to say, 'Don't worry. You will all marry rich men and they will have servants.' That was nonsense. None of us did, although she seemed to think that this would happen automatically because we were so attractive. As I said, she told me that I would marry a duke. What I had, chiefly, was vitality. I was supposed to be the beauty, and Nicolette, too, but Brigid rather less, which was unfortunate. It was a very open-air childhood, but the bad thing about it was the lack of any proper education; this was something that Nicolette and I both missed, though Brigid never complained because she didn't have any big ambitions, and nor was she the type: she remained the saint of the family.

The first school that I went to was a tiny school in Ringwood called The Parents' Educational Union, or something like that; it was full of maiden sisters, a sort of kindergarten. We used to go for botanical walks and take down the names of flowers. After that we had a succession of French governesses: as far as education was concerned they were quite hopeless although one of them, Henriette, did marry my brother John. (John was in quite a different world from us girls; he was in the Navy and was very glamorous and good-looking. He was fond of the ladies, too, but had particular tastes; he liked tiny, charming women. They always seemed very sophisticated to me because John was ten years older than I was, and they were usually nearer his own age.) The only thing I remember about those French governesses is that we read a lot of Racine and Molière, but that wasn't exactly an education; there was no grammar or mathematics. The nearest I came to acquiring any of those was when I was sent to an awful place called Groveley Manor School in Boscombe when I was thirteen or fourteen, which was leaving it too late. It was the dreariest school in the world, a singularly uninspiring place made worse by the ugly tunics we had to wear, the awful crocodile walks, and endless sermons in the school chapel (I actually fainted in the middle of one, once). I was terribly shy and appallingly miserable; the whole first term I wept; nothing went in, and the only light relief came when my brother John arrived to take me to the *thé dansant* at the Palm Court in Bournemouth.

It was while I was still at Groveley Manor, during one school holiday, that I fell madly in love with Caspar John. His sister Vivien had been my closest friend all through childhood, and both my parents had known Augustus long before I was born. Augustus had travelled around Ireland in a gypsy caravan in the days when my father was living at Doolin, and I think that was when the friendship started. There are family photographs of our family playing with his when I was just a baby. Later Augustus asked Francis to teach his son Romilly how to write and he was employed as a kind of tutor. Augustus was a real Bohemian, the genuine article. He and Dorelia ran a kind of hippie family at Fryern Court, where there was a carefree air of sexual abandon, with people falling in and out of love, and Augustus presiding over it all. He was an exceptional man, a great figure who fancied himself as a king of the gypsies; he was always going on about the Romanies and claimed to know the gypsy language. I never saw him as a romantic figure; I found him an awful bore, and only half listened when he expounded his ridiculous theories about the gypsies being the descendants of primitive man.

In the evenings Augustus reigned supreme over the dinner table. We would all sit down together, guests and children, friends and family, and this introduced us to the world of ideas. Bertrand Russell and T. E. Lawrence used to come over to dinner sometimes and so did Lord David Cecil. We were slightly in awe, trying to hold our own, and finding it hard to get a word in edgeways. It was very hard to talk to the Johns. They were closed up like oysters and hardly said a word when there was no one else there to provoke them. It was a grim atmosphere; I can't think why; it was as if they had nothing to say unless someone else was leading the conversation. Bertrand Russell was very charming, always neat, tidy and fastidious; a very sympathetic listener. I remember him saying once that he had found the secret of happiness and didn't want to die. Lawrence used to arrive on his huge black motorbike. He lived by very spartan rules: he once said that he hardly ever ate, and that all he needed was one light meal a day; this impressed me, because he seemed to be glowing and full of life. David Cecil was such an ethereal creature; no body at all, and he had a tiny little wife who was equally fairy-like.

I was just drifting along in those days, and I am very bitter about that. We were all so strong and healthy because of the awful goats' milk that my mother made us drink, and were all predestined victims for alcoholism and decadence because we had nothing to hold us. In the John house there was always drink, and I could hardly bring myself to speak at dinner unless I'd had some of their beautiful wine. I found wine immediately pleasant. I didn't have to go through the trauma most people go through of getting sick and then trying again. Later, when I was married to Dylan and we were in Brown's Hotel in Laugharne, it was double whiskies. I don't know how we managed that because we never had any money, but we did, and it all started with that wine at the Johns.

Augustus had seven beautiful sons. On those evenings together we all sat down in a row on the sofa with our boyfriends, drinking before the meal. Poppet, the most glamorous of all the John children, always had different boyfriends; Vivien had hers and I had Caspar, who was quite a bit older than I was. I was then about fifteen and this was the first time I had fallen in love. I have never felt like that about anybody else. I suppose it was his looks, chiefly. He was tall, dark and handsome, and already a sailor; he was beautiful, unbelievably good-looking, with a voice that was low and enchanting. The boys were the only ones that got any education in the John family, but the girls got even less than we did. Caspar must have had some or he wouldn't have got into the Admiralty; everybody thought he was dumb, so it was quite a revelation when Caspar finally became an Admiral. I never thought he was a great wit, and to me it was an advantage that he never said much because then we were both mute.

That romance must have lasted for about two years. We used to go on midnight picnics on the Downs, and I was completely infatuated. We were both unbelievably innocent. My mother had told us very little about sex other than that it was 'quite a pleasurable sensation' – by then she was living with Norah Summers. I was completely unskilled and didn't know what to do with men. I think I had a very romantic view of love then, although I was desperate for him to make love to me. Then one night we got the chance. I was staying at their house, Caspar was in bed, and I had got myself all beautiful in a frilly nightgown and was clinging to him. I wanted him passionately at that moment, but he wouldn't respond at all. I tried pulling him to me, but it was no good: whether he was being virtuous in not making love to such a young girl, or had some sexual problem of his own, I just don't know.

22

He never proposed to me. I wanted him to, although I never thought in terms of marriage; I was just loving him, that was all. We went to bed, but he never made love to me. We didn't get beyond kissing and hugging and rolling around on the Downs, and I think it was all the more passionate for that, in a sense; it was my first teenage romance.

What happened eventually was that my mother broke up the romance in a very cruel way, although I didn't know that she was behind it all at the time. Caspar and I were due to meet in Norah Summers' house at Ferndown, and usually when we met we would fly into each other's arms. This time, Caspar just looked at me coldly and turned away. I was completely shattered, and I could never find out why. I remember writing to him twice, asking him to tell me why he was taking no notice of me, and that I just wanted to know because I was so distraught. I even thought of throwing myself out of the window, and then decided that it wasn't a big enough drop. Caspar never answered my letters, and then years later my sister Brigid told me that my mother had written to him to say that I was much too young for him and that he wasn't to go near me again; she advised him to go out with Brigid instead. When she told me about my mother's role, I was even madder; it seemed a very Jane Austen thing for my mother to do, trying to marry her daughters off in the right order.

I could never feel the same kind of passion for Dylan that I had felt for Caspar, chiefly because of Caspar's looks, I think: as far as I was concerned I was Caspar's. If at any time during my marriage to Dylan, Caspar had come along on a great white horse, I am sure that I would have let him carry me off. I always compared the two of them, to Dylan's disadvantage, although I never told Dylan that. I was carrying this torch for Caspar all through the years of my marriage. The feeling is still there now. Every now and then I hear something about him and I get a little twinge when his name is mentioned. He was the great love of my life, and he remains a dream figure.

I saw him a few years later in a pub and Caspar made a few superficial jokes about me acquiring an Irish brogue. As I listened to him I kept looking at his face and wondering whether I could bring myself to make the first move and open it all up again. Looking back now, I think it's very sad. Anyway, he suffered for hurting me: he lost both his legs, and I couldn't help thinking that it was

God punishing him. I have noticed that in my life: if I do something good, something good happens to me, and if I do something bad, something bad happens. It seems to work every time. My way of reacting is completely opposite to the Christian way of turning the other cheek. I think the old primitive idea of a tooth for a tooth and an eye for an eye is much more logical.

At that time I had an almost perfect figure, except for my knees, which seemed to stick out too much, and my legs, which should have been longer. As far back as I can remember, I had always wanted to be a dancer. Even at Groveley Manor I can remember standing on the bed holding the bars around it and trying ballet exercises and *pliés*. I had seen Pavlova in *Swan Lake* and was convinced that this was the life for me; that whole world exercised a tremendous fascination, and I kept begging my mother to let me go off to London and train as a dancer. I yearned for that twilight lighting and sense of artificiality because it was in total contrast to the frightful open-air childhood that I had had. I knew it was a disciplined life: that attracted me, too, because I knew that it was what I needed – neither at Blashford nor in Ireland had there ever been any kind of discipline. I was dying to be sucked into one of those groups – a ballet company or a chorus line – that had caught my imagination, and I kept on nagging until my mother eventually sent me off to a tap and acrobatic dancing school in Rupert Street, off Shaftesbury Avenue. I went there for a couple of years with Vivien John.

I was very innocent when we went to London. Vivien may have been more experienced than I was, but that's not saying a great deal. She was beautiful, full of life, and we had great fun together. She was always sketching. All the John children drew with the greatest ease; they didn't produce anything lasting, but the facility was there. We stayed in a hostel for quite a long time, a very homely, virtuous place with no flashy girls, and we went to classes together until Vivien gave it up and went back to her Spanish dancing. When I was in London in 1982, Vivien rang up and said, 'Shall we meet?' but we'd had such a strong emotional bond that I said, 'No.' I find it upsetting to think about her now. I don't know why. I should have met her; it was cowardly not to, but I am always afraid of being fond of someone and then seeing them again and finding that it's all different – which it always is.

Tap and acrobatic wasn't the dancing that I would have chosen had I made the right decisions about a dancing career early in my childhood, but I loved it all the same. With the acrobatic training I became incredibly supple and could bend right over backwards, touch my heels and do walk-overs and cart-wheels, and if I hadn't been so stupid as to start drinking so much with Dylan I think I would have become exceptional.

While we were at dancing school, my father moved back to London. He had a very nice flat in Regent's Square, and Vivien and I stayed there for a while. We had bunk beds in a small bedroom piled up high with frivolous clothes that Vivien and I somehow managed to acquire: brassières, tutus, panties and so on. My father used to give dinner parties (to which we were not invited), and spent his days writing letters to my mother, anything up to fifty pages long, explaining his philosophy and begging her to have him back. At other times I stayed at home in Blashford with my mother and commuted to London by train, sometimes staying overnight with my elder sister Nicolette, who was studying at the Slade.

According to Nicolette, I stood out from the other two sisters and I had a very high opinion of myself. I had high expectations. I thought I was going to be one of the world's greatest dancers, and I was mad about the stage. Nicolette says in her book *Two Flamboyant Fathers* that I was always being pursued by men and besieged by love letters, and that is true as well, although they usually happened to be the lowest of men. I have always found that the men who want to make love to you are never the ones that you want: it's always some frightful little worm who cowers and grovels and lays himself out. Whenever I met a man like that I wanted to kick him.

There was one very dark little Italian, Gabriello, who committed suicide because I wouldn't have anything to do with him.

I met him at a party of Nicolette's. He was small and curly-headed, a smaller version of Dylan, in a sense. He pursued me with great persistence. I didn't have the slightest interest in him, but he was very insistent. He used to follow me about and find which buses I was travelling on. He discovered which dancing school I was at and started waiting for me outside. I used to sweep past him whenever I saw him. It was cruel, but he had no rights over me. Then one day I was told he had shot himself out of desperation because I could not return his affection. I had to have one rather painful meeting with his parents. They didn't blame me for his death, although they were very upset. Nicolette told me that I ought to see them because they wanted me to know that they bore me no ill feelings and they realised that I hadn't encouraged him. I felt perfectly detached. I thought, 'Thank God, I've got rid of him!' I felt absolutely no pity or compassion because he had been such an awful nuisance.

All through that period my one burning ambition was to find myself a permanent job with a dancing troupe. I wanted to go to Paris as one of the Bluebells in the Folies Bergères but my mother wouldn't let me go, and then I ran away from home with Vivien hoping to get a job in one of Charles Cochran's revues. We did get as far as the audition, which was quite an achievement, but soon came home with our tails between our legs.

One day Augustus said, 'Come over to the studio. I want to paint you.' So I did. It seemed quite an honour, although I didn't think of it like that because I had known him since my earliest childhood.

Augustus was then at the height of his fame; in fact, his reputation had become somewhat inflated because of his notorious lifestyle. As an artist I thought he had a great talent, especially with his drawings and some of his portraits. His portraits of men were usually better than his ones of women: I think this was probably because he was trying to woo the women at the same time. He would give them necks a yard long and huge eyes in order to flatter them, seducing them with paint, then flinging them immediately on to his couch. He was much more exact with men, and his portrait of my father – whom Augustus called a professional eccentric – brought out his real character. Augustus' problem as an artist was that he never knew when to stop. He did several colossal canvases with groups of different figures in gypsy clothing, and just when he had the perfect picture Augustus would ruin it by filling in so much detail that he lost that initial spontaneous feeling.

The first time I went to sit for him he didn't speak to me or say anything to put me at my ease: he just glared most ferociously, without the trace of a smile, with his long black hair and long black beard accentuating his fierceness. He usually offered his models £1, but he didn't pay me a penny, and then right at the end of the session he suddenly leapt on me, pulling up my dress and tearing off my pants, and made love to me, although you could hardly call it love. It was totally unexpected and I was still a virgin. He didn't ask for my consent or even try to woo me; he just pounced and I couldn't fight because he was an enormous, strong, bestial man. I was cowed and too frightened to resist. What drove me nearly crazy was that I had wanted Caspar and now I had his hairy animal of a father on top of me instead.

I was petrified. When he had finished (and it didn't take long) Augustus just got up, adjusted his clothes, and left the room. He didn't say anything to me, not even 'Sorry'. I didn't burst out crying. I just got dressed myself, thinking how disgusting he was. I suppose it was rape, but that thought didn't enter my mind; he was a very old friend of my father's. It taught me that there is no such thing as a gentleman's law among men.

Augustus used to have lots of Society women. I tried to imagine him pouncing on *them*. My mind boggled at the idea, and then I thought, maybe they enjoyed it; it must have been quite a novelty for them. I had no knowledge of the world and thought perhaps that this was all part of it. I also wanted to be an experienced woman. I wanted to try everything, to know what it was like, and not only in the sexual sense. I do have an inbred, bitter view of men: I don't trust them. In a roundabout way this probably started with Francis, but in a physical way I think it started with Augustus.

I went and posed for Augustus again the next day – I had to, the painting wasn't finished – and the same thing happened.

Augustus did have a reputation for behaving like that, but nobody had warned me in advance. In the end I was more disgusted than frightened. Every time I did a sitting I knew what was coming at the end – the big leap. I just waited for it, thinking, 'Oh my God! If only I could escape.' He could see that I was miserable because he would ask me sometimes, 'What are you so sad about?' But I couldn't tell him. Sometimes, I tried to push him away but I didn't want to offend him, and eventually I think he became quite fond of me. He painted several portraits of me in oils: one is well-known, but I don't know what happened to the others. He also did many drawings, which I hated sitting for because he did most of those nude. I used to die a thousand deaths because he would sit me down on a divan and tear my legs apart until I was in the position he wanted.

Augustus made me very anti-sex: you couldn't call his man-handling making love; there was no tenderness at all. It was horrible, with his great hairy face: I don't know why I didn't fight it; why I just let him get on with it when I certainly had no pleasure myself – it was like being attacked by a goat. The saddest thing is that my whole sexual development happened the wrong way round. It was a catastrophe from which I have never quite recovered.

I never became fond of Augustus, although he did start taking me around a bit. He took me out to lunch and dinner, introducing me to people as Francis's daughter. Afterwards we used to stay the night at his flat in Fitzroy Square: I didn't enjoy the love-making part, but I liked going out with him because he would take me off to the Eiffel Tower and other restaurants where the food was good, and I came to look upon the sexual side of it as a necessary sacrifice.

I don't think my mother knew he had raped me. She wouldn't have cared, anyway, because she was so immoral herself. I didn't really feel that he had offended me, and I rather think that Augustus thought that I ought to be grateful that such a famous painter had wanted me: he was like that.

3

In one sense Dylan and I were hardly made for each other. He needed someone with simple values to provide that sheltered, secure, deadly dull and warmly protective small-town Welsh home background in which his best work was always done, and I could only go so far. I was just as bad as he was when it came to drinking; and my mother had brought us up never to think about money. We never talked it: she thought the subject was vulgar.

Although I wanted money very badly, it burnt a hole in my pocket. When I came up to London to train as a dancer, sometimes I went down to Waterloo Station late at night to catch the last train home to Ringwood, and I would see people sleeping in the subways – the down-and-outs. I had never seen anything like that before and it moved me.

Once I had four £5 notes which Augustus had given to me. It was a very large sum of money, and I'd come up to London hoping to buy some clothes. (I was always seeing beautiful things in the shops that I couldn't afford, and I was desperate to have nice clothes.) I wandered up Oxford Street towards Marble Arch, and there, just by Speakers' Corner, I saw more down-and-outs, fast asleep, stretched out on benches. They were low, horrible types, but I thought, 'Poor devils!' and started tucking my £5 notes inside their jackets. It was a silly thing to do because I had never had £20 before, and yet I felt that I had to do it, something compelled me to.

Dylan was just the same. If he had money, he gave it away – he was the kindest and most generous of men – and if he didn't have money, then he thought it only natural that other people should give it to him. The thought of saving money never occurred to him, and throughout his life he never owned a house or a car and rarely more than one suit at a time. He just didn't need them, and although I can understand it, and know how he felt and often agreed with him, it was fatal having the two of us living together under one roof. But that's the way we were. When people told me that Dylan was penniless it didn't deter me; it just added to the glamour.

In between my sittings for Augustus, I had found some work as a dancer, had been over to Ireland and had lived in Paris; I was still convinced that I would become as famous as Isadora Duncan.

That was my whole reason for going over to Paris. I thought that if I went there I would be able to develop my own style of dancing and that this was the way to stardom. While in Dublin, staying in the basement flat at my father's house, I met Vera Gribben, who had been a pupil of Isadora Duncan. She gave me private dancing lessons. When she returned to Paris with her husband I went over there, too, and rented a little studio, just a room with a few steps up to a balcony where the bed was. I used to practise every day in the studio, dancing to a recording of *The Blue Danube*. I didn't do any jazz dancing, which was all the rage in Paris then, because Vera Gribben looked down on it and thought I was worth something better.

I had no introductions to any of the English or American writers then living in Paris. The only affair I had there was with a painter named Segall. It lasted some months. I can't remember how I met him unless it was through Vera Gribben. He was a small man, quite a bit older than I was. I didn't model for him, but we went to bed together. He was rather charming, kind, quite ugly with a Jewish nose and brown hair. What I liked about him was that he liked me – I responded to that: he was very warm. We didn't go anywhere together, to the restaurants or round the galleries, because he was much too poor.

I had sympathy for him because he was gentle and, I thought, a good but unrecognised artist. I have never seen an attic as wretched as the one he lived in. He made it plain enough that so far as he was concerned this was just a passing affair and that was all – just a little sexual incident.

I have no particularly happy memories of Paris, though it was quite interesting going to the Raymond Duncan school: he was the brother of Isadora and I thought him something of a freak. I did some dancing there on a little stage, but I never really thought it through; I was still on my way, climbing upwards to fame and fortune, or so I believed. I didn't think much in those days, and it was all the wrong sort of dancing, really, for me. It was much too monotonous. I was dancing at private little gatherings for the so-called élite. It was all very artificial, with people dressing up for the occasion and sitting around in groups at smart salons. I made a lot of stupid mistakes. That kind of Isadora Duncan, self-expression dancing had no rules at all; you just did more or less as you and the music felt together, and if you didn't feel it, that was just too bad. I felt that I was interpreting the music of Mozart and Schubert and a few people responded to it, but it was never very popular. Sometimes I would put the wrong record on for a dance, and nobody seemed to notice; no one was any the wiser. It's all a hazy memory now. I don't know how I managed to survive there for a year because I had hardly any money: my mother was sending me £1 a week and somehow I managed to get by on that, living on simple things – wine, bread and a little salami.

Only one thing came out of my year in Paris and that was a lesson taught me by Vera Gribben: she made me change my whole approach to dancing. 'You use too many movements. All that could have been said with one gesture,' she said, when I had done about ten hundred somersaults during one routine. I really did learn something from that.

The one breakthrough I had on returning from Paris was an engagement with the chorus line at the London Palladium, earning around £8 a week, which seemed a lot of money in those days – I thought I was well off. I was in the chorus for one of the Crazy Gang's seasons, and I was a really good dancer, the only one who had been properly trained. But by then I was already going around with Dylan and one night, when it came to the high kicks, I forgot which leg should go up next; it all seemed to go dead on me, and I just stood completely still, which must have looked very odd for the audience. Very soon after this an awful man, Mr Fisher, who was in charge of the girls, said, 'You're fired!' I was tremendously upset because I couldn't think why, and I pleaded with him: 'For goodness' sake, tell me why?' He didn't say anything about the mistake I had made, but ever after I kept wondering what it could have been. I think I have answered the question now, after my years with Alcoholics Anonymous: I must have been drinking and that was why I forgot the legs.

My dancing really came to an end with Dylan. I was still sharing a room with Vivien, but she could never get a job in the chorus because she couldn't keep time. During one Christmas season I had a job in a pantomime at the Lyric Theatre in Hammersmith, hopping around, and I did a small cabaret act around the night clubs. After that I was reduced to a job at Peter Robinson, demonstrating Charnelle rubber corsets, doing back-bends and walk-overs and splits to show how supple they were. It's sad because I still believe that I had a natural talent to become a good dancer.

I had never had much sense of direction, but I seemed to lose it all when I met Dylan: I loved him and that was enough. It wasn't his appearance that attracted me; it was what I heard more than what I saw: his voice going on and on, often speaking so softly that I could hardly hear a word, with those pop-eyes and that funny nose. It was quite a long time before he went to fat, and what I remember now is that never-ending, non-stop flow of words, nice sweet compliments which sounded all right at the time but are now impossible to reproduce; that and the feeling that he really did care about me, right from the very first moment in the Wheatsheaf; he said it was 'nice to have a bit of class for a change'.

At the time that I met him he had had a long, sexless relationship with Pamela Hansford Johnson, and the odd brief affair, but apart from that I think he was fairly innocent: he certainly seemed to be, and yet at the same time he claimed to have been to bed with several different women, including the Millie who was with him when we first met. She was an ordinary pub girl – nothing special about her – and she seemed quite pleased that he'd found me. I don't think she'd wanted a penniless poet; she'd had enough of him being a terrible slob around the house and always wanting money for drink. I don't suppose any other woman would have been so crazy as to marry a penniless poet, but I thought it was rather a splendid thing to do. I had a lot of funny ideas. I didn't want to get into the grand, classy world: my only ideas were for the stage; and I had a feeling for the down-trodden; they were the real people and they had to be helped. Dylan came into that category.

Those other women had all been very different, and often much older than he was. He had an affair with Veronica Sibthorp, who had a flat in Great Ormond Street and a cottage in Cornwall. His relationship with Wyn Henderson went quite deep, too, though she later became a friend to both of us. They were both mothering types and that was what he wanted. Perhaps this was the reason why his romance with Pamela Hansford Johnson failed to mature.

Dylan talked a lot about Pamela Hansford Johnson. Their relationship was quite intense, although it hadn't gone very far physically. He told me she would never go to bed with him; she was very respectable and I don't think she would ever have dreamt of marrying him. To me, she sounded like the worst kind of woman, playing the lady writer and dressing the part. When Dylan's father read her books he said he thought they were 'absolute muck'. I only read one and I agreed with him.

Dylan's letters to her are very strange, long teenage intellectual outpourings with the occasional protestation of love, totally different from his letters to me, which were often very passionate. When I read them years later, when Constantine FitzGibbon gathered them together in the *Selected Letters* (1966), I could see that Dylan had used her as someone to pour out to, a sort of confessor for all his views on poetry, philosophy and Life with a capital L. I think she probably lapped them up. To me they were deadly boring, but Dylan was always like that: he would gear his letters to what he thought the recipient wanted. All his letters have to be taken with a pinch of salt (especially his begging letters, which were worst of all – they were deliberately calculated). He wrote once that he had been to bed with another woman: Pamela was absolutely horrified. I remember him telling me about it, and when the *Selected Letters* came out I read the actual letter. Dylan told everybody about that encounter; it became one of his favourite stories, because the woman was apparently very lascivious. Dylan used to dress the story up and talk about her red mouth, and it all sounded so sickly that I thought the whole incident was an absurd exaggeration on Dylan's part. It was rather stupid of him to have written a letter like that to Pamela Hansford Johnson, but perhaps it was as well; it showed her what kind of person he really was and her reaction shows me what kind of person *she* was. She comes through in their correspondence as a rather stiff young lady, prim and proper and not his type at all. One reason their romance came to an end was because he had told her that he was two years older than he really was. Then, when she went down to stay with Dylan's family in Swansea and found out that he was only nineteen, she had a fit of hysterics and the doctor had to be called in. But it was that letter that finally ended the relationship: she was very wary of him after that. By the time Dylan met me and told me all about her, he said he was no longer in love with her, if indeed he ever had been. Soon after we met she gave a party and invited Dylan. I was invited to go along and I would've loved to have gone, out of curiosity, to see what she was like, but Dylan steered me well clear of that, saying how provincial and snobbish she was. I think the chief thing which must have stopped any idea of marriage was that Dylan had absolutely no money. Eventually she married C. P. Snow, and I thought that was probably the best place for her.

After that first meeting in the Wheatsheaf, and then the few days at the Eiffel Tower, I went back home to Ringwood and then took off to Ireland for quite a long visit without telling Dylan where I had gone. I didn't fall out with him, but one night we were in a pub and he was the centre of attention as always, telling stories, and I was on the fringe, being ignored by everyone and beginning to resent it. I thought, 'To hell with it,' and walked off and caught the next train home. I felt hurt. He was being neglectful. I wasn't sure that I was in love with him, but he seemed to be taking it all too lightly. I just couldn't bear it any more, and I thought, 'Well, that's just one of those things; another passing incident.' Dylan didn't write to me: he didn't know my address, and so far as I was aware he made no great attempt to find me. I went to Dublin and then to Doolin, dancing again around the cottages. I was very proud. I didn't ever want to give the impression that I was clinging to a man: the man had to follow me. I was playing hard to get. This may be something that I learnt from my mother in a roundabout way; what with the lesbianism and all those women alone in the house without a man, there was a great feeling against men, a kind of contempt for men that may have been working on me. Deep down I wasn't like that; I like men's bodies very much. But there is another side, that crops up now and then, of thinking men contemptible. Even when I've been infatuated by a man it is always there at the back of my mind – I don't trust them. Even though Dylan had said that he loved me, had told me that he would marry me and had made love to me, I still wanted to be sure that he meant it. I always felt that he did really love me, but the thought of him drinking so much and talking so much – that worried me. I didn't think so much in those days about where I was going or what I was doing – I just went along on a wave, and for a while the wave took us apart.

It would be no good trying to place the events of that year before we married in any kind of logical sequence: there wasn't one. We lived together for most of that year, but we weren't together all the time, and we didn't have a place of our own. He would go back to Swansea and I to Blashford, and then we would be together again.

Dylan was never aware that I had been to bed with Augustus. I didn't tell him and Augustus wouldn't. Augustus was very angry with Dylan, but not with me. Dylan had pinched me from him, which was a blow to his pride, but I had never been attached to Augustus in any kind of binding way. He may have been trying to protect me from Dylan, but really *I* needed protection from Augustus. FitzGibbon suggests that Augustus was trying to guard me from Dylan because Dylan had had VD, but I don't believe that. I know that Dylan did have the disease because he told me about it, and soon after I met him I had to go into hospital myself when I caught gonorrhoea, but I didn't catch that from Dylan: I caught it at some party I went to; I have no idea from whom. I was in no condition to notice such insignificant details . . . Augustus came to visit me in hospital and he was very jocular about it. The treatment didn't last long, only a few days.

It was while I was there that Dylan wrote me one of his earliest letters – it may have been the first:

Nice, lovely, faraway Caitlin my darling,
Are you better, and please God you aren't too miserable in the horrible hospital? Tell me everything, when you'll be out again, where you'll be at Christmas, and that you think of me and love me. And when you're in the world again, we'll both be useful if you like, trot around, do things, compromise with the They people, find a place with a bath and no bugs in Bloomsbury, and be happy there. It's that – the *thought* of the few simple things we want and the *knowledge* that we're going to get them in spite of you know Who and His spites and tempers – that keeps us living I think. It keeps *me* living. I don't want you for a day (though I'd sell my toes to see you now my dear, only for a minute, to kiss you once, and make a funny face at you): a day is the length of a gnat's life: I want you for the lifetime of a big, mad animal, like an elephant. I've been indoors all this week, with a wicked cold, coughing and

35

snivelling, too full of phlegm and aspirins to write to a girl in hospital, because my letter would be sad and despairing, & even the ink would carry sadness & influenza. Should I make you sad, darling, when you're in bed with rice pudding in Marlborough Ward? I want so very much to look at you again; I love you; you're weeks older now; is your hair grey? have you put your hair up, and do you look like a real adult person, not at all anymore beautiful and barmy like the proper daughters of God? You mustn't look too grown-up, because you'd look older than me; and you'll never, I'll never let you, grow wise, and I'll never, you shall never let me, grow wise, and we'll always be young and unwise together. There is, I suppose, in the eyes of the They, a sort of sweet madness about you and me, a sort of mad bewilderment and astonishment oblivious to the Nasties and the Meanies; you're the only person, of course, you're the only person from here to Aldebaran and back, with whom I'm free entirely; and I think it's because you're as innocent as me. Oh I know we're not saints or virgins or lunatics; we know all the lust and lavatory jokes, and most of the dirty people; we can catch buses and count our change and cross the roads and talk real sentences. But our innocence goes awfully deep, and our discreditable secret is that we don't know anything at all, and our horrid *inner* secret is that we don't care that we don't. I've just read an Irish book called Rory and Bran, and it's a bad charming book: innocent Rory falls in love with innocent Oriana, and, though they're both whimsy and talk about the secret of the language of the hills and though Rory worships the moon and Oriana glides about in her garden listening to the legendary birds, they're not as mad as we are, nor as innocent. I love you so much I'll never be able to tell you; I'm frightened to tell you. I can always feel your heart. Dance tunes are always right: I love you body and soul: – and I suppose body means that I want to touch you & be in bed with you & I suppose soul means that I can hear you & see you & love you in every single, single thing in the whole world asleep or awake

Dylan X

I wanted this to be a letter full of news, but there isn't any yet. It's just a letter full of what I think about you and me. You're not empty, empty still, are you? Have you got love to send me?

I went into a pub one night and there was Dylan. The moment he saw me he was immediately all over me again, and we seemed to go back to our previous relationship, although we still had nowhere to live. It was the spring of 1937. For some months we stayed at Veronica Sibthorp's flat in Great Ormond Street, and from there we went down to her cottage in Cornwall, just to get away from London and all the boozing. It was a general move down to

36

Cornwall with various friends: Wyn Henderson had a cottage at Polgigga; Oswell Blakiston came down and so did Wyn's son, Nigel, and Rayner Heppenstall, and several others. We had so few possessions – just some clothes and Dylan's notebooks – and no children, and we were able to move anywhere, just when we wanted to.

There was something magic between us then: an affinity of souls, perhaps. I felt it right from the moment that I met Dylan, and although I didn't think then that he was a great poet, I knew that he would become one and that his gifts were quite out of the ordinary. I felt intuitively that he had this magic casket in him. He seldom read poetry to me: it was all talk, about love and us and me, and we slipped into a life together, revolving around the pubs, as though we had done it all our lives. I didn't talk much; he did all the talking. I was never a good listener, always switching off, but I could feel that he changed once we were away from London. This was to be the pattern: he needed London for talk and pubbing – for stimulation – but he could only write away from it. He wrote well in Cornwall. As soon as I could get him away into my little dull country places he would settle down and start working. Nicolette says that I used to lock him up in his shed to make him work, but this isn't true. The truth is that once he was in an environment where he could work, Dylan was extremely disciplined, writing to a strict routine no matter where he was, and that continued right to the end.

We spent several months down in Cornwall, staying at Polgigga, and then in Mousehole (where Wyn Henderson had bought the Lobster Pot and was running the restaurant, with her mother working in the kitchens), and later at Newlyn, where we rented a studio from the painter Max Chapman. It was while we were there that we decided to marry. By then we had spent a year together, and we had become nomadic, moving from place to place with our few possessions in a bag. We wrote to our parents to tell them of our plans. Years later – nearly twenty-five years after Dylan's death – I heard that his father was most unhappy about the marriage. Dylan didn't tell me at the time, and when I first met his parents later that year they made me very welcome. It was only when Ferris's biography was published in 1977 that I read for the first time of his father's anguished appeals to different members of the family in an attempt to stop the wedding. I can only guess now that Dylan kept it from me because he knew that marriage as such didn't mean all that much to me; it was just a piece of paper as far as I was concerned. Dylan was probably afraid that I would have been influenced by his father's attitude, and would have said, 'Well, perhaps we shouldn't get married, then.' He was quite determined to marry me, although I was quite happy to carry on as we were without all that nonsense. I didn't really believe in marriage. I was anti all the conventions. I believed in free love, and had absorbed all Francis's half-baked ideas, but underneath, Dylan wasn't like that at all. He was much more conventional than I was, a typical Welsh Nonconformist at heart. He was always talking of finding our ideal, beautiful little house and being happy ever after, and I never believed him for a second. I quite liked the idea of being married, but I couldn't see the point of it.

On my wedding day I wore a simple little blue cotton dress and no hat. Dylan wore his usual corduroy trousers, tweed jacket, check shirt and no tie. We had had quite a lot to drink before we went down to the Penzance Register Office for the ceremony, and my main memory of it is the feeling of being lightly bemused. We had already postponed the wedding twice, having drunk the money that we had set aside for the day. Then, when we did eventually arrive before the Registrar on 11 July 1937 (after Wyn Henderson had paid for the marriage licence), I was amazed how soon it was all over. The Registrar was stony-faced, and it seemed to be over in about two minutes. Neither of us was particularly excited; we were pretty well primed up, and I think the drink was predominant. Dylan was very romantic. Without telling me, he had gone off to Penzance and bought two little Cornish silver rings for about six shillings (30p) each, and we went through a ceremony of exchanging them. I kept that ring for quite a long time, but have no idea now what happened to it. I lost everything; whatever I had, I lost. A friend of mine brought me some nice gold earrings from Ceylon once and was very offended to find me not wearing them. 'For God's sake, I lost those ages ago,' I told her. I found it impossible to hang on to things. I don't know how I lost my wedding ring – it must have fallen off some time. It had no kind of significance for me at all. I think Dylan kept his longer than I kept mine; he was more conventional in that sense, and loved all that whimsical stuff.

Wyn Henderson was there at the wedding. She must have been because she paid for it, and she would never have allowed us to get married without her being there, but I don't have a clear recollection of her being there. We spent our honeymoon first at the Lobster Pot and then at Max Chapman's studio in the nearby fishing village of Newlyn. He had all his gloomy paintings hanging on the wall, terrible dark-coloured things.

Wyn Henderson became a lifelong friend. Later she married a priest who left the priesthood for her; I think she pretty well defrocked him. She was a huge woman, and when she came out to stay with Giuseppe and me in Rome after Dylan's death, he nicknamed her 'Moby Dick'. She was always very unconventional. One day, soon after we married, Wyn asked if we would mind if she got underneath while we were making love – she said she would make a comfortable mattress. I said I didn't mind, but Dylan objected very strongly.

At that time, I think Dylan and I were faithful to each other; it was right at the beginning and anyway there weren't many practical opportunities to be anything other than faithful. I was half in love with one of Wyn Henderson's sons, Nigel, but nothing came of that. I used to get these regular infatuations, but I don't think Dylan had anybody then. It all started when he began making periodic visits to London: I am positive now that, almost from the beginning, whenever he went away he was unfaithful, but I never thought it then – I stupidly believed whatever he told me. 'You are the only woman for me,' he would say. It took me quite a long time to realise that he had been doing it all the time.

We spent most of that summer down in Cornwall, walking the cliffs and the country lanes, pubbing and making love. Dylan was writing well, but it had to come to an end: the money had run out. He took me to Swansea to stay with his parents. By then his father had retired from his teaching post at Swansea Grammar School, and they had moved from the house at 5 Cwmdonkin Drive, where Dylan was born, to a smaller house in Bishopston.

His parents made me very welcome, but it was the kind of house, place and attitude which I dislike most: all that petty wrangling about pennies and nagging about dust, all the things that free-thinking artists (which was how we thought of ourselves in those days) never bothered about. My mother had never made any of us dust or clean so I was horrified at all this neatness and tidiness, and it was certainly no background for all my brilliance, or so I thought.

By then Dylan and I had been together for almost eighteen

months, and this was the first time that I had seen him with his mother and father. To me, he was slightly diminished by his parents. He behaved much more conventionally, always calling his father 'Dad' and his mother 'Mother' and never using the kind of swear words that he used normally. It was chiefly because of his mother. She was a typical Welsh farmer's daughter, a complete non-stop talker and basically a very stupid woman, although she had a kind heart. She would fuss and nag and play mother, getting on Dylan's nerves about him being warm enough and clean enough. She had coddled him so much that he didn't even know how to take the top off an egg.

Every night she prepared his bath for him. When Dylan had a hangover (she never called it that; she always said he was 'sick with the 'flu', or something) she would take him bowls of bread and milk. Dylan adored bread and milk with salt on it (he had to have the salt); he thought that it was the cure for everything, and I had to administer it throughout our marriage. She fussed about every little detail, and I can't begin to imagine what she was like when he was a baby. Dylan got extremely irritated, and as soon as he possibly could he would head for the nearest pub. He didn't spend much time at home at all.

We usually went out in the morning and came back for some kind of lunch. Then we went to bed in the afternoon, together, and out again in the evening to the pubs. Dylan had a lot of Swansea friends. Actually, in the morning we didn't go straight to the pub but usually caught a bus into town, where all his friends used to congregate at the Kardomah coffee house, which they had all gone to in the days when Dylan worked on the *South Wales Evening Post*. There was Charlie Fisher, who was a smart-alec, much more dressed-up than the others, although not madly good-looking: very neat, dapper and chatty. He was rather despised because he had lots of ideas which never came off. Fred Janes was different. He was a simple, lovable man and Dylan was very fond of him. I liked him, too. The family had a greengrocer's shop and Fred spent quite a lot of his time there. He was a painter, specialising then in still-lifes of fishes, spending ages getting all the scales and fins just right. Dylan used to joke about Fred being so meticulous and hardly ever writing a letter, but he always talked about him affectionately. When Dylan first moved to London he shared various lodgings with Fred and Mervyn Levy, always living in stinking squalor in one room with none of them doing a thing about cleaning. Mervyn was always so full of himself; he was really funny, a true comic. Then there was Tom Warner, a musician and composer, who was always quiet.

Dan Jones was Dylan's special friend in Swansea: he and Fred Janes and Vernon Watkins were the close ones. Dan had a lot of character and personality. He looked like a stronger version of Dylan, a bit taller and more manly. He always made a big show of drinking, and he could be quite aggressive. I think he probably resented me because until Dylan met Vernon, and I came along, Dan had been Dylan's closest friend. Dan wrote a book *My Friend Dylan Thomas* (1977), and didn't mention my name once. I thought it strange. I don't know whether he had a personal dislike for me – if so, he never showed it – but I never got much into conversation with him, because he and Dylan were so busy together. They were like teenagers, hitting each other with rolled-up newspapers and playing all the old games they had played as children. It became very irritating for anyone looking on, especially for me as the only woman. Then Dan married Irene. I liked her. She was a classy girl with a great sense of fun. She drank, too. She was high-spirited and full of bounce. I think Dan was jealous of Dylan's success: he undoubtedly was, because, according to Dan, *he* was the superior one of that whole Swansea group. He had an extraordinary amount of knowledge on all kinds of subjects. He was a clever musician and an able composer, winning scholarships and travelling through Europe. He could write, too, but it never quite came off. He also knew a number of obscure languages, and he certainly thought the world of himself. Dan must have had a very good scholastic brain, but he didn't have the necessary sparkle or whatever is needed to write anything outstandingly creative. He was too concentrated on knowledge and too conceited. I believe one needs a lot of humility to develop creatively. This was where he and Dylan were so different. In many ways, Dan had the wider range of knowledge, but whatever Dylan had, he concealed: he never boasted. Dylan very rarely spoke about his poems to me or to anyone else; he didn't like talking about his work. He did occasionally open out to me, when he had finished a poem, perhaps, and he would come into the kitchen and boom it at me while I was doing the washing-up or the ironing, but that was all: he liked to keep that side of his life completely private.

The closest of all those Swansea friends was Vernon Watkins. I met Vernon on that first visit to Dylan's parents. We used to walk along the Gower to the house where Vernon lived with his mother. Mrs Watkins would serve us colossal teas with scones and cream and at least six delicious home-made cakes, all in a row on the table. Those teas were enough to feed you for a year. Then we would have a game of croquet and go down to the pub, where Dylan would try to get poor Vernon drunk; Vernon seldom drank and his tolerance was very low. Dylan used to delight in trying to take him over the edge – one of the nastier traits in his personality. Years later he would get Vernon crawling down the path to the Boat House on his hands and knees, while Dylan burst his guts laughing, although this was often his own way of getting home.

Apart from Henry Treece, who later based a book upon their conversations, Vernon was the only person to whom Dylan would talk about the different styles and techniques of poetry. He was suspiciously closed-up with Treece, but there was something in his relationship with Vernon that made Dylan open up; they had a real rapport. Yet at the same time I think the friendship was more important to Vernon than it ever was to Dylan.

When I first met Vernon I thought he might be gay; he did act in a feminine way. We were always rather curious about his sex life and surprised when he said he was getting married. We couldn't imagine that any girl would want to marry him because we didn't think him the least bit sexually attractive: he was thin and fey, with a high-pitched voice. He obviously adored Dylan and Dylan was fond of him, although he could be a bit condescending at times. With Vernon, it was hero-worship. Presumably, he saw something in Dylan that he hadn't got himself: he was a sensitive poet but his body of work was rather limited. I didn't imagine that he would ever be able to produce many really good poems, although he did manage one or two; according to Dylan the rest were rather pedestrian. His real strength was his criticism; he had all the understanding of technique to have become a major critic, if he had applied himself to it. I think Dylan recognised that quality in him, although sometimes he found it irksome.

Whenever we went to their house, the point would always come when Vernon would invite Dylan into his study to talk about poetry. Dylan found it something of an ordeal, and when the invitation came his eyes would roll skywards and he would give me a quick, fleeting glance before the study door closed behind them. Sometimes they would be gone for four or five hours, and Dylan would reappear almost squashed to the ground.

In spite of this, Dylan must have gained a certain good from those discussions. He must have learned a few things, too, because Vernon was much more educated than he was and had quite an extensive knowledge of European literature. They were quite harsh with each other in their criticism, which was good for Dylan, who would hardly listen to other poets in the same kind of way. While they talked, I resented being stuck with Vernon's mother. I would be glued to a chair, surrounded by cakes, while she rambled on. 'You can't go through the rest of your life being decorative, you know,' she used to tell me, obviously thinking that I, too, should be bustling around making cakes.

Dylan and Vernon kept a correspondence going for years, which is partly why I think the relationship was much more important to Vernon than it was to Dylan: Vernon kept most of the letters that he received, but Dylan kept none; he just dropped them into the wastepaper basket with the rest of his morning mail, and he always treated his own letters to Vernon as though they were a kind of duty. It was chiefly gratitude, because Vernon (who had a steady job with Lloyds Bank in Swansea and therefore a financial security which we never had) was always kind and generous to us when we had hardly any money. But Dylan could be condescending, too, because Vernon wasn't exactly his kind of friend: his closest friends were usually much more rumbustious, whereas Vernon was proper by instinct – very delicate and sensitive, and never a drinking man. 'Poor Vernon,' said Dylan to me, on more than one occasion, 'he knows a lot about poetry, but he writes pretty boring stuff . . .'

Dylan had a very strange sense of his own ability. He knew that with him words would suddenly spurt out without him having any idea where they had come from. Like most highly analytical people, Vernon lacked that magical quality. But I will say this for him, he was the best of friends. As Llewelyn's godfather he never failed to remember Christmas and birthdays; he never ignored Dylan's requests for money, which were often quite desperate, and although he had a special feeling for Dylan which was probably quite close to love, he was always very sweet and polite to me.

Dylan's other great friendship from the Swansea days was one that had little to do with the Kardomah, Dan Jones, Mervyn Levy

43

and the rest. It was a very strange relationship because the person concerned, Bert Trick, was a much older man. Dylan used to talk about him a lot. Bert Trick was a Communist who had thought his philosophy right through, who was keen on poetry but put his politics first. Of all the friends that Dylan had acquired in his Swansea days, Bert Trick was the one with mettle: he was tough, and it was through him that Dylan developed his hatred of Fascism. There was a period during the Spanish Civil War when Dylan seriously thought of going off to fight; that war caught his imagination far more than the Second World War ever did, and although he was a natural pacifist he saw the issues in Spain and strongly supported the Republican side. A lot of his friends went out there, and at one time Dylan thought quite seriously about joining the Communist Party (which he never did, mainly, I think, because he just wasn't the kind of man to join a political party).

These political views didn't come from his father. D. J. Thomas was an obscure man, the most unhappy man I have ever met, and it showed in his face. He was unhappy with his life. It was exactly the kind of life that he had hoped not to have, and by the end he could feel himself sinking back into the very existence that he had sought to escape. He practically never opened his mouth, and he was also maddened by Granny Thomas, who never stopped saying, 'Daddy this' or 'Daddy that' or 'Daddy likes his dinner'. She took the words out of his mouth. At first I thought what a miserable man his father was: a complete hypochondriac, always taking pills and medicines, hating the country he lived in, and occupied by the thought that he was made for much better posts than he had ever held, which he undoubtedly was. He was a fine teacher, apparently. They all said he was brilliant. English Literature was his subject. He had a very good collection of books and nearly always read in the evenings. All through his early years, poor old D.J. had been dying for the university life. He wanted very badly to go to Aberystwyth, and although he was good enough he felt that they had ignored him; he felt that he had had nothing but frightful blows throughout his life. Later, he became even more unhappy, moving to Laugharne. He felt that this was the final straw of degradation for him, and I don't blame him, either.

Although D.J. was always very polite to me, he never showed me any affection. He would never kiss me on the cheek or greet me warmly. He was much too reserved for that, completely self-controlled. As a family, they were very undemonstrative.

Dylan became closer to his father later in life. He had a deep admiration for him, although Dylan didn't talk about it a lot. He was very influenced by him, by his knowledge of Shakespeare and everything else. Dylan adored Dickens and Jane Austen, Hardy and Trollope, and so did his father. Dylan had always had that library to grow up on, and his parents used to say that Dylan could read by the age of three. Although I took that with a pinch of incredulity, I could see that Dylan had grown up with books, and to love books, in much the same way that I had. My mother also had a marvellous collection of books, with beautiful sets of Hardy, the whole of Jane Austen and Proust, all carefully arranged on shelves, and she always read aloud to us as children.

I think his parents must have been rather shocked by me, and certainly they disapproved of the way Dylan was living. After all, it was their son who had gone off to London and brought back this rather Bohemian dancer, and there I was, sleeping with him in their house. They didn't say anything to me; they didn't want to discuss intimate subjects. I think they were afraid to, perhaps, or too shy. The Welsh are very narrow. Dylan's mother was narrow in her whole outlook, but D.J. was quite a different proposition, and I began to appreciate him much more later on when I could see what an unhappy man he was.

D.J.'s reading went way beyond the classics. He knew his Shakespeare and his Milton, but he had read the latest poets as well and all the contemporary Welsh poets, and he thought highly of D. H. Lawrence at a time when Lawrence hadn't been fully accepted. His problem was that he had never had anyone to share these passions with, and one can imagine the pain he went through towards the end when he was living among all the philistines of Laugharne. He liked his drink, too, and Dylan told me that years before, as a younger man, D.J. had been a heavy drinker with a beer belly. He described his father as looking like a human beer barrel, and there were family tales of his coming home drunk, although I never saw him like that. The drink may have been the reason why his career never took off, although I don't know that for certain. Behind the neat façade of that Swansea suburban life there were many tensions. D.J.'s life was so dull that he had to drink – it was a valid reason.

In those early days of our marriage, when I first stayed at Bishopston, D.J. used to go out every night for a drink, although seldom for more than two or three pints. He was known around the pubs as 'The Professor'. Granny Thomas always used to say, 'I've never seen Daddy the worse for drink . . .' In point of fact, he was the worse for drink many times but she would never have seen it, and I think D.J. would have been careful not to get too drunk. There were tales of him waiting in Cwmdonkin Park until he had sobered up or she had gone to bed. He was very conventional and would never have wanted the neighbours to see him obviously drunk.

D.J. always kept his hat on, because he went completely bald at the age of twenty-six. He even went up to bed in his hat and always sat down to meals with it on. He used to avoid us like the plague, taking great care not to go to the pubs that he knew we went to. I think he thought we were going to make fools of ourselves and behave scandalously and God knows what, and he wasn't going to get involved in any of that Bohemian tomfoolery.

Dylan's father rarely laid down the law in the home, although Granny Thomas treated him as though he did so he may have been different when I wasn't around. I heard later that he had been quite a tyrant in his younger days, with a fine range of swear words, but that was a side of him that I never saw and which he may have been careful to keep hidden from me, for reasons of convention.

When I first went to Bishopston, it was Granny Thomas who kept lecturing Dylan about his drinking. Sometimes he used to come back on the bus from Swansea completely drunk, and she would tell him the obvious things – 'You are spending far too much', 'You are ruining your health', 'Spending all your money' – all the old clichés, which were true enough. Dylan didn't like that at all. When he married, she expected him to turn over a new leaf, she thought that I would save him, although she should have had more sense than that. Maybe she thought that I would start nagging him when we needed more money for the children, but I didn't want to become a nagging wife. We used to have huge rows, but never about drinking. I didn't want to row with him about little things, and anyway, I was hardly in a position to do so. The rows were always about his 'ladies'.

Granny Thomas never saw that side of him because we would never have that sort of row in front of her, and Dylan would never misbehave on his own doorstep, in Bishopston, or in Laugharne, or in front of the neighbours. They all thought that he was a proper little gentleman and that I was a trollop. I became the target for abuse in Laugharne because whatever I did could be seen as clear as daylight.

Dylan's sister Nancy was hardly ever there. I found her cold. She was in the respectable world, eight years older than he was. She looked like Dylan, her face, her hair, everything: a sort of polished-up Dylan. She was quite a pretty girl, but we had little in common. Before Dylan left for London, she had also been in the Swansea Little Theatre company and had been expected to become an actress. A lot of men were chasing her. I can't remember her first husband, Haydn Taylor, or why they divorced; they both seemed the same type, typically British, rather dumb, and I preferred her second husband, Gordon Summersby. They lived down in Devon, lobster-potting off Lundy Island. I saw another side of Nancy then, a more open-air, tomboyish side, but we never really got through to each other and never shared any confidences. Dylan always spoke badly of her, but I thought there must be *something* between them. He always said she lacked imagination and was a typical hockey-girl, and gave one to understand that it was he who had inherited all the beautiful, dream-like qualities that should have gone to her; but I don't believe that, either. There must have been more to Nancy than met the eye, being the daughter of the same parents; it couldn't have been all Dylan the bad boy and she the virtuous angel.

Nancy must have seen that her mother loved Dylan much more than she loved her daughter. She was spiteful to her mother and seemed ashamed of her insensitivity and lack of knowledge about how to treat people. She behaved towards her mother with an undisguised disdain, but she and D.J. were very fond of each other. They had much more in common, and would sit together in the evenings by a blazing fire with Nancy on a stool at his feet, reading, while we were roistering around the pubs. Nancy was very protective towards her father. She was conformist, and rather smart, dressing respectably without going in for ostentatious elegance.

Dylan's father hardly ever talked to Granny Thomas because he considered she knew nothing whatsoever about literature or anything intellectual. There was no exchange of ideas, and very little mental contact between them. In her youth, Granny Thomas had been very attractive. She came from a Welsh chapel background; her father had been a deacon. I did hear once that she and D.J. had had a passionate affair, and that they had to get married (though the baby died), but there was very little of that passion left when I knew them, and a total lack of intellectual contact. I don't think there was much of that between Dylan and me, really, because he had been brought up not to expect it; that wasn't what he was looking for, and he wasn't the least bit interested in what went on inside me. This was no surprise to me because I think all creative people are incredibly egotistical or they couldn't create (and I, incidentally, am quite as egotistical as any of the rest).

I came to realise as I knew D.J. better that he had a genuine love of literature and was proud of Dylan, too, though he would never admit it or give a word of praise to Dylan, who was doing exactly what he had wished to do but had never had the courage to try. D.J. had got half-way out of his peasant background and then seemed to falter and was never able to carry it through. I think he did write some poems, but Dylan used to say they were not great; they were just attempts. D.J. couldn't have made any actual blunders – he was too good a scholar – but I don't think that the creative thing was there. What interested me was his character.

All the acidity in the family came from his father; Dylan respected this a lot. At Swansea Grammar School, the boys were terrified of D.J. when he was in full cry; he used to lash out verbally at boys who might have moved or said something while he was talking, and the reaction would be out of all proportion to the offence. He would send them to hell or out of the room. He didn't apply any corporal punishment because he didn't need to: his words were like whipcord and the boys were petrified of him. He was a great teacher, too. He didn't have to apply authority because his mere presence was enough for them all to quail – even the worst boys, the hooligans and the ones who didn't give a damn about literature anyway. He had a very thin face, always wore glasses, and always kept that hat on, and yet he had a kind of distinction of his own. It was rather pathetic to think that anybody's ambition could be to want to be a gentleman, and yet that, for him, was always the first step, and Granny Thomas was always ruining it for him by being too enthusiastic, bursting out laughing at all the wrong times, and yakking away with her peasant friends.

The Rimbaud of Cwmdonkin Drive. Sent by Dylan to Pamela Hansford Johnson in 1933

Portrait of Dylan in 1934 by Alfred Janes

Augustus John in the 1920s

Portrait of Caitlin by Augustus John

Dylan and Caitlin at Blashford

Dylan in thoughtful mood at Blashford, 1937

D.J. never told *me* that he wanted to be a gentleman; Dylan told me. He said that in his father's eyes a true literary man was a gentleman with all the other accoutrements, like being discreetly well dressed, with his suit, his trilby, his umbrella and *The Times* under his arm. He certainly kept his distance as a gentleman would, and his manners were very formal. Occasionally when I was doing the washing-up, he would come along and do some drying-up, and I used to think how embarrassing it was for this perfect gentleman to be standing there with a tea-towel in his hand; I used to wish that he wouldn't do it because he really didn't fit the part at all and was obviously unhappy, talking to me about utterly unimportant things like the pattern on a plate just to be able to say something. We never got into any big literary conversation at all, apart from agreeing that Pamela Hansford Johnson was nil. Nobody gives praise more than I do when it's due, but it certainly wasn't due there, and D.J. could see this at once because he was so knowledgeable.

Apparently, to hear D.J. interpreting Shakespeare was one of the great experiences at Swansea Grammar School because he had a quite magnificent vocal range, quite as good as Dylan's, if not better. Talking about him still makes me cry; I don't know why. D.J. should not be someone to cry over, but in fact he is. He had nothing that was his own. It is sad to think how misplaced some people are when they have a great gift: he had so much hidden away inside him and he couldn't pass it on. He did pass it on to Dylan in a roundabout way, through ordinary talking, but even when he became proud of Dylan's achievements – as I know he was – he still couldn't bring himself to talk to me or anyone else about them.

Just a month or so before D.J. died, Dylan's *Collected Poems* were published and the critics hailed him as 'a genius', and 'the greatest living poet'. I am sure D.J. was proud of him, and yet at the same time it was a kind of thorn in his flesh because D.J. felt that all that fame should have gone to him – that his gifts didn't emerge until they came out in Dylan. It was a great satisfaction to him, of course, but it's not the same as doing it oneself. Poor old D.J. lived such a boring life, with only one or two friends to talk to, and then none at all when he ended up in Laugharne.

In those last years, the only thing he did outside his home was occasionally to walk down the hill to the Cross House for a couple of pints, and he only went there because he knew that we would either be in Brown's Hotel or the Corporation Arms. This was his only real pleasure, and while I think he quite enjoyed an argument with Phil Richards, the landlord at the Cross House, he couldn't make it very high-class or high-brow, as he would have wished. Since he couldn't, he tended to be a bit crotchety, not so much in what he said as in his outlook. Sometimes, when people come into a room, you feel they are overflowing with joy and love and you want to hug them. D.J. was the opposite of that, pushing people away; and yet my feelings for him grew.

I remember the other relatives whom we met on family occasions or when staying at Blaen Cwm in Llangain, where Dylan's aunts lived and where his parents moved during the war; all as provincial as his parents. There was Uncle Bob, who never said anything: he used to sit on a chair all day, and then sometimes he would get up, stretch his legs, walk out of the front door and sit on a wall, always with his hat on. There was Aunt Polly, who also had never married. She was like Granny Thomas, she never stopped talking. And then there was Aunt Dosie, the superior one, who thought she was more refined because she was the wife of Uncle Dai (the Rev. David Rees, Minister at the Paraclete Chapel). Dai was the one who told D.J. that Dylan ought to be locked up in the madhouse. Dylan tolerated them all, and wrote about them in his short stories, but he couldn't stand their company for more than five minutes.

Yet Dylan couldn't break away from them, either. They were the background from which he had sprung, and he needed that background all his life, like a tree needs roots. It was the cramped atmosphere that got me down: cramped houses and cramped attitudes. The parents' house at Bishopston was a tiny semi-detached house, three up and three down, with all the books packed into the front parlour, where the only people allowed in by D.J. were Dylan and Vernon. There was a room behind where we ate. As soon as we went in the door I had a feeling of excessive tidiness all around me. It's a good thing to be tidy, but this was too exaggerated. Granny Thomas couldn't walk past a surface without giving it a dust.

When we went there that first time, Dylan greeted his parents quite effusively, though he was always formal with his father, never kissing him on the cheek or putting his arms around him. That didn't surprise me. I was living among the English; it would have surprised me if he *had* kissed him. Granny Thomas would get a hug or a peck on the cheek, but it was just a formal shake of the hand for poor old D.J.

Over the years we spent quite long periods with the parents. Granny Thomas tried to make me feel at home by giving me little jobs to do – dusting and washing-up, or taking my turn with the carpet-sweeper. But I could never get really close to her. She wasn't outwardly disapproving, but both parents could see that I was a different kind of animal from those they had seen before. With me, nothing ever went together and, although I was very fussy about clothes and wanted beautiful clothes more than anything, I would just put on anything that I had at random, whereas Granny Thomas thought I ought to be wearing stockings, shoes and a handbag every time we caught the bus into Swansea.

They only began to appreciate me, I think, when I started having babies, and they saw what a lot of care I took. I don't think that they ever expected that a real mother would emerge from what their son had brought home, when in fact the mother-part of me was stronger than the Dylan-part, and they were a bit surprised by that. I remember overhearing Granny Thomas once, talking to her cronies when one of them was running me down: 'But she's very good with the children, mind. You can't take that away from her.' Granny Thomas really came into her own when the children were born: she was a great extrovert, whereas D.J. was an introvert – she was good with the children, especially Aeron, because that was her line.

4

Dylan was right about our innocence. That was what we had to share, and we didn't care what others thought. We were inseparable. Our families could see that. Most people could. And Dylan was very careful. He never said a word against me to anyone. His parents would never have dared to criticise: they knew Dylan adored me, and wouldn't have wanted to hurt his feelings. They saw us together all the time – a pair of lambkins.

Those first months after our marriage we spent with his parents at Bishopston, and then with my mother down at Blashford, where we lived for six months through the winter of 1937/38 before making our home in Laugharne.

My mother was so broad-minded; she accepted everything. The first time I took Dylan home to meet her, she quite liked him, I think; she found him polite and charming, but they didn't really get on and he didn't really like her, although he told me at first that he did. Of course, she wouldn't tell me what her reservations were, but I think she was sorry that he had no money. Those famous rich men who were going to marry her daughters had not appeared. Dylan suffered in that house, but he can't have suffered as much as I did when I went to his. He said he felt free and independent at Blashford; but there was always the money problem underneath it all, and my mother handing out the odd pound which she couldn't afford. It must have been difficult for him. I imagine he was swamped, with no other man in the place and all those women – it was the thing that practically drowned my brother John. They were all strong-minded, opinionated women; they weren't little docile mice. It got him down because he liked the company of men, for drinking and so forth.

Dylan had a room of his own to work in, and at first he worked quite well there, but he would get very morose if he wasn't writing. Usually it was the booze that stopped him, but sometimes he would try and the words wouldn't come. He would talk about books with my mother, but I don't think there was ever any kind of an understanding between them, because she used to make snappish, acid remarks. She probably found Dylan hard to take. She was used to having scruffy artists around so it wasn't so much that. No, she had hoped I would do better, although she never told me so in so many words; Dylan didn't quite come up to her ducal expectations.

My mother was casual in her manners. She would never try to get really close to anyone, but would just say polite things and drift away, unlike the Welsh, who want to know everything about you from the day you were born. She spoke to Dylan politely and kept it all on the surface. We stayed with her for quite long periods; six months that first autumn and winter and then the next two Christmases as well. We would ride our bicycles into the New Forest every day, to Bluebell Wood or Cuckoo Hill; and we'd spend hours walking. The marriage was young and fresh and Dylan was very sweet and nice. We were both about the same size, still not much more than seven stone, but I was much stronger than he was and could pick him up in both arms and carry him over the streams. He liked that, though it was all the wrong way round. I was being the man and he was quite happy to be the woman. In the evenings we would go down to the Ringwood pubs – usually the George, sometimes the White Hart or the Crown, which were all pretty dull.

In April 1938 we returned to Bishopston and then went to stay with Richard and Frances Hughes in Laugharne – Dylan was hoping that he would find a cottage there. We always thought that we would be better off in the country, in a romantic little place, by water. I always wanted water. I was crazy about the sea and the estuary. I liked swimming, cockling and stabbing for fish. I never got on with Hughes. He was very kind to us, to Dylan especially, but I found him an awfully artificial, affected man, and I couldn't stand the way he kept talking about his children as though he understood child psychology better than anyone had ever done: the success of *A High Wind in Jamaica* seemed to have gone to his head.

To be fair to him, it must have been an inconvenience to have us staying in Castle House. They were very good; they let us stay for a month or two until we found a small fisherman's cottage in Gosport Street with the unlikely name of Eros. But Hughes was so mean at table that he would only produce a bottle of wine if there was someone important dining with them. He would pour them a glass and then one for himself, and not offer a glass to us. It caused great resentment.

Castle House adjoined the grounds of the old Laugharne Castle, a romantic ruin with just its walls left standing. Up on the battlements there was a tiny one-roomed gazebo where Hughes sometimes wrote and where he also allowed Dylan to work. It was very pretty there, with a lovely view. I don't think those places are usually conducive to working or thinking about words, but it was there that Hughes wrote one of his better novels, *In Hazard*, and Dylan compiled the short stories in *Portrait of the Artist as a Young Dog*.

We had a stroke of luck there. One day we were both up in that little gazebo, which had windows looking out over the estuary, when we saw Hughes going down some steps into the bowels of the castle. We watched, and saw him return with a bottle of wine in his hand. Needless to say, as soon as he had gone we went down the steps to see what was there and found he had constructed his own private wine cellar. At first we were very careful, creeping down there when it was dark and taking the odd bottle. Hughes didn't seem to notice so we started taking risks and would come back sometimes with our arms full of bottles, laughing at the cheek of it all because Hughes had laid down some really good stuff.

One afternoon, Dylan was sitting in the gazebo, gently sipping wine in a slightly dreamy state, when Hughes came prancing across the castle yard: there was nowhere to put the bottle, so Dylan whisked it under his bum. There was no cushion; he just sat on it, whereupon Hughes, who always had a lot to say for himself, launched into one of his great tirades, with Dylan looking more and more uncomfortable as he started to drip. It looked as though he was peeing on the floor. Dylan had quite a scare, and when Hughes eventually went he quickly polished off the bottle. Then one day Hughes appeared, full of righteous indignation; he had been robbed; his best bottles had gone. We made horrified noises of sympathy, with Dylan saying, 'Now, who the hell could have done that?' Luckily for us, there were some Territorial Army soldiers camping nearby, and Hughes soon accepted that some of them must have raided his cellar during the night.

We disliked Eros intensely. It was a tiny two-bedroomed cottage with a ghastly little velvety parlour which I was supposed to clean with a feather duster, no bathroom and an outside lavatory. The only nice thing about it, like all the houses down that side of Gosport Street, was that it had a long, narrow back garden, almost down to the estuary. I used to go for a swim there when I felt in need of a bath, or when Dylan was working on the table in the parlour. In those days I wasn't as fanatical about washing as I am now. I think I must have got up in the morning and put my clothes on straight away, like most people do. I wouldn't dream of doing that now.

It was while we were living at that little cottage that Henry Treece first came down to stay with us. He had written to Dylan saying that he wanted to write a book about Dylan's poetry. At first Dylan was rather flattered and wrote him long explanatory letters, but that soon wore off. I didn't like Treece and Dylan came rather to despise him. 'That bloody Treece is coming down again; can't you get rid of him?' he would say, expecting me to protect his privacy. Dylan found Treece rather boring, always putting stodgy analytical questions of the kind which Dylan hated to answer: he never liked intellectualising, and when the book eventually appeared nearly ten years later, *Dylan Thomas: Dog Among the Fairies* (1949), it was just as dull as we thought it would be.

By then, Dylan had established himself as a poet of some importance. His first two volumes had been published – *18 Poems* (1934) and *Twenty-five Poems* (1936). His work was appearing regularly in the literary magazines of the period – *New Verse, Adelphi, Criterion, Contemporary Poetry and Prose, New English Weekly, Seven* and *Life and Letters Today*. He was being invited to give occasional readings, and several of the older-established writers were taking an interest in his work, although he didn't talk very much about these aspects of the career that he was carving out for himself. We lived on hope most of the time; often he would only get £2–£3 for a poem that might have taken him weeks to perfect.

Dylan hadn't got his life mapped out by any means. He wanted to write, and knew that that was all he could do. Being a poet for him was working; it never occurred to him that he may have been forsaking some other form of work to be a poet. He did not want a humdrum job in an office: he told me that it would be much too boring, and made out that he despised people who clocked into jobs every day, taking the Tube backwards and forwards. He spoke about them with real contempt, saying how miserable their lives were: not miserable in the sense of being unhappy, but wretched, whereas ours might be penniless but it had a purpose. When he had money, he would always give me some; he was never stingy, just careless. Any money of his own went on drink and this was something that he never regretted; it was his life-blood, and Dylan genuinely believed that the drinking life was the best way to live.

I don't think he was ever totally honest, even with me. His way of impressing people was to invent things. When we first met, he invented a lot of whimsical fantasies about himself which I didn't take in much. Because it was Dylan I was very tolerant. To me, he was so endearing, lovable and comforting that I could overlook this unreality, but I think many people were deceived by the stories he told. He was always careful with his fantasies; there was cunning as well. He chose his targets, and he was never a name-dropper. Dylan was totally classless, and he got on just as well with the grand, snobbish people (whom I disliked) as he did with the oafs of Laugharne.

We went a few times to the parties that Edith Sitwell used to arrange at the Sesame Club. He didn't tell me at first that she had taken him up in a big way and had defended him against his critics in the *Sunday Times*. Dylan was wary of her when they met but he soon got round her, and she was very fond of him. It became a human relationship, and although he didn't think much of her poems he always managed to talk about them in a nice way. Eventually, I think he may have started having the kind of conversations with her that he had with Vernon, although I can't say that with certainty because Dylan seldom repeated that kind of conversation – it was a very private side of his life.

To begin with, he was always on his best behaviour with Edith, but then he became more relaxed with her, although she would never have seen the Dylan that his pub friends knew because he kept all those different sides of his personality in separate boxes, for separate occasions and friendships. That pub personality of his was like a mask, a clown's mask, and I think he needed it and maintained it so that he could preserve his privacy, and avoid talking about the things that really mattered to him. Basically he was, as I was, a born egotist, and very selfish. I don't mean that in any material sense – he would share anything he had, always – but he wouldn't share his real self with anyone, and that is the mark of the supreme artist.

Edith Sitwell was quite extraordinary, dressed in turbans and bangles and long oriental gowns – a grand eccentric. At her lunch parties she would usually have a guest of honour like T. S. Eliot or Marianne Moore, and she introduced Dylan to all these people. Eliot was kind to Dylan. He was dignified, a bit pompous, very courteous. (He had once been in the audience for one of my eurhythmic dances, and I was told afterwards that he sat there looking at his feet and never said a word.) Osbert and Sacheverell Sitwell were sometimes there as well. This was a world that I hadn't come across before; I knew the artists, but not the poets. I was a bit intimidated when Edith Sitwell gave us those minute glasses of sherry; and I never ate much on those occasions – I was too paralysed with fright.

Dylan admired Eliot, but it wasn't his kind of poetry. He told me he thought Eliot was much too materialistic, and that as a man he found him rather stiff. Dylan also admired W. H. Auden, but he didn't like him, either, and he couldn't stand Geoffrey Grigson.

We would meet all these people when we went up to London, but at that time Dylan was anxious not to make his home there. He had already discovered that London held too many distractions. He could meet editors there and be introduced to visiting writers like Henry Miller or Lawrence Durrell, but he couldn't settle down to write. For that he had to be in Laugharne, where we soon found ourselves a much grander house, Sea View, at the higher end of town, also overlooking the estuary and just a minute or two's walk from the Hughes'. It was a tall, dignified, cream-washed house of fairly odd proportions (when Augustus came to see us, he said it looked just like a doll's house), and we rented it for 7s 6d a week. Our landlord there was Tudor Williams, brother of Ebie of Brown's Hotel.

We immediately liked Sea View; it was much more friendly. To begin with we only used two rooms, the kitchen and the room above, but there were another six or seven rooms as well. We bought ourselves a very nice, large double bed on the instalment system, religiously putting aside seven shillings a week in our tea caddy. We made the first payments, but then we started drinking them instead. After we had had every kind of warning in the post some little black-beetle men came and took away the bed. We didn't mind all that much because we still had the mattress. It wasn't the sort of thing that upset Dylan; he laughed – but we didn't buy anything else on HP. Then we had a bit of luck when one of my aunts, my mother's sister Suzette, died. My mother sent all her furniture down to us. Suzette had married Roger de Cassilis, but he left her as husbands will (apparently he thought he was much too grand for her), and she went to live with my mother. They had spent some years out in Africa, and the furniture that was sent down included some nice cane chairs and so forth. In the end we were able to furnish Sea View quite nicely – my mother sent us pretty well everything we needed.

We settled down to a simple, domesticated life, and I think Dylan was fairly content with that. Vernon came to stay with us sometimes, and he said later that this was the happiest period of our lives together. I think he was right.

Dylan liked the domestic life, not that he would ever do anything himself. I discovered that even though I had always thought I had no housewifely gifts whatsoever, I couldn't bear squalor or dirty things being left around the house, so our life fell into a comfortable rhythm, with Dylan going off to see Ivy Williams at Brown's every morning and then working through the afternoon, and me looking after the home and Llewelyn (who was born a few months later). In the evenings Dylan would return to Brown's without fail, seldom paying, usually getting his beer on tick. Throughout the whole of our marriage he never spent a single evening at home, not one. When Vernon gave us a radio, Dylan would always follow the cricket scores (he was a great cricket enthusiast), but he never allowed this to interfere with his drinking, and he hadn't the patience to settle down and listen to a concert or a play. Later in the evenings, around seven o'clock, I would join him at Brown's. (We had a little girl who came in during the evenings to give Llewelyn his bottle.)

Although we had very little money, we seemed to live quite well, most of the time. Occasionally Dylan would sell a poem or a short story; sometimes my mother would send us a little money, and Vernon was very kind, but mostly we lived on credit. There was a very good butcher, Mr Gleed, who would always let me have huge piles of bones for our broth. All the other shops gave us credit, too. Periodically we would get a large cheque or one of our patrons would come down and help us pay off the debts – it was to become the pattern of our lives. We never starved. I had a huge black cooking range with hobs on top, which was very nice and homely when it was going well on coke or anthracite. We had a huge black iron cooking pot that was permanently full of broth. I would chuck in everything I could find – turnips, carrots, potatoes and leeks; those butcher's bones – and it would simmer gently from one week's end to the next, sometimes going a rather nasty shade of blue.

Every Wednesday we put on our best clothes and caught the bus into Carmarthen for the market. This was where I got all our china, blankets, and nice clothes for Llewelyn. It wasn't all that cheap, but I liked the atmosphere of market day, all the colours and the people pushing and bustling. We would go in together, and then meet up again at the Whore's Bed (as the Boar's Head was known to everyone in the town). It was always a good day because on the market day the pubs of Carmarthen stay open all day. By the time I met up with Dylan again, he was always at the centre of a crowd; within two minutes he seemed to know everyone in the pub, often farmers and tradesmen that he had met some other market day and who now knew him.

In those early days of our marriage, Dylan was much simpler and more straightforward; we were more in harmony and there were none of the rows that we had towards the end. He liked our simple routine – it was very important to him – and he particularly liked his friendship with Ivy Williams, who ran Brown's Hotel with her husband Ebie. (Her sister married Billy, who was the most jolly of the Williams brothers.) I don't know where Ivy came from originally, but she was always talking about her 'Deddy' being a sea captain. Dylan adored her: they both loved gossip and scandal; they would spend the whole morning in her kitchen talking about the awful things people were doing, who was sleeping with whom, who had been fighting or poaching or up in court.

Ivy thought Dylan was a painted saint who could do no wrong. She had no idea how he behaved when he was away from Laugharne; to her he was always the perfect little gentleman. In later years she would have all my crimes lined up to tell him when he returned; that I had been to bed with so-and-so and was carrying

59

on, and so on. Dylan just rose above it and said, 'That's absolute nonsense; my wife would never do that,' and left it at that. He deliberately blinded himself: he must have known there was some truth in it. I've always found that what the Welsh don't want to see, they don't see.

One time Dylan went up to London for a few days to meet Henry Miller, whom he described to Vernon as a dear mad mild man, bald and fifty with great enthusiasm for commonplaces. I was prejudiced against Miller for writing all that filth – I don't like that kind of thing – but Dylan loved what he called 'good fucking books', and brought some back for Ivy, really dirty stuff that Miller had had published in Paris. She hid them in the oven so that Ebie wouldn't find them. Ebie would have been livid, because he could be terribly jealous.

Dylan couldn't keep away from London. It was as important to him in one way as Laugharne was in another, and yet he could write to Vernon:

> I've just come back from three dark days in London, city of the restless dead. It really is an insane city, & filled me with terror. Every pavement drills through your soles to your scalp, and out pops a lamp-post covered with hair. I'm not going to London again for years; its intelligentsia is so hurried in the head that nothing stays there; its glamour smells of goat; there's no difference between good & bad.

I quote that letter because that was how Dylan always spoke to me; London was an ordeal that he had to go through; he didn't want to go; it was a pain that he had to endure because it was only by going to London that he could sell his work and make some money. At first I believed it – but then he started coming back penniless and in a bad physical state, completely laid out with booze, having usually spent a few days with Norman Cameron, who was a great friend of his at that time. Dylan had a great respect for Norman as a poet (although I didn't think he was half as great as Dylan made out). Although he once brought a glamorous-looking girl down to stay in Laugharne, I thought he was probably homosexual. It seemed to me that he had too much of a passion for Dylan, and that Dylan was cowed by him. One day, when I was in London as well, he invited us both to lunch at Simpsons, and then didn't say one single word to me throughout the meal. I couldn't forgive him for that.

In those days I didn't worry when Dylan went away for a few days. I accepted that drinking with his buddies was an essential part of his life and it didn't upset me too much. Also, shortly before we moved from Eros to Sea View I found myself pregnant, which was totally unexpected. It gave me an enormous sense of calm. I felt as placid as a cow – most unlike me – and absolutely unworried by material things, except that I was a bit anxious about getting the baby's nappies and clothes. As it happened, I didn't have to do much about that myself; soon gifts came rolling in from friends and family. I hardly felt morning sickness because I was so used to hangovers.

We stayed with my mother at Blashford over Christmas of 1938 and during the weeks before the baby was born. No one had prepared me for the mechanics of childbirth. I had no idea how appalling the pain would be. I went into Poole General Hospital, where I was in labour for forty-eight hours before Llewelyn was born. I had a frightful time and was terribly shocked, and afterwards I felt stripped of all my flesh, like Christ crucified. How I survived I shall never know. I had had no instruction on what one was supposed to do and I kept screaming for anaesthetic. They put some wretched little thing under my nose, but it didn't make the slightest bit of difference. The people in the wards said they had never in their lives heard anyone scream like I did, but I was in agony. The nurses kept coming in to say, 'Push down, push,' and I kept squeezing back. I thought, 'My God! I'll shit the bed if I push down!' It was grotesque. The nurses were horribly brutal: they kept telling me to 'Stop that awful noise,' and said that I was disturbing the ward.

Dylan wasn't present at the birth of any of his children; some men can't face it and I don't think he could, and I wouldn't have wanted him there, watching me writhe and scream. The baby was very small, just over six pounds, and I chose the names myself – Llewelyn because I liked the sound of it and Edouard after my French grandfather. For the first fortnight my mother brought in an old nanny, who had worked for her before and knew all about babies, and she saved my life because she looked after Llewelyn beautifully and showed me how everything should be done.

Dylan was nowhere to be seen the night the baby was born, and I am absolutely convinced that he spent the night with a girl we had nicknamed Joey the Ravisher. She had gone to the dancing school with me and I was very much aware of her at the time. She was an ostentatiously flashy piece of goods, tall and glamorous. Dylan had always lusted after tall women. When I saw them together I could see that there was a smell of passion between them, and when I heard that he had disappeared while I was in hospital I realised at once where he had gone. It didn't distress me then, because I was totally preoccupied with having the baby, and afterwards I was so happy to have Llewelyn after having had such a frightful time. But when I thought about it later, I realised that was where he had been, because I knew he was seeing her on his visits to London. It gave me my first feelings of jealousy. He didn't come to see me in hosptial, and I don't think I saw him again until I was back home with my mother. Nor did he bring me flowers (Dylan would never think of flowers): Llewelyn was the gift.

Everyone thought that Llewelyn looked like a wizened old man; he had practically no hair and looked a bit like Dylan's father. He was like a piece of raw meat, very red, and I could see that he wasn't beautiful, but my God, he was to me – I thought he was the most wonderful object on earth. Dylan called him 'the Mongolian monkey'.

I didn't see many signs of pride or joy in Dylan. He looked upon the baby, as many fathers do, as a rival; I was quite conscious of that. Dylan was jealous of the attention the baby was getting, and I could see when he first saw the baby that he didn't want to gaze at him or touch him, and he never dreamt of picking him up. (That may have been my fault; I wanted Llewelyn entirely to myself and didn't want to share him with anyone; had Dylan been more loving with him I think I would have been jealous myself, but there was never any danger of that.) It was the old, classic thing of the husband feeling pushed into the background. At first Dylan was everything and now the baby was everything. He must have felt it very strongly because he started behaving extra badly, going with other women flagrantly, but at the time I was so engrossed with the baby that I didn't care, and I thought, 'He can bloody well go to bed with whoever he likes,' because I much preferred the baby. Loving the baby was the strongest feeling I had ever had (Caspar apart), a much stronger feeling than going with a man. I should have been more tactful with Dylan, I suppose, but I did look on him as rather a nuisance when he came into the house, and I had all this paraphernalia for the baby, all laid out beautifully by mother's blissful old nanny.

I really adored Llewelyn. I didn't spend every minute of the day with him, because the nanny had taught me a rigid discipline: put them down for four hours, get them up, feed them, and don't pick them up like gypsies, up and down all the time. I had trouble getting him to take the nipple because my breasts got like two little crystal balls; they were so hard you could tap them like marble before the milk came through. I thought it was the most marvellous thing in the world, suckling a baby; I became terribly sentimental, which I had never been before.

I was afraid to stop breast-feeding because I had no idea what to give Llewelyn to eat when it came to the next stage; I didn't like to ask people because it seemed such disgraceful ignorance – I thought I ought to know – so for a time I gave Llewelyn only cow's milk diluted with water (and was told afterwards that that was the last thing I should have done). For a long time I just used to give him two rusks soaked in boiled water with a little brown sugar, which he seemed to like, and I can remember once giving him beetroot, which was certainly not the right food for a baby. I boiled it and mashed it up – and then his shit came out all pink. I thought I had poisoned him, but he survived.

Dylan's reaction to the birth of Llewelyn didn't surprise me very much because I had already come to realise that in many ways he was immature, acting like a child without thinking of the consequences. In fact he was always like a child, even in bed – to me, a most gifted child.

In bed, it was like embracing a child rather than a man; he felt so young and tender, so soft and sweet. He wasn't aggressive in a masculine sense; he wasn't strong enough. He was able to make love; he functioned, but I can't remember much about it because it didn't make much impression on me: somehow, the actual fucking didn't touch me. His sweetness and kindness and lovableness was child-like and that was how I loved him. I don't think I ever felt as you are supposed to feel with a man, that he dominates you; he never gave me that surrendering feeling at all, and yet I had the old-fashioned idea that the man dominates and the woman surrenders. With us, it was the other way round.

But I loved Dylan, even though I never felt that he was a full-grown man. (When I went to bed with other men, they were always big, strong and masculine men, but I didn't come with them either – it would have been more logical if I had.) I wasn't living with Dylan and going to bed with him for a sexual reason, I suppose. I think it was love. It was a strange relationship because our minds were certainly not the same. When he went off with other women, I think he must have done his stuff, but he can't have satisfied them very much unless they were very clever women and were able to handle him better than I could: I never went in for any of that refinement – I always waited for the man to make love to me.

Though Dylan was precocious in many ways, he had not had much sexual experience; he appeared timid and inhibited, depending on how many drinks he'd had (I don't think we ever made love without having a lot to drink first), and he had an almost juvenile approach to sex. I noticed that this kept cropping up in his early poems and short stories, often unnecessarily, with constant allusions to 'French letters' in his own correspondence. I rather blame myself for this ignorance about sex. Had he been with a really knowledgeable woman before me, perhaps it would have been better, but we were both much too innocent. I don't know if it worried him very seriously, for he was certainly interested in all the primal sexual instincts. I think he wanted a full sexual relationship, but he didn't know how to make the woman want it. I don't think he was neurotic about it because I would have felt that, and perhaps I should have said more. I was very embarrassed to talk about sexual matters; that was why I always took so much to drink before going to bed with a man, and I was like that with him. I should have had a little more education, I suppose. I wanted the sex but it never seemed to come right, or at the right moment, and I put the blame chiefly on my own embarrassment. I never felt able to discuss this with anyone and Dylan and I never discussed our own sexual relationship. It wasn't a forbidden subject; we would talk about other people's sex lives, but never ours. On my part, it was shyness, and I think Dylan may have been too much under his mother's influence; as I've said, she used to treat him as a child right until the time he married me, giving him sweets, preparing his bath for him, fussing over his clothes and his underwear, making him his bread and milk when he said he didn't feel well, and cuddling him for years longer than most mothers do. I think that may have had a lot to do with it.

But there are many things about Dylan that are hard to explain. It is strange that a full-grown man should have wanted baby comforts so much and should have been so lacking in sexual drive, and yet he had an innate wisdom that is rarely given to any man. How can one explain that? He may have intellectualised it all too much in his writing; for him, *his* world became the real world. I think he glorified sex and made it more powerful than it really was. Often men who are obsessed by sex are not very good at it because it's a thing in the mind, the obsession: those who are very potent don't have to be obsessed. They just do it, and then forget about it and smoke a fag. Ours was a more harmonious relationship, then, because we were close in other ways: we touched each other, we clung together and were very close. But Dylan didn't have whatever was needed to arrive at that ecstatic stage one is supposed to achieve with orgasms, and I didn't even know what an orgasm was. Yet I was aware that there was something missing, not only in the marriage but in my life.

5

Looking back now through the mists of nearly half a century, I can
see that Vernon was right: those two years we spent at Sea View
were the happiest period of our life together. It was also the simplest
part of our life. We didn't seem to be overwhelmed or cluttered
up with too many debts, and even when the bailiff's beetles had
come to take the bed away, we were able to laugh: Dylan laughed
a lot and I laughed too, then, although I haven't laughed much
since.

One is never really aware of happiness at the time; at least, I'm
not: the only times I think about it are in retrospect – 'I was happy
then,' or, 'I was happy there.' My trouble is that I don't feel things
spontaneously, but I realise now that we were having a pretty good
life, and the happiest time of all came when Llewelyn was born. I
always had a sense of wonder with my babies, owing to the fact,
I now believe, that I'd never had a good sexual relationship; my
happiness came from the children.

The sexual side of our marriage was still important to me, and
not having a climax was rather sad, but I didn't know enough about
love-making then to bring it off. I think it was because of this
deficiency that I was so happy when Llewelyn was born; he was a
real climax in himself – a tremendous sense of fulfilment and
happiness. I felt that this was my real best self, particularly when I
was cuddling and looking after him – an overpowering sense of
love which I had not experienced before with a man. I was in love
with Dylan, but it wasn't one of those knock-out feelings, and it
was hardly a marriage of minds because he was much more

intellectual than I was, although he used to read to me and I read, too. I wasn't a complete cretin.

Late at night, when we hadn't had too much to drink, he would read to me in bed before going to sleep; not much Shakespeare (that was too heavy-going), but extracts from Dickens (for whom Dylan had a passion), T. F. Powys, Hardy, Thackeray and Lawrence. I enjoyed this because Dylan read so gently; he never boomed out loud when he was reading to me, and he read very well.

Vernon came to stay with us one weekend, and Dylan was very thrilled because he recited some poems by W. B. Yeats that had been printed in the *London Mercury* after Yeats' death; the poems were 'Lapis Lazuli', 'The Statues', 'Long-Legged Fly' and 'News from the Delphic Oracle'.

By then, Dylan had a clearly defined idea of what he liked and what he didn't like; the kind of poems or stories that he read to me in bed, or would recite with Vernon, sitting perched on the castle walls by the gazebo, were the ones that he later used in his American lecture tours: extracts from those authors that I've mentioned and also Auden, Spender, Hart Crane, Henry Miller, and especially *Nightwood* by Djuna Barnes, which he raved about, arguing that this was the finest work of literature ever written by a woman.

By now I was beginning to realise that underneath all the external flamboyance, Dylan was a fairly conventional man. He'd had a lot of rules bred into him in childhood, and he liked all the traditional highlights of a year – Christmas and birthdays. I don't think we ever had a Christmas at home; they were always spent with the parents, so we never got round to anything as ambitious as roasting a turkey, but wherever we were, I had to look after the tree, stockings had to be hung the night before, and special presents opened at breakfast: he liked all that paraphernalia.

In so many ways, other than sexual, Dylan was like a big baby. He was used to being waited on, and never thought of doing anything for himself. Much of his life was an act, like pretending to be sick. He always made out that he was terribly delicate, and had this myth about being tubercular (which many people believed), but in point of fact he must have been jolly tough to survive all he went through; the only times he ever went to a doctor were for bone-setting after he'd broken an arm or a collarbone. (He had incredibly brittle bones.) In the mornings, he would have these coughing fits when he was always trying to cough up blood to convince me that he really had something serious; but I never saw it, and always scoffed at him for being a hypochondriac. He was perfectly all right, just lazy. It was partly attention-seeking; all that he really had wrong with him was damage caused by drink and smoking, and even that he exaggerated, though it may have caused all that coughing. He was constantly smoking – Woodbines, because they were cheapest. If he was talking to someone in Brown's, Dylan would rarely take his cigarette out of his mouth; he just left it hanging there.

Dylan had a romantic view of the poet as a rebel; it was a very conventional perception and an old-fashioned one, almost nineteenth-century. He often used to talk about Keats and he may have been measuring himself against him, in their stature as poets, and in the idea of an early death, which just fitted in with his legend. Dylan had this rather odd view that all the best poets died young and that he himself would never make forty, and there were times when he almost seemed to live his life by that. But at the same time there were all those other contradictions; he was such an old-fashioned man, believing in old-fashioned things about the rules of the house, the way the children should be brought up, and that the wife's position should be either at the sink or in bed.

I was firmer with him than Granny Thomas had been; she had treated him like a baby all his life. I still hugged and kissed him in bed, but I didn't make as much fuss of him as she had. I used to hold him in my arms and cradle him, wrap him up and keep him warm, pile sweaters on him, one on top of the other. Dylan would put on a sweater if he had to, but he preferred to have someone put it on for him, and he was like his father in that he had to have his slippers laid out by the armchair in the evening, when he'd finished writing for the day or when he came back home from Brown's. He did follow in his father's footsteps in those little ways. He was very fond of his creature comforts – sitting next to the fire in an armchair, reading, newspapers mostly or detective stories, with plates of savoury titbits to pick at. In the summer months, he would sit listening to the radio, following the cricket scores. He was passionate about cricket, and although he could seldom get to a match because the grounds were too far away, he would follow all the games on the radio and fancied himself as a fast bowler. He always listened to John Arlott's commentaries (because he liked Arlott, who was also a poet and became a close friend), and took it all very seriously, insisting that nobody disturbed him. I always had to keep well out of the way when there was a Test Match on.

I can't say that my sexual life with Dylan was unimportant because it was always important to me to have a good relationship with him, but something wasn't right. He may not have been a good lover, and maybe I wasn't either; it does take two. I don't want to suggest that he was impotent or anything like that, or that because he was a hard drinker he was incapable of making love. Many hard drinkers are incapable of making love, but it was not the case with Dylan.

There were suggestions that he might have had homosexual relationships with Max Chapman and Oswell Blakeston, but I think it highly unlikely. At the time it did faintly worry me because he was effeminate, in some ways, but I would have thought that of his male relationships that with Norman Cameron was much more likely to have been homosexual. I don't think they went to bed together, but nevertheless they had some kind of relationship, and when they were together they were always talking familiarly about things I didn't understand. I don't think Dylan was ever a practising homosexual; when he talked about homosexuality, he always said how much the physical side of it revolted him, and I think he probably talked about that too much. If he had had homosexual relationships, they would have been occasional or under protest; they certainly hadn't become a habit. I don't think he was ever buggered. He was both randy and soft, and it was hard to separate the two, but when he was being chased sexually, in London as well as in America, it was always by women, not men.

These sexual doubts were never a problem in our marriage in those early Laugharne years, partly, I think, because Dylan didn't know what he wanted any more than I did. We would spend hours together, mapping out our plans for the future, and Dylan would paint very romantic pictures of our life together. We were going to live by the sea in faraway places where the sun always shone – Spain, or one of those other cheap, sunny countries – and we were so far removed from the rest of the world that the growing threat of war in Europe hardly seemed to touch us. Life in Laugharne went on in its own eccentric way, and it was only when our friends there started getting called up and appearing in uniform that the war seemed to get close.

★

We didn't know it then, but the life that we had made for ourselves was coming to an end. Dylan was still working to his old routine: Brown's in the morning, where Ivy allowed him more tick than she ever allowed anyone else, and writing during the afternoons. Dylan was pleased when *Portrait of the Artist as a Young Dog* came out, but he didn't show much excitement. He looked upon it as a lesser work than the poetry; he didn't regard his prose as being as important. After that he worked on *The Map of Love*, but that was a disaster. The book was published just ten days before war was declared, and got completely lost in the confusion. Only 280 copies were sold by the publishers. I hated *The Map of Love* and told Dylan so. He had put short stories and poems together in one book, which was a mistake, and I couldn't bear the kind of story he wrote in that book; he got so muddled up with surrealism and pornography – I didn't like it at all. His poems had become much too complicated. I liked his short, passionate poems like 'And Death Shall Have No Dominion' or 'The Force That Through the Green Fuse Drives the Flower'; those real, pounding poems. Sometimes he would read those to me, but never the short stories. I don't think that his short stories are all that good, although I liked 'Extraordinary Little Cough' and 'A Visit to Grandpa's'.

I did tell him time and again that he was making his work too complicated, piling on too many words. Sometimes he made his poems completely unintelligible, and he'd joke afterwards that he couldn't understand them himself. If I said something like that, Dylan would always listen. He didn't mind my criticism, and occasionally he would ask me which alternative word I thought was better, or what other word could be used in a certain line – small things like that.

His writing changed a lot after we met. Many of those early poems were largely taken from ideas that he had developed in his teens and then stored away in his notebooks. He had quite a long period in Laugharne when he concentrated more on the short stories, but then he put the notebooks behind him, psychologically. A serenity came, and out of it, simplicity and beauty. I was never one for only beauty; it was another thing I distrusted. I thought truth was the important thing. I always told him that truth was so much more interesting. It was always one of my principles and passions: to speak it on all occasions, however painful.

Time was running out for us. The war was getting nearer and

nearer; the literary magazines that Dylan had written for were closing, and we were more in debt than ever. The shopkeepers and Ivy had all been very good to us in Laugharne, allowing us far more credit than they really should have done, but everyone wants to be paid eventually, and so did they. Dylan begged money from friends, and tried (and failed) to get a grant from the Royal Literary Fund. Many people tried to help us, but I won't go through all that again because it's all documented in the *Collected Letters* (1985), but we just couldn't go on as we were.

And then there was the war itself.

Dylan's politics had always been on the far Left. Through that friendship with Bert Trick he had seriously considered joining the Communist Party at one stage, but, for some reason that I still can't understand, he never saw the Second World War in political terms. Dylan's philosophy was really that of the man who sympathises with the poor and downtrodden and looks to the Left for an answer; it didn't go far beyond that, and he never read any of the political books of the time. In one of his letters he wrote, 'What are you doing for your country? I'm letting mine rot.' But that was just Dylan trying to come up with the clever phrase that would rock the reader back on his heels; he often did that, just to shock people.

The truth of it was that he hated the thought of war. The whole idea was an abomination to him.

Dylan was a very gentle man with quite enough fears of his own. He had an absolute horror of mice and rodents, and went hysterical at the sight of them. If he heard just the scraping of mice behind the skirting boards in the bedroom he became mad with terror (and we couldn't have cats because he didn't like those either). He hated moths and bats, and believed all those stories of bats getting in your hair and sucking your blood. There used to be bats in Laugharne and if he saw one as he was walking home from Brown's, he would run down the street in terror with his hands over his head; they were his paramount horror. Yet he would never have been able to bring himself to kill a mouse or a bat. He was the total pacifist.

Early in the war, Dylan thought of registering as a conscientious objector, but he dropped that idea after going to sit in the public gallery at an objectors' tribunal in Carmarthen: they were mean little chapel men, refusing to fight for all the wrong reasons, and he preferred the company of the real, natural fighting men to the pacifists. Later, he thought briefly of trying to join Victor Cazalet's anti-aircraft battery (which seemed to be a way of joining the army without having to leave the country). He even got to the point of going for an army medical at Llandeilo, but that was very much the second-best option. His first choice was not to sign up at all. The night before the medical, he drank himself silly in Brown's Hotel, mixing beer with sherry, whisky and gin, deliberately trying to give himself a hangover. The next morning he came out in spots, and was shaking and coughing his guts up. At one stage, he even fainted. They classified him C3, right down at the bottom of the list.

Dylan was delighted: 'I've done it; I've done it; I've got away with it,' he said excitedly when he got back to Laugharne, and he got drunk again that night to celebrate it. Many of his friends were envious and kept asking him how he managed it, because they also wanted to avoid going into the Services. Whenever he described what he had done to himself it sounded pitifully painful, and for years afterwards that was one of his pub stories.

There was more to it than that. Dylan wasn't just a coward, although he could be weak at times. He had a total lack of hatred, and couldn't share the feelings that people had at the time. He didn't believe in all those false heroics, patriotism and all that nonsense. He thought there was nothing glorious about war, and he couldn't bring himself to write poems about its causes or its purpose. To him no one country was better than another: all men were equal, regardless of race or religion, and he recognised no boundaries between people. He bore no enmity against people because they were black or because they were German. The whole notion of war was ridiculous to him, and he told me that he would never ever, under any circumstances, kill a human being; he took very little interest in the course of the war, and had hardly any respect for Churchill or any of the other war leaders; he appeared totally unmoved by it all; he had too great a sense of eternity to contemplate such minor things. Yet he found it hard to write during the war, particularly the early part, and by the time it was ended, his whole attitude had changed. He had put nearly all his earlier work behind him, and in its place there was a serenity and a confidence that had never been there before, and which was evident throughout *Deaths and Entrances* (1946).

Our trouble in Laugharne was that we couldn't go on as we were without any income; we had run out of credit and were being threatened with writs of every kind. In May 1940, we went to stay with Dylan's parents at Bishopston to avoid the daily evasion of creditors. (Stephen Spender helped us to raise the £100 we needed to pay them all off.) Then, in the July, we left Sea View for Marshfield, and didn't return to Laugharne to live until 1949.

This strange interlude came about through Dylan's friendship with John Davenport, who was another of those men like Dan Jones; he had been brilliant at school and was a highly accomplished critic, but he could never bring off a book of his own; he didn't have that little extra spark. Davenport had inherited a large sum of money, had bought a very fine house, The Maltings, at Marshfield, a small town in Gloucestershire, and had invited various friends in the arts – writers, painters and musicians – to join him there to escape the first bombing raids on London. It was a very odd set-up, with Davenport playing the *grand seigneur*, a role which he carried off rather well because he was an imposing figure; he wasn't very tall, but was enormously fat, and also enormously snobbish.

Among the other people staying there that summer were Benjamin Britten, Antonia White, William Glock and Lennox Berkeley. They were all quiet, civilised people, and although there were a lot of affairs going on it was all very discreet. Quite a lot of pubbing went on in the mornings; in the afternoons we would all do our own things, and then we'd all get pretty jolly over dinner, finishing off the cellar that Davenport had accumulated during the pre-war years. In spite of the wartime restrictions, we ate very well and always had wine with our dinner, and port and brandy afterwards.

At times, the war seemed very far away, but some nights we would hear enemy planes going over. Dylan was terrified and would immediately put his head down the bottom of the bed, underneath the sheets, while I sat up in bed reading. I thought I was impregnable, and never dreamt that they might drop one on us. Dylan was whimpering, and stayed there whimpering until it was all over; it was all part of his babyishness. Some might say he didn't have much guts, but that's not true; he did for certain things. He was always picking fights in pubs with men about six times larger than he was.

During the day Dylan was working with Davenport on *The Death of the King's Canary*, which they wrote together, largely in the local pub. I used to practise my dancing in the private chapel, where

Davenport provided me with a record player. They left me on my own for quite long periods, and it was then that I had my first serious affair since marrying Dylan: I fell in love with Glock.

It was chiefly his talent that attracted me, but Glock was an impressive-looking man, too. Although I usually prefer very dark men, I thought Glock looked rather beautiful and imposing. He was very fair. I had always had a prejudice against blond men, the blond and fleshy, but I was rather taken with him. He was a fine pianist and I used to sit in the bay window, listening to all that beautiful music, Schubert and Mozart, which was very flattering to him. Occasionally, we would meet in the garden and he would hold my hand and be very tender. There was a feeling between us when we were together like falling in love, and we conceived this idea of having one night of love in Cardiff: it was the first time I had ever calculated an infidelity.

I told Dylan that I was going down to Swansea to see his parents (we hadn't seen them for a long time and he seemed to swallow that) and would also go over to Laugharne. I hadn't any proper clothes for the night in Cardiff and was very worried about it: I wanted to get all dressed up, so I decided that the only thing to do (because we never had any money) was to sell up all our possessions in Laugharne, and use that cash to buy some posh clothes.

It was all carefully planned. I went back to Laugharne, and Ivy helped me sell off all those Welsh blankets and the beautiful crockery that I had bought in Carmarthen market, which I sold for practically nothing to anyone in sight. Then I went to Cardiff and bought myself a super outfit. The shopping part of it was the only bit that I enjoyed, because I bought all sorts of lovely things that matched and were in the right colours, which I had never had before. These weren't Bohemian clothes; they were smart things, but at the same time very noticeable because I wanted to create a sensation. Eventually I went to the hotel where we were supposed to meet, and there was Glock, waiting for me in the lounge. We had a few drinks and then had dinner together, and it was all very strained and embarrassed. Then came the worst part of all – bed.

I was feeling very amorous. Glock got into bed first, and lay there, stretched out in his pyjamas like a stick. This didn't surprise me; I would have been rather overcome had he been naked. I perfumed myself, put\on my Isadora Duncan tunic, which seemed to be just right for the occasion, and climbed into bed – and nothing happened. I just lay there. And he just lay there. I was getting more and more worried. What did he mean? Was he hesitating or waiting for me to start? Glock didn't say anything and neither did I. There was total silence between us. Nobody will ever believe it, but we never touched each other all night: we just lay there, looking at the ceiling and watching the shadows.

Eventually I fell asleep. I don't know what happened to Glock. I was terribly upset and nervous, but beyond anger. I was completely baffled and disappointed; my only sexual education had come from my mother, who had told us that 'the woman lies back supine while the man warms her up'. I lay back all right, but nothing happened, and next morning we got dressed and disappeared in opposite directions as soon as we could, without talking about it.

I had told Dylan that I would spend three nights in Swansea, and this farce turned into a real drama when his wretched mother gave the game away by telling him that I had only spent two nights there. The Welsh mind is like that, noticing everything, taking it all in. She wrote to Dylan, and he *realised*. He was very upset and started cursing me. I was never planning to leave Dylan: it was just intended to be one night of love, and I thought I was getting my revenge because Dylan was always going off to London and having affairs. It was all agonisingly painful. Dylan threw a knife at me (which missed me by miles), and for a long time after that he wouldn't come near me. He just turned his back on me, and it was ages before we sorted ourselves out.

That was the end of our summer in Marshfield. Immediately after that incident, Dylan took me down to my mother's in Blashford and it was then, by coincidence, that he got himself a job in films in London, which was to give us the first real financial security that we'd ever had. He started going up to London and not coming back for days at a time, and I realised then that we were on the brink; if I didn't stay with him now, we might never see each other again; it could be the end of our marriage.

Eventually, we abandoned Llewelyn, leaving him with my mother, and moved together to a small one-roomed studio in Manresa Road. I didn't want to do it, but we had nowhere else to live and I was convinced by now (this was 1941) that if I didn't stay with Dylan I would lose him. Leaving Llewelyn was very traumatic, quite the most painful thing that ever happened to me,

75

because I had been so in love with this baby and so possessive. It was a frightful wrench leaving him with my mother – though the fact that Brigid was there as well eased the pain a little – but I felt that if I didn't do it Dylan would drift back into that pub life that he had before he met me, and would soon forget all about me. Dylan treated me badly; I know that now, but I was in love with him, and usually one falls in love with the worst kinds of people. Virtue in a man doesn't make you want to grab him. I loved Dylan more the worse he treated me. One always searches for something one can't get, and if someone is too easy you start to undervalue them. I've always had that kind of twist about men. Dylan didn't change after he married me; he just carried on living in the same way that he had lived before we met. He was always telling me how much he loved me; he never stopped saying that, right through to the end. He was sincere in loving me, but he couldn't help his character, and even now I find this hard to explain, and painful, too.

6

Had we known then that Llewelyn wouldn't come back to live with us until after the war, I don't know that I could have gone through with it. Given that choice, I might have stayed with Llewelyn at my mother's; I just don't know. At the time I felt that I was doing something wrong, but didn't know what else I could do. Even now I have terrible feelings of guilt.

All through the war I kept wanting to get Llewelyn back, but our circumstances were always so bad that I never seemed to be able to manage it. After leaving Sea View in the summer of 1940, we didn't have a proper home of our own again until we moved to South Leigh in Oxfordshire in September 1947. We moved around quite a lot during the war, partly to avoid the bombing (and Llewelyn was safe from that), keeping that one room at Manresa Road as a London base and staying sometimes with Dylan's parents, with Frances Hughes in Laugharne, with an old Swansea friend of Dylan's, Vera Killick, at Talsarn in Cardiganshire, and then for a year at New Quay, also Cardiganshire, where we rented a bungalow overlooking the sea. For much of that time I had my daughter Aeron with me (she was born while we were living at Manresa Road in March 1943). She stayed with us wherever we moved, which only made it worse for Llewelyn, who must have felt that I loved her more than I loved him, which just wasn't true.

We had left Marshfield in a hurry with a bad feeling between us, and it was quite some time before Dylan would sleep with me after that. He was jealous, and what hurt him even more was the realisation that the other house guests knew that I had spent that night in a Cardiff hotel with Glock. John Davenport's wife Clement certainly knew because she rather fancied Glock herself, and when she found a letter from him to me, she tore it up angrily. Davenport himself obtained £50 for Dylan from Lord Howard de Walden, who was himself a writer, and with this money, and an introduction from Davenport to the film director Ivan Moffatt, we set off first for Blashford and then for London; that was the beginning of Dylan's work in film-making.

Dylan had always been fascinated by films, and it just so happened – as these things often do – that Moffatt was working with the producer Donald Taylor, who was producing high-quality documentaries for the Ministry of Information. Moffatt introduced Dylan to Donald and they took an instant liking to each other. Ivan and Donald both admired Dylan's work, and were also drinkers.

Constantine FitzGibbon, who was friendly with them all, and often saw more of Dylan than I did during those periods in the war when I was down in the country escaping the air raids, described the relationship that developed thus:

Ivan Moffatt appealed to the generosity and kindliness of Donald Taylor's nature. Not only, he said, was Dylan penniless: he was also too sick to be in the Army. It was essential that something had to be done for him at once. They met in a pub in St Martin's Lane one warm September evening . . . Donald and Dylan took an immediate liking to one another, which grew stronger with the years. The relationship between employer and employee is not always an easy one, and with so touchy, proud and self-conscious an artist as was Dylan its difficulties might easily have led to disaster. Instead it became one of close friendship and mutual understanding. Donald soon realised that Dylan was not only a fine poet but also a fine film craftsman. Dylan for his part, while not infrequently bored by the scripts on which he was asked to work, never made the cardinal error of many writers new to films: he did not regard his work as a prostitution of his talents, nor did he believe that he should assert his artist's needs by adopting a patronising attitude towards his employer's needs. On the contrary, Dylan was fascinated by films – had he not been film-struck all his life? – and he was in this, as in all other aspects of his work, whether reader, actor or writer, a pro. Donald Taylor recognised this rapidly and with delight. Dylan was soon on the payroll of Strand Films, first at eight pounds and later at ten pounds a week, and throughout the war this was his financial anchor . . . Nor was that the end of it. Donald Taylor did not insist that the writers he employed kept any sort of office hours. Provided that they did their work, and met their date-lines, he was quite uninterested in how they did it or where. When Dylan was in London there was an office for him if he wanted it. If he preferred to be in Wales, or anywhere else, Donald had no objection . . .

The Life of Dylan Thomas
by Constantine FitzGibbon

I have quoted this paragraph from FitzGibbon's biography because it describes what happened from a different angle to my own: the relationship was man-to-man, like so many of Dylan's closer friendships; and FitzGibbon was correct in his description of Dylan's attitude to the work he did for Strand Films. He never took the job lightly; he was keenly interested in the new techniques that he was learning, and he was hoping to move on to other forms of film writing when, as he expected, the film industry revived after the war. This whole period of Dylan's writing career is largely undocumented. I couldn't describe it in any detail because he was so often working in London while I was down in the country with Aeron, and even when we were down in Wales together and Dylan was working there on a script, I would only be able to see what he had written and not how he visualised it as a film. But I can confirm that FitzGibbon was correct – Dylan was as conscientious about his writing for Donald Taylor and later for Sidney Box at Gains-borough Films as he was in his other literary work.

It was Donald who commissioned Dylan to write a script for *The Doctor and the Devils*, which has only recently been made into a film, some forty years later. He also commissioned him to write *Twenty Years A'Growing*, an adaptation of Maurice Sullivan's book about the Blasket Islands off Kerry, for which Dylan wrote 130 pages of script towards the end of the war, which has still not been filmed (although it has been published as a book). Dylan also scripted about a dozen other films that were produced by either Strand or Gryphon (Donald Taylor's other film company) for government departments during the war. These included *Is Your Ernie Really Necessary?*, which was thought to be much too flippant and was never released; a film about Wales, *Green Mountain, Black Mountain*, which the British Council distributed overseas, and *Our Country*, a film for the Ministry of Information about life in wartime Britain. He also worked on scripts based on the lives of Robert Burns and Dr Crippen, but both projects were abandoned.

While he was working on those films, Dylan wrote hardly any poetry. When he was writing he always had to keep to his routine, which meant mornings pottering about, afternoons writing without interruption, and then off to the pub in the evening, often with the new friends he had made through working for Strand. Graham Greene wrote for Strand, and so did Philip Lindsay, who became one of Dylan's great pals. He was a big drinker, and he would stream off novels when he was drunk in the night (the novels often looked like it, too!). Dylan went through periods of seeing Philip Lindsay almost daily. He was very poor, and never had enough money, like Dylan. His brother, Jack Lindsay, was another friend, but a duller man altogether.

Our closest friends during this period were Constantine and Theodora FitzGibbon, and most evenings when I was in London we would meet early and go to the Chelsea pubs, the Cross Keys or the Six Bells. Constantine was also a very heavy drinker and eventually went into a home for treatment for alcoholism, although I never noticed him drinking more than anybody else.

This was the first time in our lives that we had ever had a regular income, and with our rent at Manresa Road only £1 a week we should have been able to manage quite comfortably, but we never did: whenever Dylan had money he drank it, and always wanted more.

Dylan was still the generous friend whenever he had cash in his pocket, but he would now steal if he had to without the slightest qualm. He had no conscience whatever about other people's possessions: he was aware that they belonged to them, but he just preferred to convert them into money for himself.

On one occasion, before my sister Nicolette married the artist Rupert Shephard, he and his first wife Lorna lent us their flat while they were away for a short time. Dylan pawned her fur coat, a gramophone and the family silver (which he carefully polished before taking down to the pawnbroker). On another, Theodora FitzGibbon was walking down the street towards their home in Chelsea when she met Dylan carrying her sewing machine. I did tell him that I thought this was going too far, but he thought it rather funny. He never stole money, so far as I know: it was always goods that he could take down to the pawn-shop, because he thought that he would be able to reclaim them before anyone had noticed. Dylan used the pawn-shop quite a lot.

Caitlin at Blashford

Caitlin as Isadora Duncan, on the banks of the River Avon, Hampshire

Brown's Hotel, Laugharne

Dylan plays nap with Ivy and Ebie's brother Billy in Brown's. Note the photograph to the left

Caitlin with Llewelyn in 1939

Dylan and Caitlin at the round table in Manresa Road, Chelsea, in the early 1940s

Sea View, Laugharne: Tudor Williams in the foreground

The Town Hall, Laugharne, with the Hughes' home, Castle House, to the right

When we went to a party, Dylan would often leave with a better coat than the one he was wearing when he arrived, and quite often he took people's shirts and left his own dirty ones behind. He didn't really believe in right and wrong: he thought there were some special rules for him, that he was one of the chosen ones. Some people became very angry with him. Norman Cameron even wrote a poem about those rather unusual habits of Dylan's, and it was published in *Horizon*:

THE DIRTY LITTLE ACCUSER

Who invited him in? What was he doing here,
That insolent little ruffian, that crapulous lout?
When he quitted a sofa, he left behind him a smear.
My wife says he even tried to paw her about.

What was worse, if, as so often happened, we caught him out
Stealing or pinching the maid's backside, he would leer,
With a cigarette on his lip and a shiny snout,
With a hint: 'You and I are all in the same *galère*.'

Yesterday we ejected him, nearly by force,
To go on the parish, perhaps, or die of starvation;
As to that, we agreed, we felt no kind of remorse.

Yet there's this check on our righteous jubilation:
Now that the little accuser is gone, of course,
We shall never be able to answer his accusation.

Though some people were furious with Dylan, no one ever called the police. On the whole people were very patient with him. I can't remember anyone bawling him out (although they wouldn't have known he had stolen their shirts until after he had gone!). It was all very strange for someone from a Welsh chapel background. At times he seemed to think it was his duty to relieve the rich of their shirts or their clothes; anyone who was rich was fair game, and I had as big a prejudice against the rich as he had. Most rich people are so smug and mean: their houses are cold and they give out no warmth. It must have been desperation that drove Dylan to do it, because he did it for drink. He certainly thought the wrong people had possessions and wealth (we shared that together), but there was nothing truly rebellious in his character. I was the rebellious one. Dylan was just taking what he thought was his due.

His pubbing became relentless. He would go out in the evenings with a chrysanthemum in his lapel, pretending to be a queen. He would dress up in fancy clothes, saying that he was 'an actor from the BBC', then offer to bite the caps off bottles of beer if he could have the beer. Some of his pub games were incredibly childish, if not embarrassing. One was called 'cats and dogs': he would get down on his hands and knees and crawl round a bar, biting people's ankles and howling like a dog (which I don't consider funny in any circumstances). He would pour drinks into other people's pockets; and once I heard that he unbuttoned his trousers and offered a girl his penis (although I never saw him do that myself; he would never have behaved like that in front of me). Dylan also had an enormous repertoire of obscene songs, dirty limericks and 'blue' stories, which he would tell when he had a helpless audience. Most of them have gone for ever, because no one can remember that sort of thing the morning after, but Rayner Heppenstall recalled one:

> There was a young bugger called God
> Who put a young virgin in pod.
> This amazing behaviour
> Produced Christ our Saviour
> Who died on a cross, the poor sod.

Dylan had acquired a reputation as the pub fool and he had to keep it up at all costs. I always thought he went too far. He monopolised every conversation, and it was difficult for anyone else to get a word in edgeways. Sometimes he would keep on going, drinking all the time, until he became painfully tedious. He was partly singing for his supper, though he would never have admitted this – so long as he kept up the performance, people would keep buying him drinks.

The strange thing (and I think people find this hard to believe) was that Dylan was never like that at home, in Laugharne, or with his closest friends. He seemed to have created two personalities for himself, and he kept them both leading quite separate lives – and those who knew the one didn't know the other existed. Right to the end of his life, he still worked to the strict routine he had always adhered to: mornings spent pottering about, reading letters or doing the *Times* crossword, followed by a quiet drink with Ivy, and afternoons spent working. Only at night would the other Dylan emerge – and then only when he was in London or America.

It was during this early part of the war that Dylan decided to sell the notebooks in which he had drafted many of his early poems, and which he mined constantly during the late Thirties, re-working some of the poems. The London bookseller, Bertram Rota, bought the four poetry notebooks, a prose notebook and the work-sheets of 'Ballad of the Long-legged Bait' for £41.10s and sold them to the Lockwood Library of the State University of New York at Buffalo. Dylan's biographers and critics have since assumed that he was so desperate for money that he sold them for drink; but that wasn't so at all. What really happened – and this is where the two Dylans become confused by those who do not know how he was living his life – was that the calm, rational, literary Dylan decided that he didn't want to refer to them any more. He wasn't desperate for money then – he had landed the job with Donald Taylor, which was bringing in a regular income. He was now thinking about, and discussing with me, the writing he had done before the war. *The Map of Love* had done very badly. He knew that I didn't like its whimsical short stories and was none too keen on some of the poems, which I thought were over-written: he blamed much of that on his notebooks, and he said that he had been using them far too much while we were living at Sea View.

'I've pretty well exhausted all the stuff in there; there's nothing more I want to use,' he told me, and he agreed that there had been too much diving into childhood memories and fantasy. The drinking Dylan may have drunk those notebooks (and I wouldn't be surprised if he did), but it was the creative Dylan who decided to sell them. This, of course, was in the early stages of the war, when things were looking black, which may have affected the way he was looking at his poetry. And he was finding it hard to write poems when his script-writing was absorbing so much of his creative energy.

We were then living at Manresa Road, and while we were there my daughter Aeron (or Aeronwy, as she was christened) was born, during a tremendous air raid. I had gone into Mary Abbotts Hospital for the birth, and I can remember a frightful noise in the skies, which seemed to be just above the labour ward. In some strange way it was a kind of comfort – the thought that, out there, there was something worse than childbirth. Every time there was a vast explosion I felt the baby was going to explode out of me. I was really beyond fear. The birth was predictably awful, but nothing like the horror of the first one.

The thing that upset me was that, once again, Dylan was nowhere to be seen. He first came to visit me in hospital about a week after the baby was born. It was very embarrassing for me because he missed the mothers' visiting day. This was chiefly a parade of the fathers rather than a showing-off of the babies, because all the women wanted to find out what kind of man the other mothers had married, and I was the only woman there with no man to parade.

I felt very bad about it. When Dylan did arrive, a week late, he shuffled in wearing an old dressing-gown, which was obviously not his own, and bedroom slippers: he was unshaven and his hair was all over the place; he looked completely shagged out. Dylan had had one hell of a week of dissipation while I was going through my labour. I took one look at him and rather hoped he wouldn't recognise me, but he made a beeline for the bed. I can't remember the exact words I used, but I'm sure I started ticking him off and asking where on earth he'd been. He didn't seem very concerned, either for me or the baby.

Dylan didn't come to collect me when the time came for me to be discharged from the hospital, so I ordered a taxi and had myself driven back to Manresa Road, which was a terrible dump at the best of times, with a foul stink coming from the thirty bedraggled Siamese cats that were owned by the woman in the flat next to ours. We just had the one room, which had a bed in one corner and a round table (which made the room look much grander than it really was when we were photographed there by Bill Brandt), a very primitive stove behind a curtain, and a bath which was covered by some wooden planking.

I walked into the room with Aeron in my arms, and there was nowhere to put her down. I had never seen such a mess in my life. She was so beautiful, cocooned in white baby clothes, that I just couldn't put her down in all that filth. Dylan had done no washing-up all the time I had been in hospital. There were dirty dishes everywhere, empty beer bottles, cigarette ends strewn all over the carpet, old newspapers thrown here, there and everywhere; I only had to take one look at our crumpled bed to realise that Dylan had had some other woman in it while I'd been in hospital.

I was still feeling weak and miserable after having had the baby and I found this homecoming harrowing. I couldn't have felt worse, and when he arrived back home later that evening, like all cowardly people he came in with his buddies, Constantine and Theodora FitzGibbon. They had obviously been down to the pub and had had a few drinks to get the courage to face me. It was all rather embarrassing because I couldn't do my cursing in peace, and that he knew. I had to be fairly polite to them as they, too, sat around in embarrassment. It was a deplorable situation, and there wasn't much anyone could say to alleviate it. I was almost speechless and near to tears.

Thinking about it makes me feel miserable, even now. But I am the kind of person who rides over these things, somehow, and next day I pulled myself together. I am a fighter. I don't just accept any situation in which I find myself, so I set to and started cleaning up the place.

Eventually we got together again and peace was made, but this time it took longer for us to re-establish our loving relationship than it had done before. We'd had so many violent rows, but this went deeper. I'd felt neglected both while I was in hospital and when I came home. I don't know how I put up with it, but what alternative did I have? To go home to my mother's? I could have done, but I was still very attached to Dylan, and when the man you are living with is the father of your child it gives him a much greater hold over you. It may be entirely symbolic but it's a very strong link. I did think of leaving Dylan sometimes, especially when he was away from me for anything up to three weeks or more, and I used to think to myself, 'My God! If I had the money I would book myself straight into a very expensive hotel so that he wouldn't find me, and disappear myself.'

In the period after the birth I think it was Aeron who kept me from leaving because I had to look after her. My feelings for Aeron were quite different from those I had felt for Llewelyn. I marvelled at how beautiful she was and how a little baby could be so feminine, exactly like a little woman, perfectly angelic, with such beautiful curly hair, even then. When I was bathing her I used to look at her with wonder, and I still hold that strong image of Aeron. It's hard for me to talk about my children because, in spite of all that tenderness (which was genuine), I still left them alone in the evenings to go drinking with Dylan. It was a habit of years, like getting up in the morning and having a cup of strong tea. Had I not gone to the pub with Dylan, I would have been left there, sitting like a fool. Nevertheless, the children were mine and my duty. I suppose most good women would have remained at home with their children with the bombs falling all around. I left Aeron alone in that flat with its glass roof to go down to the pub, and I still feel guilty about it. I used to go about seven o'clock and then come back around ten. I remember coming back once and finding my Dutch woman neighbour who had the cats holding Aeron in her arms. She meant well, but there was this filthy woman with my child in her arms. I felt such disgust with myself that it was through me that it had happened.

At that time I wasn't so badly affected by my surroundings as I would be now. Now I would never, never share a lavatory with people like that, as we had to. The whole place was so squalid, but I kept Aeron clean. I was very fussy about that. I remember all those piles of nappies, which had to be done by hand in those days, and which I hung up in the bombed-out building opposite.

My only happy memories of the war years relate to Aeron. She gave me a feeling of wonder. It lasted until she was nine or ten years old, and then she became a little fiend and turned against me, like all daughters do. Aeron says now that she realises I did adore her until then, 'but after that you suddenly stopped' – and it's true. I spoilt her. I spent hours brushing her hair. Aeron has a strong nature, too; she is not docile now; she can be positively aggressive (like I was, in fact). She always looked very much like Dylan, but so much prettier. Later on, when she became very naughty and stubborn, I realised it was chiefly my fault for pampering her. I used to have to go to collect her from school on the train. She behaved so abominably that I would lose my temper and beat her. The other passengers were horrified. 'You can't do that to a child,' they'd say. I'd reply, 'You would if you had this one.' I could be hard with my children. I hit them, but then I adored them, too. I used to slap her around the head occasionally and I hit the other children when I had to. I rather believe in hitting children. Even Dylan, who would never hit a flea, was enraged by her once. (That was another thing about Dylan; although he was so soft, he could also be fairly pugnacious, and he would spring to my defence if he thought that someone had said something that would offend me, though I didn't offend easily. These incidents always began with something small and unnecessary. Mostly he didn't notice if someone, say, made a pass at me.)

It was Donald Taylor who suggested that I should take Aeron away from London to avoid the air raids and then the flying bombs. He said to Dylan, 'Why don't you bring your wife and child down to my place?' Of course, we leapt at that. We stayed at his house near Beaconsfield for a couple of months and later in the war we spent a few months down at Bosham in Sussex. Bosham was quite a pretty little place in a highly conventional way; typically English with water and sailing boats, untouched by the war, with a chi-chi rustic pub. We stayed in a cottage there for three months with a revolting outside lavatory. Most of the time, though, we stayed either with Dylan's parents at Blaen Cwm or with Vera Killick at Talsarn.

Dylan's parents had moved to Blaen Cwm because they could live there cheaply, and much more safely now that the Germans were regularly bombing the Swansea docks. Granny Thomas' sister Dosie and her husband the Rev David Rees had been living there, but they had both died, so D.J. and Florence were able to move into one of the semi-detached pair of cottages. The thought horrified poor old D.J. He was growing old and felt he was sinking. 'God, here's that bitch,' he would say when Aunt Polly approached from the cottage next door, where she lived with her brother Bob. The two adjoining cottages were both tiny, cramped and gloomy. Dylan was always scathing about the place (although he did begin 'Fern Hill' there). We had a tiny little room at the top of the house, and the only nice thing about it was listening to the brook babbling by. We hardly ever saw Uncle Bob. Aunt Polly was a terrible nuisance, always asking questions and chattering. She was a tiny little shrivelled-up creature, and she used to spend her days looking at *Vogue* and imagining herself in velvet gowns, which was a grotesque fantasy. They were simple country folk, and Dylan had a vague affection for them, but I had nothing in common with them at all, and there were times when they drove us both mad.

Dylan was very affected as D.J. aged and, later, began approaching death, because he had been such a great figure when Dylan was younger and going to school. D.J. had suffered too much. Cwmdonkin Drive was already a come-down in his eyes; then Bishopston was another step down, and Blaen Cwm lower still. He used to curse that place. He was a strong atheist. He saw nothing in his life to prove the existence of God. Everything bad had happened to him. (Dylan had a simple religious faith of his own, but it wasn't an orthodox religion. He seldom went to church, but he insisted on having all his children baptised. That was important to him, even though he didn't feel the need for regular contact with the Church.)

Our visits to Talsarn began when Dylan met an old friend, Vera Killick, whom he had known in Swansea. She had straight blonde hair and was pretty, and they met again when she was working as a waitress in a Chelsea restaurant. She was very emancipated and was in with the Chelsea bunch. She had this family home down in Talsarn where she invited us to stay to avoid the worst of the bombing. I sometimes went down there on my own with Aeron, with Dylan coming down occasionally. The cottage was in the valley of the River Aeron, and we had given her that name because that was where she was conceived.

Sometimes Dylan would return to London and say he'd be back again at the weekend, and then not return for two or three weeks, always with some excuse – that he had a writing deadline to meet or money to earn. I think this was the time when he started going off with women more or less regularly, and drinking more heavily than he had ever done, although I wasn't fully aware of it then. During this period his physical appearance changed; he became fat and flabby, and by the end of the war he looked very debauched. I was slow to realise about the women, although I could see the state he was in, and I used to think he would be all right as soon as we had a home together. He was tortured and tormented, because he had to make the money to live. I think he just needed women to boost his self-esteem. I never thought he was a genuine womaniser at all.

In London, Dylan had been working on the film treatment for *The Doctor and the Devils*, but for some reason he could never settle down to write poetry there: the distractions were too many. As long as he was in company he was in company, and he couldn't do anything else, but as soon as he was away from London, initially at Talsarn and Blaen Cwm and then at New Quay, he started his real writing again with a sort of driving, pent-up energy; there was so much that he wanted to say. He hadn't been writing poems during our time in London. The poems he wrote then must have been bottled up inside him while he was writing all those film scripts for Donald Taylor.

Dylan was never consciously happy while engaged on film scripts or, later, radio work, because he always found it a struggle.

He *knew* that poetry was his thing, what he had to do, so naturally it brought him more satisfaction. I wouldn't describe the poetry as his happiest work because happy is a word that I don't like to use much in describing Dylan. (I am rather afraid of the word, anyway, because I don't think happiness exists on its own. I am wary of people who say that they are happy or have never felt such happiness in their lives before: it's rather like love – it either doesn't exist at all, or if it does, you only realise its existence after it's happened. I always react retrospectively.)

Our move to New Quay came through the friendship with Vera, which went back a long way with Dylan. He had known her in Swansea before she married, when her name was Phillips. They liked each other, and I liked her, too: I never suspected any sort of an affair there. Dylan described her as 'a girl who lives on cocoa and books on third-century brass'. We had been hoping to move back to Laugharne, and while we were staying at Blaen Cwm (which is just across the river from Laugharne) we tried to rent another cottage there, but we couldn't find one. Vera's family had a place in New Quay, right up on the cliffs, and we rented the bungalow next door. It was more like a wooden shed than a bungalow, with paper-thin asbestos-sheeting walls, lighting by Calor gas, and a paraffin stove. It had two bedrooms and was cheaply primitive, and though made to look dainty in the English sense, it wasn't a solid building at all.

Our bungalow was called Majoda and we rented it for a year. New Quay was beautiful, but it didn't have the intimacy of Laugharne, and for long periods there I felt lonely. Dylan kept going up to London, where he stayed with Bill and Helen McAlpine, who were among our closest friends. I only had Vera, who moved in next door with her husband – 'Drunken Waistcoat' we called him, because he always looked so fancy and he liked his drink.

My mother came to stay with us once, which I think was brave of her, because she knew the kind of people we were: 'artistic', we called it. Right below us was the roaring ocean. I used to have a marvellous time down there in the waves, and one day she decided to go for a swim as well; I really am the most egotistical person in the world because I never thought to accompany the poor woman, and she could easily have drowned.

Superficially, she and Dylan now got on quite well, but I think that underneath, Dylan didn't like her much: he didn't like women to be too intelligent or too intellectual, and my mother was exceptionally bright. She was widely read and did that impossible *Times* crossword with the greatest of ease (she was the only one of the Majolier daughters who had been given a proper education, being the eldest, and she had been presented at Court). She had been well set up, but she really came down in the world after Francis left us, and she didn't think much of Dylan going off to London and leaving me alone, because that was exactly what Francis had done. I was careful not to get involved in any conversations along those lines, and I didn't tell her that Dylan had been going off with other women because she was less approachable than Granny Thomas: she was cool and cold, as classy women often are.

Dylan would never tell me when he was going off again: he would just leave with some very plausible excuse. It was always to make money, by going to see a publisher or an editor, but somehow the money was all drunk away – he always came back broke, and broken in health as well. Dylan was said to have had a chest haemorrhage at the age of sixteen, and to have been sent to a farm in West Wales to recuperate by his mother; and he claimed to have been told once that he had only four years to live. His father used to say that Dylan would never make forty. His father was right. I heard Dylan say that, too, but usually when he was suffering from a hangover.

To Dylan the idea of old age was appalling, and he was right about that, too: it is. I told him that we should both arrange to go before we were forty, that I didn't want to go on getting older and uglier on my own, but I turned out to be very hard to kill because I had such good health. I couldn't go along with all the hypochondria that Dylan indulged in; I had too many other things to do. Dylan was perversely strong underneath; those claims of ill-health were mainly attempts to get sympathy, which he was always after.

The strangest thing that happened at New Quay involved Vera and Drunken Waistcoat. It's a story that has been told several times before: the shooting incident at Majoda that ended up with Drunken Waistcoat being prosecuted for attempted murder and Dylan giving evidence in the court case.

It was all very odd.

Dylan was late with his script for *The Doctor and the Devils*, which had been commissioned by Donald Taylor on behalf of Gryphon Films, and Donald was anxious to get the film into production. To help Dylan, Donald sent down a Russian-born secretary who worked at Gryphon, with whom Dylan was friendly; she had mothered him a lot, and helped him out with his typing.

One evening, after Dylan had worked all day on the script, we went down to the Black Lion, the pub we used every day in New Quay. Vera and her husband were there as well, and there were several other people in the crowd at the bar. A lot of drinking was done, and at some point the Russian secretary made several remarks that upset Drunken Waistcoat, who lost his temper. He was very rude and made some stupid comments about her being Jewish, which, in 1944, was rotten timing. She clawed at his face and he hit back, whereupon Dylan and the other men present threw him out of the pub. What none of them knew was that Drunken Waistcoat had recently returned from a very hazardous mission as a Commando officer, and he was more than a little battle-weary. What's more, he had brought some of his weapons back, including a Sten gun and several hand grenades.

Drunken Waistcoat was also nursing a grudge: he was convinced that his wife had been living with us in a *ménage-à-trois* (which was a ridiculous thought) while he had been away, and that we had been drinking too much of their money (there may have been some truth in that). Anyway, he went off to another pub and brooded while we carried on drinking.

We returned to Majoda with Mary Keene, a friend of ours who was staying with us with her baby (she was the wife of Ralph, or 'Bunny', Keene, but at the time she was living with the painter Matthew Smith), and we settled down in front of the fire with some bottles of beer that Dylan had brought back from the pub. Suddenly, we heard some shouting outside the house and then a violent commotion, followed by a hail of bullets which ripped through those paper-thin walls. Mary and I dived into the room next door to see if the children were all right (they were fast asleep), and, moments later, the front door was kicked down and in burst Drunken Waistcoat, with his Sten gun under his arm.

Somehow, Dylan – who was unusually calm on this occasion – managed to take the gun away from him, at which point Drunken Waistcoat produced a hand grenade and threatened to blow us all to smithereens unless his gun was returned to him immediately. When he was later asked at the trial what he did then, Dylan replied, 'Naturally – I handed it back to him.'

There needn't have been any trial. Peace had been restored and tempers had cooled, and we were all settling down again when the police suddenly arrived (one of the neighbours had heard the shots and had dialled 999). So then, of course, there was a big investigation and Drunken Waistcoat was charged with attempted murder and we were all required to give evidence. It was one of those crazy things that happen in wartime; poor old Drunken Waistcoat was obviously in a bad state because of what he had been through, and none of us said very much against him. We all went to court and gave fairly weak evidence. I said that he had appeared very nervous and out of control. Eventually, he was found not guilty on the grounds that the provocation had been such as to temporarily deprive him of his reason.

The incident distressed Dylan, who didn't like any kind of violence. He was calm at the time, but he realised afterwards that we could all have been killed, and our friendship with Vera petered out after that.

Dylan was anxious to leave New Quay after the shooting incident, but looking back now it is easy to see that those twelve months were one of the most important creative periods of his life. He had started writing again at Blaen Cwm, and then, once we had settled at Majoda, Dylan rented a room nearby where he worked on *The Doctor and the Devils*, his radio talk *Quite Early One Morning*, the script for *Twenty Years A'Growing* and some of his finest poems – 'Fern Hill' and 'Poem in October' (both of which he had begun at Blaen Cwm), 'This Side of Truth', 'Vision and Prayer', 'A Winter's Tale', 'A Refusal to Mourn the Death, by Fire, of a Child in London', 'The Conversation of Prayer' and 'In My Craft or Sullen Art'.

New Quay was just exactly his kind of background, with the ocean in front of him as it later was in Laugharne, and a pub where he felt at home in the evenings. Dylan needed that combination of circumstances before he could work well: the further away we were from London and the bleaker the landscape, the better it was for him. In London there were too many distractions, not only the drink but the company, the intellectual chit-chat as well as the carousing and story-telling. When he got back to New Quay, and later Laugharne, Dylan still had his drinking, but it was normal, everyday drinking and conversation, and his thoughts were channelled into his writing. The strange thing was that he always wrote better when he had no intellectual stimulation: he was always at his best when alone with his own resources.

One of the poems he wrote at New Quay, 'This Side of Truth', was written for Llewelyn. It is not a very clear poem and I was a bit surprised that he wrote it, but pleased that he did. I think Dylan was disappointed that Llewelyn wasn't more of a natural boy. He was always brooding and introspective, sensitive and vulnerable. Dylan wanted a straightforward boy who kicked a ball. (Our third child, Colm, was much more like that, although I still think Llewelyn may prove to have more stuff in him in the end. I've always thought that Llewelyn had a very good brain, but he's been terribly hurt in life, and by the way he was brought up. When he stayed with us recently in Sicily I deliberately held his arm and touched him – as the Italians do. At first he backed away and shuddered, but then he got used to it and liked it. Our relationship is a lot better than it was.)

I can't remember what led Dylan to write that poem, although I imagine that there must have been a certain amount of guilt, because Llewelyn had not had decent treatment. Dylan must have been aware of this because, when we saw Llewelyn again, after all those years with my mother at Blashford, he seemed very lost and he didn't fit into any of the age groups of the other children. But after a while he settled back in with us again.

When I read those poems now, which he gathered together for *Deaths and Entrances* (1946), I can see that he was mellowing out and becoming more mature. I liked 'Fern Hill' and 'Poem in October' very much. He was simplifying. It was part of his growth, I think, now that he had put the notebooks and *The Map of Love* behind him. This new maturity was only in his work, in that other, hidden Dylan: he wasn't changing much as a man or in his habits. I think he realised that he had made a mess of his life and that there was nothing to come back to; nothing to do next or to live on; no means of supporting his family. At the back of his mind he was always thinking about death and the possibility of suicide and not living beyond the age of forty, which he used to say quite often, sober or drunk, even when he was writing those serene poems. He always felt that he was doomed to die early. He said he wanted to. Like me, he didn't want to get old and ugly, and he realised that he was getting that way, flabby and fat, with a beer belly. He had completely let himself go, physically.

While one side of Dylan was now working better and more serenely, the other side was as unreliable as ever. It was then that he treated Vernon most cruelly, which was strange, because the writing Dylan was communicating still with Vernon. They had been the closest of friends, and when we had been in dire straits financially Vernon had always helped us out. So far as I know, Vernon had never turned Dylan down. At the same time, it was a deep, literary friendship, with them both turning to each other for advice, though, as I have explained, it was a relationship that meant more to Vernon than it did to Dylan. Vernon had kept in touch with us throughout the war, visiting the flat at Manresa Road. Then Dylan failed to turn up at Vernon's wedding when he was supposed to be best man. It really was unforgivable. Vernon was very hurt, as he had every right to be.

Although Dylan later claimed that he had forgotten the name of the church, had had a series of mishaps on the railway, had been driving around London in a taxi without knowing where to go, and had then forgotten to post his letter of apology, I suspect the real truth was that he was standing in a London pub, glanced at the clock – and carried on drinking. That was what usually happened when he got drinking: everything else went by the board, and he would excuse himself by saying that it was 'too late to go now', or that he 'hadn't got the right clothes'.

Vernon and Gwen Watkins were both very upset. She didn't like him much anyway, and in that she had some sense – he wasn't very likeable. Dylan used to charm people without any conscience; he just charmed people for his own ends. I distrust charm for its own sake; I used to tell him that I was sick of all the phoney charm that he kept ladling out: it wouldn't have been so bad if he had been discriminating about it, but I found him treating other people just the same way that he treated me. If you have a quality like that, you don't have to pile it on a plate and expect everybody to eat it. He needed a good lesson from someone: he was getting so spoilt. He had been spoilt by his mother and spoilt by me, and later he was spoilt by America. Gwen Watkins said afterwards that the letter he sent to Vernon showed every sign of having been faked, with faked creases and dirt, as though it had been left in his pocket for days. It probably was faked. Dylan did admit to me afterwards that he had acted unpardonably and was ashamed.

He was in London at the time and I was down in New Quay so I couldn't get him there myself. This was part of the bad side of his character – a cruel streak. It was like the times he failed to turn up at the hospitals to see his babies, and then later when he left me to face the abortions alone: he was never there when he was really needed.

One can just about make a case for him not staying with me when the abortions took place; it is something that a great many men would find hard to face, but it's hard for me to excuse his not being there after they had happened. There was obviously some part of Dylan that could not come to terms with life – not just the unpleasant side of it, but loyalty to one woman, having babies, deaths in the family, kindness to friends. I always seemed to end up with the dirty work because he couldn't face any kind of un-pleasantness. It's quite a common thing in people, but it's strange in a poet whose finest work was analysing life, birth and death.

When you think that in some of his poems, like 'Light Breaks Where No Sun Shines' – which was clearly about the act of love, and conceiving and creating a child – and in his poems to Llewelyn, Dylan was tackling these great poetic themes in a way that few poets have tried, it becomes hard to understand this other side to his personality. As I have said before, it was as though he had become two people. The one Dylan was becoming more and more irresponsible while the other Dylan was constantly extending his literary powers. I can see that the pieces don't altogether fit, but I cannot fully explain it even though I lived with Dylan and knew him better than anyone. There is a great gulf between the really creative person and normal people. The totally creative person does not have the rest of his life in proper proportion. I suspect that the explanation with Dylan was that he was a genius with some kind of an imbalance in his personality: he was one of the chosen ones, and therefore, in his own opinion, he was allowed certain privileges.

7

The turning-point in Dylan's career as a writer came with the publication of *Deaths and Entrances* in 1946. This tiny volume of poems, designed to slip into any pocket or handbag, included that fine sequence of poems written at Blaen Cwm and New Quay: their public acclaim was immediate. From that time onwards, until the end of his life, Dylan became a public figure instead of a private one. He worked regularly as a writer, reader and actor for the BBC, and everything he did now in that area of his life had a sureness of touch. But as a man, his life was a mess.

By then we had been married for nearly nine years, and we still didn't have a home of our own. Our possessions were remarkably few: at Manresa Road, all we had owned was a large Napoleonic bed, that round table and a swinging wooden cradle – and we had to leave those behind when we moved to New Quay because it wasn't worth hiring a removal van to carry so little. Apart from that, all we had were a few clothes and some baby things which we carried around in a suitcase.

Clothes were very important to me, but I never had very many. I always wore bright, colourful ones if I could. Helen McAlpine was very clever with the needle and the sewing machine and she made up many lovely dresses for me from beautiful materials. She also bought me some pretty shoes to match. She was very generous. The McAlpines were living in Richmond then. Helen had been married to a very old man, a millionaire, and when he died she married Bill. We used to stay in their very grand house on the river: they were very close friends – our best, I would say.

There was one other beautiful dress that I bought myself. I happened to see it in the window of a theatrical shop, and the moment I saw it I had to have it; I knew it would look terrific on me. I asked the price, and it was, for me, a fabulous one – £5. Eventually, I got the money together and bought that dress. It was covered in bunches of grapes, birds and goodness knows what. I wore it one day with Dylan at the Café Royal, where everyone said how terrific it looked, but I never heard the end of that £5 from Dylan, who was horrified that a woman could spend that much on a dress. I could never afford the shoes or the bag to go with it, of course, and when I wore that dress I had to go round in black walking shoes because I had nothing else to wear. But we always had money for drink; we never went without that.

We went to Ireland with the McAlpines later in 1946, which was one of the most frightful mistakes we ever made. Dylan had been asked to go there by *Picture Post*, to write an article on the annual Puck Fair at Kerry. This fair went on for four days and nights without the pubs closing, which was fatal. Bill and Dylan, who were great pals, made a vow that they would spend the entire holiday standing at the bar, day and night, drinking until it was all over. Dylan was always keen to demonstrate his prowess and staying power as a drinker: he was always showing off in that way. (He once won a drinking contest at Brown's Hotel, sinking something like twenty pints of beer, one after the other, and he was very ill that night.)

On this occasion, they planted themselves by the bar and started on the Guinness: it was all Guinness, draught Guinness. We left them, returning now and then to see how they were getting on. We were drinking people, too, but we couldn't have stood the boredom of standing there for all that time.

To begin with, they were chatting to each other as they drank, but by the end they were practically speechless, and yet they still kept on drinking until they were literally propped against the bar, still pouring the stuff down their throats. I thought it was macabre and horrible. We couldn't stir them, and in the end we gave up. They lasted two days and two nights, I think, and by the end they couldn't speak at all and just collapsed. They were thrown into the back of a lorry with their bicycles chucked on top of them and driven back to our lodgings. They were in a hell of a state, and utterly miserable. How can anyone be so childish? They were dripping with this awful rich black draught Guinness. They were both put to bed, where they remained for about a week, both terribly sick.

In the meantime, Helen and I went off to look around, meet people and have some fun. We danced and were very frivolous, putting our best clothes on and flirting with the handsome Irish boys. It was all song, dance and flirtation – but nothing more than that.

By then, a new figure had entered our lives – Margaret Taylor, wife of the historian, A. J. P. Taylor. Dylan had known them both since before the war, but now she became our patroness, much to the distress of poor old Alan Taylor, who was beside himself with fury.

After leaving New Quay we had spent a few months at Blaen Cwm with Dylan's parents. Then we stayed with Nicolette and her husband in Markham Square, Chelsea, before going on to Oxford, where we spent Christmas 1945 with the Taylors. Dylan had stayed with them at their cottage in the Peak District back in 1935, when Alan was teaching Modern History at Manchester University, and he regarded Margaret as an old friend, although neither of us ever liked Alan. I thought he was horrible: very opinionated and mean. There were times, too, when I loathed Margaret, but when I look back on it now, I realise that she was very generous and courageous to go against Alan's preachings. She thought Dylan was a genius, but I didn't want to hear her saying that; I wanted to be the only one. Since she died, I've grown fonder of Margaret in memory; I've recognised that she did a good deal for us, but while she was doing it she managed to irritate the life out of us, and it was difficult to be properly grateful. She drove Dylan crazy – another of those female would-be intellectuals.

We went to them that Christmas with a tale of woe; we had no money and nowhere to live. It was true; we hadn't had a real home of our own for over five years and Llewelyn had been with my mother since August 1941. Maggs Taylor was charming and helpful. She was a mad organiser, and right away she wanted to rearrange our lives and take care of all the practical details. She took Aeron in to sleep with her little girls, and let us have the summerhouse in their garden, on the river bank. We used to have all our meals with them; she was a keen cook, but the meals were awful – she hadn't got the gift at all.

Maggs wasn't a stupid woman by any means, but she wasn't a creative artist, either, although she was always asking Dylan for his opinions on her writing, and he was too grateful to demur. She would come round in the mornings and knock on the door when we were still lying in a stupor in each other's arms. No matter what condition we were in, she appeared not to notice, and she started making plans for the day. She tried to plan every day for us, arranging for Dylan to meet important people in Oxford, and she talked of buying us a house.

Alan Taylor can be amusing on paper, but he wasn't fun to live with. He used to keep a barrel of beer in his house at Oxford and he tried to ration Dylan to half a pint at mealtimes. I think he hated the sight of us, right from the start, because we were taking money from Margaret. We saw no sign of affection between them at all; he was not an affectionate man. He was obviously fond of his children, but he treated them in a severe way; he was distant and unapproachable, and he disapproved strongly of pubbing. In fact, he seemed to disapprove of nearly everything, including drink, although he had his own special bottles set aside for his own cheeses, which we were forbidden to touch. Alan used to take part in the life of the University, but Dylan was never tempted by that. It seemed rather fascinating from the outside, like being in a monastery – the ideal life for a man. I think Alan was jealous of Dylan, but I don't think Margaret ever slept with Dylan. I was always asking myself that (and him), but whenever I brought it up he would shudder.

Some time later, I did find a letter that she'd written to Dylan in which she said 'to sleep with you would be like sleeping with a god'. *That* told me they hadn't got very far with it! She must have had a curious idea of the gods. I never looked upon Dylan as the great Latin lover. He used to get round women by playing the little-boy act, but being the size he was, and with that drink inside him, I just couldn't see it. To placate me, since she must have realised that I had seen the letter, Maggs sent me a beautiful waist petticoat in purple taffeta which rustled when you walked. It was just the kind of frivolous thing I fell for, but I was so mad at her for suggesting that she should go to bed with Dylan that I took a lot of trouble and got some scissors and snipped the petticoat into tiny scraps, wrapped them up in a parcel and sent them back to her. I must say that I regretted that afterwards, because it was a tempting petticoat. She never said a word about it.

99

I don't know if she ever managed to get Dylan into bed. I had my suspicions, but Dylan always swore that he wasn't attracted by her, so I thought it would have been difficult, unless he was drunk at the time.

We lived in the Taylors' summerhouse for eighteen months, and while we were there Llewelyn came back to live with us. Maggs found him a place at Magdalen College School, and Dylan started commuting regularly to London, where, after the success of *Deaths and Entrances*, he was in almost constant demand at the BBC, narrating programmes, writing scripts and acting in radio plays. Again, his poetry was having to take second place to his other writing commitments – and Dylan was never happy with that. Nonetheless, though his work for Strand and Gryphon Films had come to an end when the companies went into liquidation, he was still hoping to write a major film script.

During the years immediately after the war Dylan was always saying that the solution to our problems would be to emigrate to one of those countries where he believed writers were better appreciated. We would have long discussions as to whether we should go to San Francisco or Majorca, like Robert Graves; it had to be somewhere warm and sunny by the sea. Then, when we eventually did this, we soon found that Dylan didn't like that kind of place at all, and was homesick for the misty old bogs.

Dylan applied for a Society of Authors Travelling Scholarship. Edith Sitwell and John Lehmann were on the committee that awarded him a £150 grant, with a strong recommendation that it should be spent visiting Italy, which was how we came to go there in April 1947 with Llewelyn and Aeron. My sister Brigid brought her two children, too, so that I would have some company while Dylan was working.

This was the first time Dylan had ever travelled in search of inspiration, and he didn't find much of it. He reacted to the new experience like the English abroad will, expecting everywhere to be exactly the same as it was at home. First we travelled by train to the Italian Riviera, staying in a quite nice hotel at Positano, and then we moved on to Scandicci in the mountains above Florence, where we spent two months in a very grand villa. It was beautiful, with its own *piscina*, and a little woman to cook delicious meals for us, but Dylan wasn't happy. He didn't like the sun; he didn't like Florence, and he didn't like the Italians.

Every morning he would go by horse and trap to the village nearby and catch the tram down into Florence, where he would sit in the Giuberossa for hours drinking beer, occasionally meeting one of the Florentine intellectuals. He didn't look at many of the sights, I'm afraid; he wasn't really aware of Florence at all; he hadn't got much sense of visual beauty, and was never very interested in sight-seeing. Neither am I; when I live among things that I know are beautiful they do affect me, but at the same time I don't like going deliberately to a gallery to see paintings; after looking at a few, I switch off and don't take them in. I never knew Dylan to go round an art gallery, a castle or a museum; it just wasn't his thing. Only words caught his imagination.

When we were staying at Positano, Dylan found a room in the hotel where he could work every afternoon while Brigid and I took the children down to bathe in the sea, but the heat got him down so much he could hardly write. It was easier for him when we got to Scandicci, because, although the heat was very strong there as well, he found a small farm cottage near the house where he could work during the afternoons, and it was cooler for him there than it was outside. It was there that he wrote 'In Country Sleep'.

Some of the Florentine writers and artists came out to see us, but it was all very embarrassing because of the language problem; they couldn't speak any English and he couldn't speak any Italian, and all they could do was drink together, with Dylan trying to entertain them by standing on his head, performing his pub tricks, and then falling in the pool with all his clothes on (he did this more than once), which didn't always have the effect he intended. Wherever he went, Dylan arrived with his pockets full of beer because, he claimed, the Italians never offered you drinks, which didn't suit him at all. There was one very embarrassing evening when we were invited to dine with Montale, one of the most distinguished Italian poets: Dylan arrived half-drunk, pockets full as usual, and then put the bottles down on the table and started drinking. Of course, our hosts were horrified. Montale was very stiff and conventional and his wife was even worse. They lived in a very correct little house with maids to serve their meals, and right at the end of dinner the wife had her lipstick brought to her on a silver tray. Dylan observed this without laughing; by then, he had drunk most of his beer and was too squashed to laugh.

It was all rather pathetic. Llewelyn was miserable because he had no one to play with, and Dylan was completely lost out there until he discovered one day, fiddling about with the radio, that he could pick up John Arlott's commentaries on that summer's England – Australia Test Series. After that he hid in the cottage all day, tuned in to the radio.

Dylan wasn't very nice to me out in Italy. He was probably a little jealous because he could speak no Italian and I had just enough to get by, and all the men were paying me attention, pinching my bottom, as Italians do. I didn't have a proper affair, but I was followed constantly and I think he was jealous of the attention I was getting.

We both preferred the island of Elba, where we spent two weeks in August; the people were much more easy and friendly. It was boiling hot, and we used to go down to the sea in the scorching sun, where Dylan seemed happy enough, sitting in a rock pool with the water up to his waist and his hat on, reading the *New Statesman*, which he had flown out to him from London, the perfect Englishman abroad. The miners there were incredibly good-looking. I was bowled over by them. I had always been attracted to physical men, and these were knock-outs. I had one of them as a lover; he was sweet and nice, not a bit violent or temperamental. Later, after I had visited Elba again after Dylan's death, he wrote to me asking me to return, but I never did. It's no good trying to pursue these affairs; you just have them, and that's that.

While we were out in Italy, we received a letter from Margaret Taylor saying that she had found us somewhere to live, and we returned to our first real home as a family in seven years. It was the Manor House at South Leigh in Oxfordshire, which Margaret had partly furnished in her usual energetic way before we even moved in.

I think Margaret Taylor was besotted with Dylan primarily because he was a poet; she was attracted by his fame and his talent. Even before I found that letter I sensed that she was after him sexually, though she didn't look the type, and Dylan wasn't after her. It was a very strange relationship, but primarily it was that she thought he was a genius, and so she had to invite herself into his bed.

On one occasion, when we were living at South Leigh, she drew up detailed plans for their elopement and told Dylan that she would be waiting for him with her suitcase on the platform at Paddington Station. We often wondered if she turned up – because he didn't. Dylan found that very funny, because here was the wife of A. J. P. Taylor, whom he couldn't bear, being properly potty.

Soon after we moved to South Leigh, she brought a gypsy caravan down from Oxford so that Dylan could work in there without being disturbed by the children; it kept them away, but it didn't keep her out. Whereas I would never dream of disturbing Dylan while he was working, she would come to South Leigh every day and go straight to the caravan. It was cruel, and it drove Dylan mad. He should have kicked her out, but he was putting up with it because she was now his patron. Dylan could turn on people and get very cross sometimes, but not with Margaret, though the last thing he wanted to hear was her views on poetry. I don't know why I wasn't more brutal with her myself.

He was very busy, too, with schedules to meet. Since Strand Films had closed in 1945, Dylan had done some script-writing with the director Dan Birt at British National Pictures (they worked on two films together, *Three Weird Sisters* and *No Room at the Inn*). Then he had what we thought was another big break when his friend at Strand, Ralph Keene, recommended Dylan to the film producer Sidney Box at Gainsborough, which was one of the biggest film companies at the time (they produced the Diana Dors film *Good Time Girl*, using a script that Dylan had originally worked on for Strand). Sidney Box commissioned Dylan to write three scripts, for which he was to receive £1,000 each, which was a lot of money in those days. The money was to be paid in regular instalments, which meant that again we had a steady basic income, quite apart from all the work that Dylan was now doing for the BBC.

It seemed as though our financial problems were over for a while, and we settled down to a simple sort of life at South Leigh. Harry and Cordelia Locke, who were great friends of ours, had a cottage in the village, and our old friends Bill and Helen McAlpine also moved to South Leigh. We'd meet in the pub in the evenings and at the weekends. Harry was a proper pub friend, always telling funny stories, and – being a music-hall comedian – telling them well. He used to have an act of pretending to speak a foreign language that he didn't know which he could keep up for hours. (Our friendship with them went back many years; Dylan had known Harry before he met me, and Cordelia had known my sister Nicolette when she was at the Slade, so I'd known her before she married Harry.)

The place itself, the Manor House, was pretty bloody awful, nowhere near as grand as its description. It had a grey front, with quite large rooms either side of the front door. There was no bathroom, and we had an outside lavatory with one of those awful tin buckets that had to be emptied regularly. There was a German prisoner-of-war camp nearby. Even though the war was over they still hadn't been resettled, and we used to get them to empty the thing and do all the other dirty jobs that had to be done. We tried to treat them as well as we could, and I always cut them a lot of bread and marge and boiled them up tea. They made me feel very shy. I wanted to show them that I had nothing against them as people, because I had never associated individuals with the war, even when the Germans were fighting against us, because they had probably been forced to do it. They also did the gardening, cutting down hedges and chopping wood, which made life a lot easier for us. It was probably the woman at the pub who organised it for us; that was how we usually got things done. I couldn't help feeling sorry for them; they had no English and we had no German, and they seemed so subdued; downhearted, I suppose, silently eating what was put in front of them.

The house itself was drably unpleasant; no electricity and lit by oil lamps, with a huge old black range in the kitchen, which meant back to the Irish stew – I always seemed to be getting back to that. Even when we had a pressure cooker it always blew up on me and I was back to the stew. It was a sad place, really, with all those dismal fields and elm trees; the English countryside can be very melancholy. (I shall never forget the morning vision at my mother's house at Blashford, when you opened the curtains and saw all that mist. I associate elm trees with sadness and mist and those fields in front of the house.)

Our marriage was under no great strain there, but Dylan and I weren't particularly happy. It was toughest on me, that place. Some days we would ride our bicycles into Witney, the nearest town: it had a little market, though nowhere near as good as the one at

Carmarthen. Some evenings, we would catch the train into Oxford and go pubbing. If Dylan had promised to be on the evening train, we'd meet for a drink with Harry and Cordelia. Maggs Taylor was the only real problem. She drove me mad because she didn't give a damn about me or the children. I turned that caravan over once with Dylan inside it, so she had it moved away from the field by the house and down into an orchard near the post office, in the centre of the village. Things got worse when Dylan's parents arrived. (His mother had broken her leg and had been in hospital in Carmarthen, and his father was getting too frail to look after himself, let alone Granny Thomas.)

Dylan's sister Nancy went down to stay with them at Blaen Cwm for a few days, but she said her cottage down in Brixham – where she was living with her second husband Gordon Summersby – was too small for them to move in there, and anyway, she and Gordon were planning to go abroad. One day Dylan ordered an ambulance and arranged for his parents to move to South Leigh without even asking me; they just arrived. I thought it was very thoughtless of Dylan, mean and egotistical, to plant them on me when I already had the kids to look after. What he should have done was find a nurse for them in their own home, but I suppose he couldn't pay for a nurse, or didn't want to. Dylan was still going off – his life never changed – and he seemed to leave me alone at home more than ever after this, always with the old excuse that he was only doing it to make money for us. He had also fallen behind with the rent to Margaret Taylor, although it didn't seem to affect his relationship with her much; she kept coming to see us at South Leigh and I used to get more and more distressed, especially with Dylan's invalid parents to look after.

Things did get a bit easier when we found a local woman, Mary, to help with the housework. She was a miracle, always happy and laughing and the best worker I ever had. I loved her and don't know what I would have done without her. She was great at chatting to Granny Thomas, too. I could have coped with it all if Dylan had been fair, but he couldn't face all the problems in the house: he started vanishing again; and I then had no one to talk to, which made it worse.

Sometimes he would go off to work in the mornings and then not return at night, and I would be raging by the time he did come home. I felt quite helpless, trapped in that desolate place with his children and his parents and no money to go away myself. I did think sometimes of going back home to my mother's but thought that would probably be even worse. It's not much fun going back to your parents when you've failed. Now I think that Dylan must have been getting steadily more estranged from me, because there were very few home comforts for him when he did return, but I didn't take account of this at the time.

Granny Thomas did that Welsh trick of pretending that she didn't know Dylan drank, or, at least, to what extent. If he came home drunk she would mentally excuse him, even when he had made up some story that was impossible to believe. He'd perform the little-boy-lost act for his mother, who was stuck there in bed with her broken leg, always jolly and laughing, with me having to wait on her hand and foot. Granny Thomas hadn't got much money herself, so what could she do? All they had left was what D.J. had over from his little pension: it was a miserable amount they had between them.

In retrospect I feel rather sorry for myself, but I don't think I did then: I had an enormous amount of pride and self-will – inner resources, I called it. I was strong, and anyway, I had to put up with it; I had no choice. I had no skills; I had never been taught anything; and I wasn't in the kind of society where I could take a rich or reputable lover. I began to feel bitter.

Old D. J. was more unhappy than ever. He had always been pretty acid, but with all the moves he'd made since retirement, from Cwmdonkin Drive to South Leigh, it must have felt like downhill all the way for the poor devil. He had left all his books behind: he had no one to talk to and no comforts – none of the things that make life tolerable. He would toddle off to the pub sometimes, still anxious to be as far away from us as he could, as though expecting the worst. When Dylan came home drunk or did one of his vanishing tricks, D. J. never said a word. D. J. was a moral coward, I think – a very frightened man. Granny Thomas sometimes gave Dylan one of her lectures, though she wasn't really capable of stopping him doing anything he wanted to do. Her lectures were very mild. She would just warn him about the drinking. I don't think she ever knew about the women, certainly not then.

When my mother came down, I couldn't talk to her, either; we still never discussed any intimate things. I could see now that she wasn't very impressed by Dylan, but she had a very low opinion of men, anyway, after the way Francis had treated her. The only person I could turn to was Brigid, but she was in no better position than I was because she had been left, the only daughter in the house, alone with mother, so there really was no one. Nor was it any good me trying to plan our lives or our future, because we were both far too much under the influence of drink to think logically about such things.

We rowed, but it was difficult to find a good battleground at South Leigh because there was no privacy. We never rowed in front of the parents, though I'm sure they heard us. It must all have made a bad impression on Llewelyn, who was the eldest and the most likely to understand.

To add to our difficulties, Dylan's debts were mounting up. The Inland Revenue had discovered that he'd never filled in a tax return in his life. He would never talk about problems like that when he was with friends or drinking, but he became very depressed in the mornings. I think alcohol does that – you feel guilty and remorseful in the mornings – and my bitterness didn't help. I didn't know whether I still loved him or not, but I couldn't bear the thought of anybody else loving him. I felt indignation, resentment, fury: I just felt it wasn't fair – and it wasn't, either.

8

Early in 1948, before the parents came to South Leigh, Dylan had gone back to West Wales to see them. It was just after his mother had broken her leg. His father was in the cottage in Blaen Cwm, and Nancy was staying there, too. Dylan wrote to me:

Caitlin, my own, my dear, my darling whom I love forever: Here it's snowbound, dead, dull, damned; there's hockey-voiced Nancy being jolly over pans and primuses in the kitchen, and my father trembling and moaning all over the place, crying out sharply when the dog barks – Nancy's dog – weeping, despairing. My mother, in the Infirmary, with her leg steep-splinted up towards the ceiling and a 300lb weight hanging from it, is good and cheerful and talks without stop about the removed ovaries, dropped wombs, amputated breasts, tubercular spines, & puerperal fevers of her new friends in the women's surgical ward. She will have to lie, trussed, on her back with her leg weighted, for at least two months, and then will be a long time learning, like a child, to walk again. The doctors have stuck a great steel pin right through her knee, so that, by some method, the broken leg will grow to the same length as the other one. My father, more nervous & harrowed than I have ever seen him, cannot stay on here alone and Nancy cannot stay with him, so she [will] take him back with her to Brixham to stay, until my Mother can leave the Infirmary. My mother will therefore be alone in the infirmary for months. No-one here will look after the dog Mably, & Nancy cannot take him back to her tiny cottage as she has, already, a Labrador retriever: they don't know what to do but to have Mably destroyed, which is wrong because he is young & well and very nice. So I have said that I will take him.

My darling, I love you. I love you, if that is possible, more than ever in my life, and I have always loved you. When you left, going upstairs in the restaurant with that old horror, I sat for a long time lost lost lost, oh Caitlin sweetheart I love you. I don't understand how I can behave to you senselessly, foully, brutally, as though you were not the most beautiful person on the earth and the one I love forever. The train hourly took me further & further away from you and from the only thing I want in the world. The train was icy, and hours late. I waited hours, in Carmarthen Station in the early snowing morning, for a car to take me to Misery Cottage. All the time, without stopping, I thought of you, and of my foulness to you, and of how I have lost you. Oh Cat Cat please, my dear, don't let me lose you. Let me come back to you. Come back to me. I can't live without you. There's nothing left then. I can't ask you to forgive me, but I can say that I will never again be a senseless, horrible, dulled beast like that. I love you.

I am leaving here, snowbound or not, on Tuesday and will reach London early Tuesday evening, with bag & Mably. I could come straightaway to you if — if you will have me. Christ, aren't we each other's? This time, this last time, darling, I promise you I shall not again be like that. You're beautiful. I love you. Oh, this Blaencwm room. Fire, pipe, whining, nerves, Sunday joint, wireless, no beer until one in the morning, death. And you aren't here. I think of you all the time, in snow, in bed.

Dylan

For the life of me, I can't remember now what that row had been about (there were so many and each one merged into the next over the years), but there, in his letter, is that mixture of fantasy love and remorse that followed every argument. He loved me. Yes, he always told me that: he never stopped telling me. But now he was coming home again, and bringing that bloody mongrel Mably with him, too. (Mably had some ghastly habits. One was the bicycle: he would run in front of the wheels barking his head off and you'd have to get off it and beat him. On top of that, he would try to bugger the children, which I didn't think was a very pretty habit, either. When Dylan died I sent Mably to the gas chamber. I just got in touch with a man and he came to collect him. Dylan was madly sentimental; I was the realist.)

Dylan wrote me many letters like that, always pleading and begging forgiveness and telling me that he loved me forever and forever. It was always forever and forever. Very few of those letters survive: I had a box of them stolen when I was staying with Nicolette at Markham Square.

When I read the letter now, I can see that we had reached another crisis; but it wasn't a real crisis, nothing like the ones that came later, after he had gone to America, or even the rows that we had at South Leigh after he had dumped his parents on me, and started disappearing again. When we had those rows, Dylan said it would all be better if only we could get back to Laugharne and the life we had known before – all fantasy, but we believed it then. Within months of our arrival at the Manor House, he was telling Margaret Taylor that we really wanted to be back home in West Wales. I think he did get homesick for Laugharne, but not until he was half-dead. As long as he could keep going, he was quite happy to be somewhere else, but when things were bad he thought of Laugharne. He had soaked up all those Welsh things in childhood – the *hwyl*, the chapel passion – and there was something there that kept pulling him back; the Welsh have a word – *hiraeth* – for that deep longing they have for home, and, strangely, there's no direct, parallel word to it in the English language. Dylan had to have West Wales and the sea and that solitary abandonment; he needed that kind of background and, even more to the point, he knew that he did; and it suited me, too.

At first we hoped that we could take over the tenancy of Castle House, where we had stayed with Richard Hughes before the war, and in October 1948 Maggs Taylor went down to Laugharne to see if she could rent it for us. She took with her a letter from Dylan to Frances Hughes:

> I want very much to live in Laugharne because I know that there I can work well. Here, I am too near London; I undertake all sorts of little jobs, broadcasting etc., which hinder my own work. In Laugharne, if I could live there, I would work half the year on my film-scripts, and half on my own poems and stories: cutting out all time-wasting broadcasts, articles, useless London visits.

Maggs returned a few days later, convinced that we would be able to take a seven-year lease on Castle House, which was owned then (and still is) by the Starke family, who had owned the Castle itself since the eighteenth century. Dylan was immensely excited: he could barely contain himself. This would solve all our problems: no more rows; no more distractions; he could get on with his work, that real precious work – his poems. His delight comes shining through these extracts from the thank-you letter he immediately wrote:

Your letter, just arrived by winged messenger, has set us dreamily grinning, hopelessly shaking our heads, then beaming and gabbling together again as we think of the great house at the end of the cherrytreed best street in the world, bang next to the Utrillo tower, with its wild gardens and owly ruins, the grey estuary, forever linked to me with poems done and to be, flat and fishy below with Tom Nero Rowlands, the one last fisherman, who hates the water, trudging through it like a flatfooted cat; saying to ourselves, 'No no no, do not dream of it, never for us, too ugly too old', and then once more saying, not too loudly, 'Perhaps and perhaps, if we try, pray, whisper, fear the God, abjure drink and fighting, be humble, write poems, do not bite our nails, answer letters, collect the fallen apples for economical pulping into glass jars, do not throw her crutches at my mother, be good, be patient, sing, love one another, ask God for peace, perhaps and perhaps one day one day the owly castle and the noble house will be ours for some of the seven most heavenly years since pride fell.' Oh the kitchen for cooking and eating, for thinking Breughels! the room to the left as, praise be, you enter the house, that room for music and Caitlin dancing! the nursery for Aeronwy, that we must have more children to fill! the bedroom looking up at an unbalanced field, the field of infancy where even now we are all running so that, writing this in the rain, I can hear all our thin faraway children's voices glide over the plumtrees and through the ventilation skull-holes of this window! and the other bedroom looking out, happy as hell, at the clock of sweet Laugharne, the clock that tells the time backwards so that, soon, you walk about the town from Brown's to the gulls on the Strand in the only Golden Age! . . . I think here of the best town, the best house, the only castle, the mapped, measured, inhabited, drained, garaged, townhalled, pubbed and churched, shopped, gulled and estuaried one state of happiness!

Our hopes for leasing Castle House fell through, but Margaret Taylor did better than that: she acquired the Boat House for us, the tiny, white-painted house on stilts at the water's edge that we had longed for for years. When we were living at Sea View we'd said often, 'Now, if only *that* house would come up . . .' It was the one that we never thought would.

Once we knew we were leaving South Leigh, the tensions eased. Dylan found that he could rent a house on the main street in Laugharne for his parents, a house called Pelican, almost opposite the doors of Brown's Hotel, and we thought that once they were there and we were in the Boat House, and we didn't have Maggs Taylor on our doorstep every day, he would settle down to his writing and peace would return to the marriage. His intentions seemed good, but I do remember being very annoyed and jealous when he went off to Czechoslovakia for a writers' congress just a few weeks before we were due to move. I thought that was really too much, him having all the fun and me stuck with his parents in South Leigh. I should have gone with him.

When we moved down to the Boat House in May 1949, we had to hire a furniture van, which was something we had never done before: we had always had to leave our possessions behind because we couldn't afford to move them. I had sold up all our furniture at Sea View at the time of my 'affair' with Glock, and later, when we left Manresa Road, we had abandoned our huge Napoleonic bed, the round table and Aeron's cradle. But now we at last had some things of our own because Maggs Taylor had helped us to furnish the Manor House, and we took it all down to Laugharne – just basics like beds, chairs, tables, a wardrobe and crockery, but the beginnings of a home. I can't remember anything about the move at all. I can remember being at South Leigh and then being at the Boat House, but nothing in between. We must have travelled by train because we never owned a car, and Dylan would have arranged for Billy Williams (Ebie's brother) to meet us at the station: he used to drive us everywhere.

The Boat House had a coal-burning stove, a Rayburn, and I was back to my big pans of broth. Our lives became really organised when I found Dolly (Dolly Long, who is still alive and living in Laugharne), who helped me run the house. She was a funny, wound-up little thing. I had no idea what age she was, but she had a very attractive sister. Dolly was a great help to me and we became friends as well: without her, I don't know what I would have done.

Llewelyn was still at boarding school in Oxford; Aeron was with us and, at the time we moved back to Laugharne, I was seven months pregnant. Colm, our third and last child, was born on 24 July 1949. He was around the same birth weight as Aeron and Llewelyn, about six pounds.

Aeron was going to the local school, and I used to get up first, at about six o'clock, to get Aeron and myself ready for the day. This was a long business because I always had a bath, did my face and my

The Boat House,
Laugharne, from the front

The Boat House and the estuary

Dylan and Caitlin with Granny Thomas and their children, Llewelyn, Aeron and Colm

Pelican, Laugharne: home of D.J. and Granny Thomas

The shed, where Dylan worked in Laugharne

Dylan at his desk inside the shed

Caitlin and Aeron, with Mably in the boat, on the River Taf, Laugharne

Caitlin looks on while Dylan discusses his next American trip with John Malcolm Brinnin, 1952

hair: I had to be as perfect as I could make myself. Then I would get Aeron up, get her breakfast and wash her. Aeron got in with a gang of Laugharne children who all went round together, and in the afternoons I used to take them down on a natural lawn by the river where we would play games – hide 'n' seek, sardines and blind man's buff. Sometimes, we would take picnics, and after Colm was born I used to take him down there with us as well.

Colm was a very good baby. He was born in Carmarthen hospital after one of those silly panics that often seem to happen with babies. I don't know where Dylan was. I had four bathes in the sea at Pendine that day, and when I got back to the Boat House I went for a walk along the cliff. The pains started, and they soon began coming fast. I called Ebie Williams and told him we had better get to the hospital quickly or it would be too late. Ebie drove faster and faster; the pains were coming quicker and quicker; he was panicking because he thought I was going to have the baby in his car. When we finally got to the hospital there was some awful bureaucracy to go through – filling up forms and producing ration books – and they wouldn't let me go up to the labour ward until I yelled at them, 'For God's sake, let me have this baby!' Then they did start shaving me between the legs, with terrible rough hands and a blunt razor.

I think Colm inherited all Dylan's charm. Dylan loved him very much because he really was sweet, whereas the other two, and Llewelyn in particular, had been much more difficult. Colm looked as much like Dylan as the others: he was always cheerful, happy and amusing. Colm was definitely Dylan's favourite because he used to play and laugh, and this was Dylan's idea of how a baby ought to be. He didn't cuddle him much, though. Dylan was never very physical towards the children (unlike the Italians), but I think he must have been proud of them because he used to carry their photographs around with him all the time in his wallet, and he would often show them to friends, particularly when he was a long way from home and feeling depressed: Dylan was very sentimental about them when he was far away.

During those first months back in Laugharne, Dylan seemed happier than I had known him before. He had a shed up on the cliff where he could work, alone and well away from the children. Every morning, when it was cold, I used to go up there after I had seen Aeron off to school and light his stove so that the shed would be warm for him by the time he settled down to work. He seemed to slip back into his old way of life very happily: pottering around the town in the mornings, calling in to see his father at Pelican (where they would sometimes do the *Times* crossword together), and then over the road to see Ivy at Brown's, where he would occasionally put bets on the horses. In the afternoon he would settle down to work in the shed from two to seven. I encouraged Dylan to work by trying to make it easier for him, keeping the children out of the way and trying to remove his detective stories from the shed so that he wouldn't be distracted by them. (He loved detective stories. If ever I went up past the shed and heard no sound from within, I knew he was reading: he always read if he couldn't work.)

I am very conscious now of his greatness, though at the time perhaps I took it for granted. He was very wise and he had that gift of *knowing*: it was something that was there from the very beginning; something he was born with, part of his whole substance as a man. Many people didn't see it because when he was performing in the pubs and getting drunk they only saw that side of him. He was very aware himself that he was different from other people, that he had been given some gift that is denied to most, and yet he seemed to go out of his way to hide it, to live his life in such a way that most people would never see it other than in his writing. And for me, of course, there has been this great difference between living in a small house in Laugharne and seeing the man that I loved walk through the door with a poem in his pocket, and then finding it forty years later treated as a great literary achievement: a tremendous transition has taken place, and I have had to live through that, though some people cannot see it: many people have no sense of space or history, anyway.

I became aware that he had this greatness in him: these later poems – the ones he wrote at Blaen Cwm and New Quay towards the end of the war, and those he worked on back in Laugharne – had a serenity in them, and when he brought them to me I could hear the noise they made, which was for me a kind of music. Some of it was very powerful: I can remember him reading 'Fern Hill' to me for the first time, and I just knew the sounds were beautiful.

The things I didn't appreciate in Dylan, which I now understand much better, were his kindness, tolerance and charitableness. I have come to recognise those as rare and important qualities; but then I thought them secondary. I was struck with that old-fashioned idea of male dominance and drive. Nor did I appreciate the fact that he treated everyone with equal kindness and equal tolerance. I always thought he ought to show more discrimination between one person and another, but even if someone was an absolute bastard he never banished them. There are people who do need shoving out of the door, but he would never do that.

He was a naturally good-natured person, although not always: he could criticise someone's poetry in a very forthright way, but he would choose his victims and go for someone well-established; he would never hurt the weak if he could help it. Bill McAlpine, for example, absolutely worshipped him, and it was pathetic because when Bill wrote poems he wrote them so obviously in Dylan's style that it was quite shaming to read them. Dylan had the charity to pretend not to notice, but he could have slain him if he'd wanted to. But he could be quite scathing of someone like Stephen Spender, whom he didn't rate highly at all, or Geoffrey Grigson or Richard Church, whom he couldn't bear. On the whole I think his judgement was correct – although it was often ahead of its time. They were duds and he saw it before anyone else did. He was careful, too, with ladies' feelings, as I can see from the letters he wrote to Pamela Hansford Johnson, who was struggling so hard and wrote so badly, or Margaret Taylor, who was even worse; and he was very kind to David Gascoyne, who was neurotic and needed tenderness.

Dylan kept so much of this to himself. For all that people have said, he remained a very private man, with an awareness that could be quite startling. He was aware of every other poet of the day and how their work was developing; he had a deep sense of tradition and of all the different techniques. I was always amazed – when he sometimes opened out, alone at home in the evenings – by the range of his knowledge: he would quote from long-forgotten poets, and refer to ideas that had long gone out of favour.

If he wanted to talk about a poem, I would listen; if he didn't, I wouldn't ask. If he wanted to share a poem with me, he would come down from the workshed, read me a few lines and say there was one line that he couldn't get right. Sometimes I would suggest to him that perhaps he should 'just leave it for now, and come back to it tomorrow'. Sometimes I would suggest an alternative word, which worked occasionally. He needed solitude, but sometimes he needed to bounce ideas, to share things – it was all part of his creative process. He shared his life with me. I think he trusted me. He knew that I wouldn't flatter him, and would never say something was marvellous if I didn't think that it was. I think I'm incapable of flattery anyway; it takes a hell of a lot to make me say something nice – but he knew that one of my compliments was worth ten of anyone else's.

And I always knew that there was a great love between us, at the heart of everything he did.

Dylan may have been dissipated in his drinking and his sexual affairs, but there was nothing dissipated in his poetry; there he was very self-disciplined. Occasionally it failed him: he would go off to work in the shed, and then after a short while he would be back and he'd say, 'No, I can't do it today; it won't work.' Then he might have to wait for a day or two for it to come back again. It has been suggested that he had burnt himself out, but no one who saw him working alone in that shed could ever believe that. I used to go out along the cliff with the children, and we would tiptoe past the shed as we heard his voice, booming, muttering and mumbling as he wrestled with each word. He knew what he wanted to do and he did it. No matter what the pressures, or what other people said, Dylan always had this tremendous faith in himself, and he just kept at it, almost daily. Sometimes, I would stand outside the shed and listen as he boomed or intoned, but I never interrupted him, and I made sure that nothing else did, either. He needed his solitude, and I gave it him.

Some evenings, after he had finished writing for the day, he would come down to the house for his bath (he loved to have a bath before going back to Brown's for the evening). I would fill the bath for him and put out his sweets – dolly mixtures, boiled sweets, humbugs – and pickled onions and savoury things in little saucers, which I used to lay across the soap tray, always with a bottle of fizzy lemonade beside the bath. Dylan would settle down in there and read, until he wanted me to come in and scrub his back, by which time the water would be getting cold and he'd want me to warm it up again. This was the routine he loved and enjoyed until the end of his life.

Later, when there were tensions between us over his affairs, I would sometimes stand over the bath and look at him and ask myself, 'How the hell could I ever be jealous of this fat pig?' He looked so gross and obscene towards the end. And yet I was madly jealous. When he was dressed he wasn't so bad, but I couldn't bear to see him naked after he had been unfaithful to me; I could have skinned the whole back off him, I was so furious. I was revolted by him, then.

But that was later.

I was pleased with our new home, which was prettier than anything we'd ever had before, and I had Colm to look after. My babies always brought out the best in me, and I think those few months, through 1949 and early 1950, were the last period of happiness or near-happiness that we had together. Llewelyn came home in the holidays and we had our family around us. Dylan left most of that to me, of course. He was sentimental about the children on paper, but he couldn't stand much of their company. (Whenever we travelled anywhere by train I would have to sit with the children in one compartment, while he made his journey in another. Usually he would sit in the restaurant car, eating and drinking, while I was left alone with them, often without food or drink. I thought it was pretty awful, but there wasn't much I could do about it.)

Dylan's restlessness had gone now that we were back in Laugharne. He was commissioned to write more books and scripts than he could ever produce, and he was writing poems again. He finished 'Over Sir John's Hill' soon after we moved into the Boat House, and over the next four years – in between writing his radio play for voices, *Under Milk Wood*, and scripts for the BBC – he also completed 'In The White Giant's Thigh', 'Do Not Go Gentle Into That Good Night', 'Lament', 'Poem on His Birthday' and the 102-line Author's Prologue to his *Collected Poems*, which were published by Dent in 1952.

We felt that at last we had the ideal spot, and while he was working in the afternoons I would go out into the estuary stabbing for flat fish or picking cockles. It gave us pleasure just to stand outside, or sit on the harbour wall, watching the tide rushing in or creeping out, the herons, oyster-catchers and occasional cormorants. The morning mists drifted across the water towards Llanybri and Llangain, where we had lived at Blaen Cwm and Dylan's family had been for generations. I bought Colm a little boat, which we called *The Cuckoo*. It was a dangerous place to bring up children, with powerful tides sweeping up the river, but that didn't occur to me then. I used to dive off the garden wall into the high tide and never thought for a moment that this was a risky thing to do, although I heard later that dozens of people had been drowned in those waters.

Laugharne could be glorious in summer and an absolute bog in winter, when it never seemed to stop raining. It fitted Dylan like a glove. It was an eccentric little town with strange customs and even stranger people, an English-speaking town surrounded by Welsh-speaking Wales. It had somehow managed to preserve its traditions: a Corporation led by a Portreeve, who wore a chain of golden cockleshells; a Chancellor; a Recorder; a Court of Aldermen, and four Constables, each equipped with a wooden truncheon.

The Corporation owned much of the town's land and met once a fortnight to decide leases and rents and which hedges should be cut, and once a year – in October – all the men sat down to the Portreeve's Breakfast, which was an excuse for day-long drinking, a day when the town's pubs never closed. Every three years nearly every able-bodied citizen went out on the Common Walk, patrolling the twenty-six-mile boundary of the Corporation's lands, all of which were distinguished by strange names – and if you didn't know the names you would be turned upside down and beaten on the bottom with a Constable's truncheon.

Dylan loved all that small-town pomp and the nonsense gossip that he lapped up every morning in Ivy Williams' kitchen at Brown's Hotel: it was where she did her cooking, but she ran it like a bar. People sat around the kitchen table drinking after hours, drinking on Sundays (when the pubs were supposed to be shut under the Welsh licensing laws in force then), and drinking from early morning before the main bar opened. Dylan found it very cosy, and it was there that he picked up all the character vignettes which he moulded into *Under Milk Wood*. The folk of Laugharne were engaged in an endless wrangle of feuds, affairs, fights, frauds and practical jokes, and Dylan would return home at lunch-time for a bowl of our thick fatty stew full of the stories he had heard from Ivy.

There were the cocklewomen, his 'web foot cocklewomen', who were famous in Laugharne because they were big-hipped, huge women who would walk out with their donkeys to the Ginst Point at the end of the estuary, where they picked sacks of cockles while the tide was out. There was one famous story of a character in Laugharne who was married to a cocklewoman; he came home rolling drunk from the pub one night and threw his small change into the fire, knowing that she would bend down to pick it up – and then he had her from behind.

Then there was a real-life 'Polly Garter' who loved having babies, and had them all by different men. There was a man who was committing incest with his daughter: everyone knew that he was abusing her but, as with everything else in Laugharne, there was a lot of disapproval and talk, with nothing ever done. We had a murder, too, very close to the Boat House. One of the ferrymen, who lived next door to us, was deaf and dumb and a bit mad; one night he was said to have gone to the other end of town to this old woman's house, taken all her money and killed her. This was a big scandal. The police were brought in, which was rare, because on the whole they preferred to leave Laugharne well alone. Everyone knew that the ferryman had done it, but the police could get no answer from him because he was deaf and dumb (and played on it, too), so they had no way of condemning him, and he ended his days in an old folks' home. There were always stories about mysteries that hadn't been solved, bodies that had disappeared, women who had gone off with other men and men who had gone off with other women, and Brown's was the place where the stories were told, over the beer. Dylan often came home with some shocking tale to tell me, usually stories with a sexual connotation, like all the best stories. It was a very uninhibited place and I think that was what Dylan liked about it. Neither of us had ever known anywhere else like it, and I was always happy there, providing I could get out and not be mown down by too much housework.

Whenever he was away from Laugharne, and into one of those maudlin crying bouts after he had been drinking, he would get very sentimental and start talking about the children, the Boat House and Brown's Hotel. Laugharne became his magical sea-town, the town where people had a horror of work, where even the smallest journeys were undertaken by bike, and where the local vicar had once said that the introduction of unemployment pay was the best thing that had ever happened to Laugharne because previously the people had had no visible means of support.

Ivy wanted me to join the Women's Institute, but I never did. Somehow I could never see myself making cakes and jam with all those old cocklewomen, but I do look back on Laugharne quite fondly, although I have a lot of reservations. I much preferred the hard, industrious men of the mining towns to all those feckless people, even if their towns were as ugly as hell and they lived in rows of tiny cottages: I didn't like the passivity of Laugharne. I am always terrified of getting sucked into decadent places, which is all too easy for people who are alcoholically inclined. Laugharne for me was a decadent place that never seemed to stop drinking.

Dylan was never a late drinker. He liked to go out in the early evening, after his bath and supper. Often he would be home around ten o'clock, though sometimes he wouldn't. It was always the same routine: I'd be there with him, night after night, once the children were in their beds.

All that drinking became frightfully boring after a time. I didn't mind it so much then because I was so involved with Dylan, but from a distance it sounds deadly, though I can still see its importance to him. It was the drinking that gave him a life apart from his genius; he couldn't have lived alone with that; it was more than he could bear. And his drinking in Laugharne was his contact with people. He knew he needed that. Dylan was rarely invited into anyone's house. His closest friends were the men he met in Brown's. He would sit with them in the bow window, looking up and down the street, and he more or less recreated Laugharne in *Under Milk Wood*. When it was first broadcast by the BBC after his death, Ivy recognised many of the characters in the play: she knew them better than I did because it was she who had introduced them to Dylan.

I never did get into all that pubbing with the same enthusiasm as Dylan. There wasn't much in it for me, except getting the lift of enough drink, and that usually ends fatally, anyway. I took to the drink easily, and there were times when I thought I couldn't do without it, though I never really enjoyed it as a way of life unless we had some special friends with us. Towards the end of an evening, after I'd had a few drinks, I would do anything. I'd strip and leap on the table and do crazy dances. Dylan used to bring people back to the Boat House after the pubs had closed, and by then everybody was pretty well lit. I used to throw myself off the harbour wall into the high tide. I drank this beautiful drink I had concocted – a glass of milk mixed with a double whisky – which gave me a great sense of warmth and courage.

It was a masculine world. There was nobody else like me who went around with their husbands, and I would stand at the back of the bar, sometimes, and make an acid remark like, 'How much longer is this story going to go on?' I did get to feel, rather like Dylan, that pubs were a home from home. At the same time it was not really my thing – just something that happened to me through following Dylan: I had to go with him or not see him. But to go cold-bloodedly into that miserable Brown's in the mornings: I couldn't do that; just to sit in that window through the light of the day was absolute torture. I was always wanting to move and get in the water and do physical things, and my only way to combat that was to drink until I didn't care.

The pubbing part was painful from the time we went back to Laugharne because it was bloody boring, though made more colourful by Dylan's presence, I suppose. If I wasn't there with him in the mornings he would just sit there in the window with Ivy. Dylan milked Ivy pretty effectively, but she enjoyed it. She and Brown's Hotel and that flat Buckley's beer created *Under Milk Wood*; the incidents, the quirks, the jealousies and adulteries – she knew what everybody in Laugharne was doing, and in Laugharne they do it more than most.

Dylan captured all that, and the lives of the more respectable people behind their blinds, who wouldn't come to the pub anyway, who wore their best Sunday suits, and walked to Church with a Bible under their arms: he saw it all.

9

Although Dylan always said that a wife should be at the sink or in bed, he would say it in a joking kind of way. His friends probably thought that this was the outrageous Dylan, trying to shock, but I knew he meant it and that underneath he was a very old-fashioned son of his father. 'You've married the wrong woman,' I would tell him when he spoke like that in front of other people, and yet in spite of this attitude we always shared everything, went everywhere together, and felt a closeness between us that everyone could see.

That closeness remained until after he went to America. There was still a strong bond between us even after that, but somehow our relationship wasn't its old self again, which distressed him as much as it did me. There was something happening to us that neither of us could control, and it was all the more painful because neither of us saw the warning signs.

During our first months at Laugharne in 1949, our life had a calm that we had not known since our days at Sea View ten years earlier. When Dylan received his first letter from John Malcolm Brinnin, just after we moved, inviting him to lecture in New York, neither of us saw this as a danger; it was what he had been hoping for since the success of *Deaths and Entrances* – a chance to reach a wider audience, and perhaps to work and stay in a warmer climate.

Dylan was excited by the invitation; he saw this as an opportunity to broaden his career – still writing for films and radio but performing, too, and earning enough money to be able to set time aside for the work that mattered to him more than anything else, his poetry. Brinnin's letter, and the new house, delighted Dylan. He wrote to Margaret Taylor:

> I can never thank you enough for making this fresh beginning possible by all the trust you have put in me, by all the gifts you have made me, by all your labour & anxiety in face of callous & ungrateful behaviour. I know that the only way to express my deep deep gratitude is to be happy & to write. Here I am happy and writing. All I shall write in this water and tree room on the cliff, every word, will be my thanks to you. I hope to God it will be good enough. I'll send you all I write. And ordinary letters too, full of trees & water & gossip & no news. This isn't that kind of letter. This is only the expression of the greatest gratitude in the world: you have given me a life. And now I am going to live it.

We settled down to do so, spending most of that year at the Boat House, with Dylan making only occasional visits to London to work for the BBC.

Dylan was writing well, and he was growing closer to his father now that he realised that D. J. was getting weaker and did not have many more years to live. Dylan saw his parents most mornings; Pelican was just across the road from Brown's, and if he didn't go to the house to see them his mother would see him going into the pub. Granny Thomas made herself at home. She was always cheerful wherever she was; you just couldn't keep her down. Poor old D. J. would be complaining that 'this is the end of civilisation' while she would be happily making his tea, cleaning, dusting, shopping, washing and cooking. When she had her women friends down from Carmarthen for a cup of tea and two hours of malice, poor old D. J. would lock himself away in another room until they had gone, driven mad by their jabbering. What D. J. shared with Dylan was books.

Dylan was never a collector of books. Books did not matter much to him as books; he could rarely afford them and, when he did buy them, he put his beer bottles on them (he hardly ever drank anything but beer); it was the ideas within them that he cared about, and once he had found the idea and stored it away in his mind he didn't need the book any longer. Dylan never built up a library of his own, but he could always refer to his father's books when he wanted to. Dylan always had these – and D. J. – as his personal reference system (though Dylan was always careful never to borrow more than two or three books at a time because he knew

that his father would be afraid he would eat his breakfast off them).
Dylan's memory was extraordinary; he could remember where he
had read a certain line and go straight back to it, and for any poem
that he had studied at length he had total recall. This interest was
largely restricted to the English-language poets; he was never
attracted by any of the great French, German or Italian writers: he
knew what he wanted, as always.

His knowledge of technique and the tricks of the writer's trade
was extensive; he knew all the rhymes and metres, had a wide-
ranging vocabulary, and enjoyed playing with word-sounds and
alliteration. Many times I asked him how he managed to know so
much, and, although he wouldn't refuse, he was reluctant to talk
about it. He liked to pretend that writing poetry was easy and that
it all just flowed, when the truth was that he was the most
perfectionist of writers. He spent hours and days balancing words,
lines and phrases, throwing out words that weren't right, and he
always did this noisily and alone in his shed, chanting and reciting,
making each sound fit. He was so meticulous, and yet equally
careful that no one saw him doing it; this was his secret life, the
source of his strength and confidence. I think many of his friends
were surprised to see this side of his character revealed when his
Letters to Vernon Watkins (1957) were published, because they
demonstrated how Dylan, in a detailed correspondence over a
period of twenty years, had sought advice from, and given criticism
to, this, the most painstaking of his friends. To those who knew
only the pub Dylan, the drinking Dylan, playing games and telling
dirty stories, this was another world entirely, and he was reluctant
to share this world, even with me. Vernon was one of the few
people who saw this private side of him.

It was the poetry that gave Dylan the confidence to perform on
stage to large audiences on those American tours; it was the only
area of his life where he was totally sure of himself. He had studied it
since childhood, and he must have learnt so much from D. J.: the
rhythm of words, the feeling of words, the assonance and use of
rhyme – it all meant so much to him. I am sure he never meant to
hurt me or anyone else; he was creating lasting works of literature
while hurting all around him, and at the time I couldn't understand
it. I think I do now. When you are creating it takes up all of you and
you are not aware of the way you are treating other people: you are
totally absorbed. Genius is selfish; the creative process itself is selfish.

Dylan did hurt me then, and later, but I feel that he did do justice to me in many ways. He dedicated some of his poems to me, which meant a lot. I was pleased and proud in a proper way. It is a matter for pride, when you think about it. I have been taught so much about false pride in Alcoholics Anonymous, because that is what they say alcoholics suffer. I have always been afraid to say that I am proud of something, but I do remember the day Dylan brought home his *Collected Poems* (1952) for the first time and I saw that he had dedicated what was, in effect, his life's work, to me. That pleased me very much. He didn't tell me he was going to do it so it came as a great surprise. I thought there would be the odd poem that he had written for me, but I never expected him to dedicate it all to me.

Although Dylan hurt us so much, I realise now that he was a very gentle man. There was something inside him that he could not control. He could only find the peace he was searching for when he was alone with his poetry. His tragedy was that he couldn't be like that all the time because he had to make money some other way. When people like Dylan are born, and they aren't born very often, they need special care to enable them to do their own special work. The miracle is that Dylan still did his, mostly from his own resources.

Yet even though he was so confident about his poetry, to the end of his life he always had doubts before starting a new poem; it was rather like professional actors going on stage, and still getting stage fright every night.

Dylan would spend a long time thinking about a new poem before starting to write, turning over ideas and deciding what he wanted the poem to say. The structure of the poem and its meaning were clear in his mind before he began, even though it then might take him months and months of work to find the words and the images, the rhymes and the rhythms that he later built around this structure. He rarely explained his poems to anyone (though he would sometimes run through a poem with me just as he had finished it, telling me how the ideas within it progressed as the poem developed); he always thought the poems should speak for themselves, and that it wasn't for him to explain how he had struggled with their structure, finding the right balance between the words and the rhythm, endlessly trying new combinations of words, and searching through dictionaries or Roget's *Thesaurus* to find a better-sounding word or one which expressed more clearly the ideas he was developing. Sometimes, Dylan would work through hundreds – yes, hundreds – of different work-sheets, changing a word here or a comma there, until he was satisfied. But he was a craftsman, and, like all craftsmen, he liked to keep his secrets to himself.

In our first years in Laugharne, at Sea View, Dylan had no doubts about his ability; his sureness was within himself and he never talked about it. But towards the end of his life – by the time we were living at the Boat House – he was setting such high standards for himself that he became afraid that he would never be able to keep it up and that the gift might run out. It was something that had happened to other writers and he thought it might happen to him, and the thought worried him more as he grew older and his work became more widely acclaimed. The later poems, which I have always thought were among his finest, were the ones about which he worried most, sometimes working months on end just to get one line right or to find the very word that he wanted. When I read those poems now – poems like 'Do Not Go Gentle Into That Good Night' or 'Over Sir John's Hill' – I realise how much he was suffering, and that his gift hadn't dried up at all.

Timidity, shyness and cowardice – I think Dylan had them all. In those years at the Boat House, when we often had so little money (although he was earning so much), Dylan was always frightened when he saw strangers coming to the door, in case it was someone with a writ, and he was always nervous in the mornings before the postman arrived. He didn't like getting official-looking buff envelopes; they usually ended up in the wastepaper basket without being opened. This was part of Dylan's trouble; he never replied to unpleasant letters or letters asking for debts to be paid. He often threw them away; he couldn't face them when he recognised their origin from the envelope. Dylan never had any kind of filing system. He was aware that his finances were in a mess, but something really dramatic had to happen to bring it home to him. He never kept any letters from friends like Vernon either; they were all thrown away.

At other times Dylan would open a letter to find that he was being asked to write something, and he would say 'Yes' without giving the matter a second thought, just to get the advance payment. Then he would get reproving letters from his agent, David Higham, because he was committing himself to writing books in which he hadn't the slightest interest and which therefore were unlikely ever to get written. When the publisher or editor started to complain about the non-delivery of the work, Dylan would start to get nervous. This was what happened with that awful *Peer Gynt* that he was supposed to have done for the BBC; it became a sort of family joke. He had been offered a fee of 250 guineas to do a television adaptation of Ibsen's *Peer Gynt* back in 1949; this was a very large fee indeed – the BBC were intending it to be one of their major productions. Dylan happily said that he would do it if they agreed to pay half the fee in advance, but he could never bring himself to write it. His heart wasn't in it. It dragged on for years. In the end, it became almost a music hall farce.

Dylan would come into the kitchen and tell me, 'They want that bloody *Peer Gynt* again,' and then burst out laughing.

Dylan was also asked to write a book of Welsh fairy tales; another book about his impressions of America and a third about travelling through Wales. None of them got written because, apart from the advance, he wasn't the least bit interested in any of them. Looking back now I think it was just as well that he didn't write them: they were all dull subjects and not his sort of thing at all.

Dylan hadn't the mind of a hack writer; everything he wrote he did with great care, even the simplest script for radio. It wasn't that he decided not to do these other jobs: because they didn't interest him he kept putting them off and putting them off; he was incapable of writing something that he didn't care about when he might have a poem on his mind, or another radio script that really had caught his imagination.

It was the everyday things that Dylan was frightened of – bills to be paid, debts, babies to be fed and me to be clothed. He was totally unrealistic about that sort of thing so the grocer wasn't paid; nor was the butcher, the milkman or the chemist. We ran up tick wherever we lived; you can do that for a time, but you can't do it for ever. It was hard on me because I had to clothe the children and I could never buy a new outfit for myself. I used to sneak a few clothes occasionally in Carmarthen and then feel guilty because I hadn't paid for them. I was then pursued by bills myself, which I would give to Dylan because I had no money of my own. I would say, 'For God's sake, we must pay this because they're getting really nasty about it.' He must have known that you can't live like that, because he came from a nagging Welsh family that never stopped talking about money, and penny-counting. Dylan was a coward not to face it, and yet at the same time one can't help sympathising with him if he had all that load of poetry to deliver (except that half the time he wasn't writing poetry; you can't write it continuously – the creative gift doesn't work like that).

Dylan was frightened of many things. He was afraid of flying, afraid of mice, moths, and bats worst of all. He used to dwell on these horrors, trying to shock people with stories of mice being found in sandwiches, and he was always morbidly fascinated by cripples. I think all these fears were part of his feminine side. I was aware all the time that he did not have a very strongly developed masculine character. He didn't want to dominate anyone, or even to reprove the children. He wasn't shocked if I smacked them, but he always accepted that I should do it and not him.

It was the same in the home. Everything in the Boat House was left to me. He would never go near the stove if he could possibly avoid it. He left me to cook those endless pots of bone broth, highly spiced spaghetti with onions and garlic, and the occasional flat fish which I caught myself in the estuary waters below the Boat House. I never thought to clean them. I just used to fling them in the frying pan whole. (I remember once I caught one and threw it in the pan, thinking it was dead, and it leapt straight out and flopped around the floor. I picked it up with a piece of rag and dropped it straight back into the pan, holding it down with the pan cover. It was struggling to get out so I must have cooked it alive. It was fresh, anyway. I ate it with great relish – the best fried flatfish that I have ever had.)

I could be pretty savage. Another time someone brought us a lobster and I dropped it straight into a stewpan of boiling water, and the wretched thing tried to crawl out. No one had told me that I had to tie the claws first. I pushed it back into the pan and held the lid down. Dylan was horrified, and he kept well away.

Dylan's fears were bottled up inside him. He was never the kind of man to let you see him cry, although he had plenty of reasons to. Towards the end of his life, I think he became a tormented man. His infidelities were probably part of it, because he never stopped telling me how much he loved me. He couldn't sleep at night; he used to say he had been thinking about his debts, but there may have been more to it than that.

Before he made that first trip to America, he used to go away sometimes, just for a few days, seldom for long. I had Colm to look after and I wasn't unhappy. Dylan would write me long, loving letters, even if he was only gone two or three days, interspersed with laments of woe about his latest imagined bout of 'pneumonia', which I always knew was the drink. I didn't know of any other women in particular; names were never named then. I could imagine him going around drinking, and sleeping the odd night in different beds. I thought he might hop into bed with the occasional barmaid for some drunken sex. It wasn't that I thought it didn't matter, but it mattered less, then. When he came home I was usually welcoming, unless he had been away too long.

Dylan could see that he was earning more money and that things were going better for him, but it still wasn't enough for him to be free and easy. If he had only had some little job that occupied him for part of the day, I think that it would have been better; it might have made him more stable. I think it's safe to say that Dylan *was* unstable. He was always so restless, unable to stay in one place for long, constantly thinking up excuses to go up to London again to change his background. Sometimes I think he was just drinking to be able to sleep, because by then he would usually pass out when he came home from the pub; but drunken sleep is not much good because you wake up at some awful hour and you want more.

The children never saw him drunk. He never drank heavily during the day; he was only like that when he came home from Brown's late at night, and then we came home together and they were already fast asleep. It wasn't me protecting them because I didn't make a secret of his drinking; nor was I in a position to do so, being every bit as bad as he was (enough drink will blot out the conscience).

Thinking about it now, it does sound rather pathetic, spending half one's life in Brown's Hotel, wasting precious hours playing darts and poker, nap, shove-halfpenny and table skittles. But it was his relaxation, that and the beer and the talk, and I think he needed it as a contrast to the lonely, concentrated work he did in his shed.

Dylan and I were different in many ways. If there was something I wanted to say about someone, or to someone, that I knew would be unpleasant for them, or for me, I would force myself to go through with it quite unnecessarily, thereby bringing myself a lot of enemies, but it had to do with truth. Dylan could never face these things head on. In the begging letters he would never come right out and say what he wanted, or indeed how much he wanted; instead he would make all these round-about contortions without getting to the point. I would bring the thing out brusquely right away, and get the slap in the face if refused. I preferred to get it over. Those begging letters went on and on and were supposed to soften up the recipient. With some people it may have worked, but I thought it was boring and unnecessary and almost indiscriminate. He was certainly like that in his letters to Princess Caetani and Margaret Taylor. He knew what they wanted – all the descriptive stuff – so he ladled it on, but it was a tongue-in-cheek exercise. Many of his letters were bogus and he couldn't give a fig about the people he was writing to; they were well-written, but they weren't written sincerely. He couldn't have cared less about Princess Caetani; she was just a source of money as far as he was concerned. Like so many of the recipients of his letters, she may have felt privileged to have been apparently taken into his confidence, whereas it was really a well-calculated exercise in begging.

Dylan couldn't bring himself to come right out with a request for money for fear that he might be turned down; I think he wrote the letters in such a way that anyone receiving them would still have been glad to receive them as letters, and wouldn't think any the worse of him for writing, even if they did turn him down. There was a lot of fear in those letters. He was treating people as friends when he was begging from them, even when they weren't friends and he didn't like them.

With all those complexes Dylan wasn't really the type to undertake American lecture-tours. He wasn't happy travelling from one strange town to the next, with no one to talk to on the train. He felt lonely – another fear – which he tried to control by stepping off the train and going straight into the nearest bar. That lecture-tour racket was too brutal for someone as soft as Dylan, because it didn't allow for any relaxation; but when the letter came from Brinnin he wrote back:

> I feel extremely honoured to be the first poet to be invited from abroad, who was not already a visitor, and delighted too. I've wanted, for some time, to come to the States, and there couldn't be a pleasanter way

of coming than this . . . I should like to come to New York to give my reading early in 1950, probably in January or February. I should be only too glad to accept your sponsorship and to read in other places, including California.

John Malcolm Brinnin had recently been appointed director of the Poetry Centre at the Young Men's and Young Women's Hebrew Association in New York. He had long been an admirer of Dylan's poetry, and almost his first decision in his new job was to invite Dylan to go to New York to deliver a reading for a fee of five hundred dollars plus expenses. After an exchange of letters, he agreed to go even further, and arranged for Dylan to make a tour of the United States, speaking to students at forty universities.

Dylan had never made a tour like it before, and neither had any other British poet. He was breaking entirely new ground. Eventually the dates were finalised: he would leave for the States on 20 February 1950 and give his first reading three days later at the Kaufmann Auditorium in New York.

Dylan was very excited to be going. I went up to London to see him off, and we spent a few days there together. He kept telling me that this time he would be making a lot of money. This had always been his excuse for his going away before so I didn't altogether believe him, although I could see that he was being offered higher fees for his readings in the United States than he had ever been paid before. He said he would send me back cheques. At the same time, he was also trying to underplay it all with me because he thought I would be jealous of him going away without me and would feel miserable in Laugharne, alone with the children. He sent his first letter to me three days after arriving in New York:

My darling far-away love, my precious Caitlin, my wife dear, I love you as I have never loved you, oh please remember me all day & every day as I remember you here in this terrible, beautiful, dream and nightmare city which would only be any good at all if we were together in it, if every night we clung together in it. I love you, Cat, my Cat, your body, heart, soul, everything, and I am always and entirely yours. How are you, my dear? When did you go with Ivy back to Laugharne? I hope you didn't racket about too much because that makes you as ill as racketing makes me. And how is my beloved Colum and sweet fiend Aeron? Give them my love, please. I will myself write to Llewelyn over the weekend when I temporarily leave New York and go to stay with John Brinnin – a terribly nice man – in his house in the country an hour or so away. And how are the old ones? I'll write to them, too. I love you, I can see you, now this minute, your face & body, your beautiful hair, I can hear your lovely, un-understandable voice. I love you, & I love our children & I love our house. Here, each night, I have to take things to sleep: I am staying right in the middle of Manhattan, surrounded by skyscrapers infinitely taller and stranger than one has ever known from the pictures: I am staying in a room, a hotel room for the promised flat did not come off, on the 30th floor: and the noise all day & night: without some drug, I couldn't sleep at all. The hugest, heaviest lorries, police-cars, firebrigades, ambulances, all with their banshee sirens wailing & screaming, seem never to stop; Manhattan is built on rock, a lot of demolition work is going on to take up yet another super skyscraper, & so there is almost continuous dynamite blasting. Aeroplanes just skim the tips of the great glimmering skyscrapers, some beautiful, some hellish. And I have no idea what on earth I am doing here in the very loud, mad middle of the last mad Empire on earth: – except to think of you, & love you, & to work for us. I have done two readings this week, to the Poetry Center of New York: each time there was an audience of about a thousand. I felt a very lonely, foreign midget orating up there, in a huge hall, before all those faces; but the readings went well. After this country weekend, where I arranged with Brinnin some of the rest of my appallingly extensive programme, I go to Harvard University, Cambridge, Boston, for about 2 days, then to Washington, then back to New York, then, God knows, I daren't think, but I know it includes Yale, Princeton, Vassar – 3 big universities, as you know, old know-all – & Salt Lake City, where the Mormons live, & Notre Dame, the Jesuit College, & the Middle West, Iowa, Ohio, Chicago – & Florida, the kind of exotic resort, & after that the mere thought makes my head roar like New York. To the places near to New York, Brinnin is driving me by car; to others I go by myself by train; to the more distant places, I fly. But *whatever* happens, by God I don't fly back. Including landing at Dublin, Canada, & Boston, for very short times, I was in the air, cooped up in the stratosphere, for 17 hours with 20 of the nastiest people in the sky. I had an awful hangover from our London do as well; the terrible height makes one's ears hurt like hell, one's lips chap, one's belly turn; and it went on forever. I'm coming back by boat.

I've been to a few parties, met lots of American poets, writers, critics, hangers-on, some very pleasant, all furiously polite & hospitable. But apart from on one occasion, I've stuck nearly all the time to American beer, which, though thin, I like a lot & is ice-cold. I arrived, by the way, on the coldest day New York had had for years & years: it was 4 above zero. You'd have loved it. I never thought anything could be so cold, my ears nearly fell off: the wind just whipped through that monstrous duffle. But, as soon as I got into a room, the steamed [heat?] was worse: I think I can stand zero better than that, &, to the astonishment of natives, I keep all windows open to the top. I've been, too, to lots of famous places: up the top of the Empire State Building, the tallest there is, which terrified me so much, I had to come down at once; to Greenwich Village, a feebler Soho but with stronger drinks; & this morning John Brinnin is driving us to Harlem. I say 'us', you see: in the same hotel as me is staying our old New Zealander, Allen Curnow, & I see quite a bit of him. I've met Auden, & Oscar Williams, a very odd, but kind, little man.

And now it must look to you, my Cat, as though I'm enjoying myself here. I'm not. It's nightmare, night & day; there never was such a place; I would never get used to the speed, the noise, the utter indifference of the crowds, the frightening politeness of the intellectuals, and, most of all, these huge phallic towers, up & up & up, hundreds of floors, into the impossible sky. I feel so terrified of this place, I hardly dare to leave my hotel room – luxurious – until Brinnin or someone calls for me. Everybody uses the telephone all the time: it is like breathing: it is now nine o'clock in the morning, & I've had six calls: all from people whose names I did not catch to invite me to a little poity at an address I had no idea of. And most of all most of all most of all, though, God, there's no need to say this to you who understand everything, I want to be with you. If we could be here together, everything would be all right. *Never* again would I come here, or to any far place, without you; but especially never to here. The rest of America may be all right, & perhaps I can understand it, but that is the last monument there is to the insane desire for power that shoots its buildings up to the stars & roars its engines louder & faster than they have ever been roared before and makes everything cost the earth & where the imminence of death is reflected in every last power-stroke and grab of the great money bosses, the big shots, the multis, one never sees. This morning we go down to see the other side beyond the skyscrapers: black Harlem, starving Jewish East Side. A family of four in New York is very poor on £14 a week. I'll buy some nylons all the same next week, & some tinned stuff. Anything else?

Last-minute practicalities: How does the money go? Have any new bills arrived? If so, send them, when you write (& write soon my dear love, my sweetheart, that is all I wait for except to come home to you) to the address on the kitchen wall. I enclose a cheque to Phil Raymond, & an open cheque to Gleed; pay that bill when you can.

Remember me. I love you. Write to me.

Your loving, loving Dylan

A fortnight later, on 11 March 1950, he wrote to me again, this time from Washington;

Caitlin my own own own dearest love, whom God and *my* love and *your* love for me protect, my sweet wife, my dear one, my Irish heart, my wonderful wonderful girl who is with me invisibly every second of these dreadful days, awake or sleepless, who is forever and forever with me and is my own true beloved amen – I love you, I need you, I want, want you, we have never been apart as long as this, never never, and we will never be again. I am writing to you now, lying in bed, in the Roman Princess's sister's rich social house, in a posh room that is hell on earth. Oh why, why, *didn't* we arrange it *somehow* that we came out together to this devastating, insane, demoniacally loud, roaring continent. We *could* somehow have arranged it. Why oh why did I think I could live, I could bear to live, I could think of living, for all these torturing, unending, echoing months without you, Cat, my life, my wife, my wife on earth and in God's eyes, my reason for my blood, breath and bone. Here, in this vast mad horror, that doesn't know its size, or its strength, or its weakness, or its barbaric speed, stupidity, din, selfrighteousness, this cancerous Babylon, here we could cling together, sane, safe, & warm & face, together, everything. I LOVE YOU. I have been driven for what seem like, and probably are, thousands of miles, along neoned, jerrybuilt, motel-ed, turbined, ice-cream-salooned, gigantically hoared roads of the lower region of the damned, from town to town, college to college, university to university, hotel to hotel, & all I want, before Christ, before you, is to hold you in my arms in our house in Laugharne, Carmarthenshire. And the worst, by a thousand miles – no thousands & thousands & thousands of miles – is to come. I have touched only the nearest-together of my eternally foreign dates. Tomorrow, I go back from Washington, hundreds of miles, to New York. There I talk to Columbia University. The very next day I start on my pilgrimage, my *real* pilgrimage, of the damned. I go to Iowa, Idaho, Indiana, Salt Lake City, & then a titanic distance to Chicago. All alone. Friend Brinnin leaves me at New York. And from Chicago I fly to San Francisco, & from there I lurch, blinded with smoke and noise, to Los Angeles. The distance from New York – where I shall be tomorrow – to Los Angeles is further than the distance from London to New York. Oh Cat, my beautiful, my love, what am I doing here? I am no globe-trotter, no cosmopolitan, I have no desire to hurl across the American nightmare like one of their damned motorcars. I want to live quietly, with you & Colum, & noisily with Aeronwy, & I want to see Llewelyn, & I want to sit in my hut and write & I want to eat your stews, and I want to touch your breasts and cunt, and I want every night to lie, in love & peace, close, close, close, close, close, to you, closer than the marrow of your soul. I LOVE YOU.

Everything is not terrible here. I have met many kind, intelligent, humorous people, & a few, a very few, who hate the American scene, the driving lust for success, the adulation of power, as much as I do. There is more food than I dreamt of. And I want to tell you again, my Cat, that I still drink nothing but ice-cold beer. I don't touch spirits at all, though that is all that anyone else seems to drink – in an enormous quantity. But if I touched anything else but beer I just *couldn't* manage to get along. I couldn't face this world if I were ill. I have to remain, outwardly, as strong as possible. It is only in my heart and head that the woes and the terrors burn. I miss you a million million times more than if my arms, legs, head & trunk were all cut off. You *are* my body, & I am yours. Holily & sacredly, & lovingly & lustfully, spiritually, & to the very deeps of the unconscious sea, I love you, Caitlin, my wild wise wonderful woman, my girl, the mother of our Colum cauliflower. Your letter I read ten times a day in cars, trains, pubs, in the street, in bed. I think I know it by heart. Of course I know it by heart. Your heart, alive, leaping, & loving, is in every word. Thank you, my dear, for your lovely letter. Please write as often as you can. And I will write, too. I have not written since my first letter because never for a second, except for falling, trembling & exhausted, thinking, thinking, think-ing, of you, have I stopped travelling or reading aloud on stages and platforms. This is the first day on which I have had no work to do. I waited until I was in bed until I wrote to you. I can cry on the pillow then, and say your name across the miles that sever you from me. I LOVE YOU. Please, love & remember & WAIT FOR ME. Keep the stew waiting on the fire for me. Kiss Calico Colum for me & arrant Aeron.

I hope you got the stockings I sent you. I sent a pair to Ivy too. Today I had sent from a big shop in Washington lots of chocolates, sweets, & candies, for you, for Aeron, for my mother. Darling darling, I am sorry I could do nothing for dear Aeron's birthday. Dates & time were a maze of speed & noise as I drove like a sweating, fat, redfaced comet along the *incredible* roads. But tell her many sweets & things shd reach her in a few days. From N York tomorrow, I shall also send some foodstuffs.

About the Ungoed cheque: if my chequebook is in the bottom of my suitcase, I shall write him a cheque & put it into this letter when I post it tomorrow. If it is not in my suitcase, but in my other suitcase in Brinnin's house, I shall send it separately tomorrow. I cannot look in the case now. It is downstairs. The house is dark. I shall lie here & love you. I DO Love You, Angel. Be good to me & ours.

What can I say to you that I have not said a thousand times before, dear dear Cat? It is: I love you.

On 16 March, Dylan wrote to me from Chicago:

Cat: my cat: If only you would write to me: My love, oh Cat. This is not, as it seems from the address above, a dive, joint, saloon, etc., but the honourable & dignified headquarters of the dons of the University of Chicago. I love you. That is all I know. But all I know, too, is that I am writing into space: the kind of dreadful, unknown space I am just going to enter. I am going to Iowa, Illinois, Idaho, Indiana, but these, though mis-spelt, *are* on the map. You are not. Have you forgotten me? I am the man you used to say you loved. I used to sleep in your arms – do you remember? But you never write. You are perhaps mindless of me. I am not of you. I love you. There isn't a moment of any hideous day when I do not say to myself, 'It will be alright. I shall go home. Caitlin loves me. I love Caitlin.' But perhaps you have forgotten. If you have forgotten, or lost your affection for me, please, my Cat, let me know. I Love You.

> Dylan

The next letter that has survived was written nearly three weeks later when Dylan was staying with Ruth Witt-Diamant in San Francisco. She became a friend to both of us. The letter was dated 5 April:

My love my Caitlin my love my love
thank you (I love you) for your beautiful beautiful beautiful letter and (my love) for the love you sent. Please forgive me, Cat dear, the nasty little note I sent about your not-writing: it was only because I was so worried and so deeply in love with you. This is going to be the shortest letter because I am writing it on a rocking train that is taking me from San Francisco – the best city on earth – to Vancouver in Canada. And with this tiny, but profoundly loving letter, I also send you a cheque to Magdalen College for £50 & a cheque for £15 to you: that £15 seems an odd amount, but God knows how much is in the Chelsea bank. I unfortunately can't find the Dathan Davies bill you sent, so can you pay it out of this. Please, my own sweetheart, send all the bills & troubles to me after this. And I hope the cheques are met. The train is going so fast through wonderful country along the Pacific coast that I can write no more. As soon as I get on stationary land I will write longly. I said San Francisco was the best city on earth. It is incredibly beautiful, all hills and bridges and blinding blue sky, and boats and the Pacific ocean. I am trying – & there's every reason to believe it will succeed – to arrange that you & me & Colum (my Colum, your Colum) come to

San Francisco next spring when I will become, for six months, a professor in the English department of the University. You will love it here. I am madly unhappy but I love it here. I am desperate for you but I *know* that we can, together, come here. I love you. I love you. I love you. I am glad you are stiff and staid. I am rather overwrought but am so much in love with you that it does not matter. I spent last evening with Varda, the Greek painter, who remembers you when you were fifteen. I wish I did. A long letter tomorrow. O my heart, my golden heart, how I miss you. There's an intolerable emptiness in me, that can be made whole only by your soul & body. I will come back alive & as deep in love with you as a cormorant dives, as an anemone grows, as Neptune breathes, as the sea is deep. God bless & protect you & Llewelyn & Aeron & Colum, my, our, Colum. I love you.

Dylan

P.S. Write, air mail, to the above address. I return to S. Francisco in a week.

P.P.S. Darling, I realise fifteen pounds is inadequate, but let that big £50 get thro' the bank alright & then I can send more. I can send you a cheque in dollars next week, which you can cash through the account of my poor old man or through Ivy.

I love you.

Two days later, Dylan wrote to me again, this time from Vancouver. The letter was dated 7 April:

Caitlin. Just to write down your name like that. Caitlin. I don't have to say My dear, My darling, my sweetheart, though I do say those words, to you in myself, all day and night. Caitlin. And all the words are in that one word. Caitlin, Caitlin, and I can see your blue eyes and your golden hair and your slow smile and your faraway voice. Your faraway voice is saying, now at my ear, the words you said in your last letter, and thank you, dear, for the love you said and sent. I love you. Never forget that, for one single moment of the long, slow, sad Laugharne day, never forget it in your mazed trances, in your womb and your bones, in our bed at night. I love you. Over this continent I take your love inside me, your love goes with me up in the aeroplaned air, into all the hotel bedrooms where momentarily I open my bag – half full, as ever, of dirty shirts – and lay down my head & do not sleep until dawn because I can hear your heart beat beside me, your voice saying my name and our love above the noise of the night-traffic, above the neon flashing, deep in my loneliness, my love.

Today is Good Friday. I am writing this in an hotel bedroom in Vancouver, British Columbia, Canada, where yesterday I gave two readings, one in the university, one in the ballroom of the Vancouver

Hotel, and made one broadcast. Vancouver is on the sea, and gigantic mountains doom above it. Behind the mountains lie other mountains, lies an unknown place, 30,000 miles of mountainous wilderness, the lost land of Columbia where cougars live and black bears. But the city of Vancouver is a quite handsome hellhole. It is, of course, being Canadian, more British than Cheltenham. I spoke last night – or read, I never lecture, how could I? – in front of two huge union jacks. The pubs – they are called beer-parlours – serve only beer, are not allowed to have whiskey or wine or any spirits at all – and are open only for a few hours a day. There are, in this monstrous hotel, two bars, one for Men, one for Women. They do not mix. Today, Good Friday, nothing is open nor will be open all day long. Everybody is pious and patriotic, apart from a few people in the university & my old friend Malcolm Lowry – do you remember *Under the Volcano* – who lives in a hut in the mountains & who came down to see me last night. Do you remember his wife Margery? We met her with Bill & Helen in Richmond, and, later, I think, in Oxford. She, anyway, remembers you well and sends you her love.

This afternoon I pick up my bag of soiled clothes and take a plane to Seattle. And thank God to be out of British Canada & back in the terrible United States of America. I read poems to the University there tonight. And then I have one day's rest in Seattle, & then on Sunday I fly to Montana, where the cowboys are, thousands of them, tell Ebie, and then on Monday I fly – it takes about 8 hours – to Los Angeles & Hollywood: the nightmare zenith of my mad, lonely tour.

But oh, San Francisco! It is and has everything. Here in Canada, five hours away by plane, you wouldn't think that such a place as San Francisco could exist. The wonderful sunlight there, the hills, the great bridges, the Pacific at your shoes. Beautiful Chinatown. Every race in the world. The sardine fleets sailing out. The little cable-car whizzing down the city hills. The lobsters, clams & crabs. Oh Cat, what food for you. Every kind of seafood there is. And all the people are open and friendly. And next year we both come to live there, you & me & Colum & maybe Aeron. This is sure. I am offered a job in two universities. When I return to San Francisco next week, after Los Angeles, for another two readings, I shall know definitely which of the jobs to take. The pay will be enough to keep us comfortably, though no more. Everyone connected with the Universities is hard-up. But that doesn't matter. Seafood is cheap. Chinese food is cheaper, & lovely. Californian wine is good. The iced bock beer is good. What more? And the city is built on hills; it dances in the sun for nine months of the year; & the Pacific Ocean never runs dry.

Last week I went to Big Sur, a mountainous region by the sea, and stayed the night with Henry Miller. Tell Ivy that; she who hid his books in the oven. He lives about 6,000ft up in the hills, over the blinding blue Pacific, in a hut of his own making. He has married a pretty young Polish girl, & they have two small children. He is gentle and mellow and gay.

I love you Caitlin.

You asked me about the shops. I only know that the shops in the big cities, in New York, Chicago, San Francisco, are full of everything you have ever heard of and also full of everything one has never heard of or seen. The foodshops knock you down. All the women are smart, as in magazines – I mean, the women in the main streets; behind, lie the eternal poor, beaten, robbed, humiliated, spat upon, done to death – and slick & groomed. But they are not as beautiful as you. And when you & me are in San Francisco, you will be smarter & slicker than them, and the sea & sun will make you jump over the roofs & the trees, & you will never be tired again. Oh, my lovely dear, how I love you. I love you for ever & ever. I see you every minute of the day & night. I see you in our little house, tending the pomegranate of your eye. I love you. Kiss Colum, kiss Aeron & Llewelyn. Is Elizabeth with you? Remember me to her. I love you. Write, write, write, write, my sweetheart Caitlin. Write to me still c/o Brinnin, though the letters come late that way, I am sure of them. Do not despair. Do not be too tired. Be always good to me. I shall one day be in your arms, my own, however shy we shall be. Be good to me, as I am always to you. I love you. Think of us together in the San Francisco sun, which we shall be. I love you. I want you. Oh, darling, when I was with you all the time, how did I ever shout at you? I love you. Think of me.

Your
Dylan

I enclose a cheque for £15.
I will write from Hollywood in three days.
I will send you some more money.
I love you.

These are some of the letters that survived, and they are now in a private collection. I decided to sell them a few years ago, when I was short of money. He wrote me many more letters, during our marriage and before, and I used to carry them with me in a lovely cardboard chocolate box, wherever we went, until they were stolen from my sister's in Markham Square. I think I know who did that, but I could never prove it. I was very annoyed because I used to preserve them carefully, and it's sad that so few of the letters he sent to me have survived. Everything got scattered in the end. When friends came to stay, they would borrow books and never return them. Photographs just seemed to vanish. Now I have nothing left apart from copies of his books, and a copy of the photograph taken of Dylan at the Salisbury pub in St Martin's Lane, which I have framed on my bedroom wall.

The letters Dylan wrote to me were very different to those that he wrote to his parents, which contained much more detail. To them he was the fond son, relating everything he had seen, recounting his successes in such a way that he always sounded enterprising and industrious. They lapped up the letters; they believed every word, and who was I to say that they should take them with a pinch of salt? But I could read between the lines of my letters. On the surface, they were passionate, loving letters, but I could tell from the way he phrased them, and made such a point of missing me, that he was having the time of his life, though I had no idea how bad his behaviour had been out there.

When he returned to Laugharne, he was tremendously excited, enormously stimulated. He had had one hell of a good time, as well as giving all those lectures and readings. He had also done some rather scandalous things, although I didn't know it then, and he had been forgiven because he was a genius – everyone forgives a genius. That new life got right under his skin without my knowing it. He had led such a boring life before; the contrast was overpowering. I understood this when I went over to the United States with him for his second tour two years later, but of course it wasn't the same for me because I wasn't the one being fêted.

He came back to Laugharne dead to the world; he was so tired he could barely talk or walk. I had been pretty selfish and mean; I had gone up to London to welcome him back, to visit friends together, go to parties and do some shopping. I was having a lovely time, and all he wanted to do was get back to Laugharne. He had been to a million parties in America, and he found all the old friends an awful nuisance, but he was careful not to overplay it. He dwelt on his loneliness away from me, although I could sense the thrill – all that lecturing, all that applause, all those students gathering around him afterwards; he felt that all the things he had been working for over the years had now been recognised, and that his beloved poetry was now being understood. It must have given him a great inner satisfaction, but the contrast with London must have been painful. In America they make too much fuss of poets; in London they make too little. I don't know whether that comes from the public schools, or from Oxford, but the English are indifferent to, and bored by, genius; they are never impressed or enthusiastic. At last he had ridden above them, but only he knew that. No one in Laugharne realised what had happened to him in the States, and even I didn't appreciate the scale of his success, because he came back home to West Wales with hardly any money at all, and was careful not to make the visit sound too glamorous because he knew what my reaction might have been. It was only when I opened a parcel that he said Brinnin had asked him to bring back as a gift for me that I found a lovely leather handbag, with eight hundred dollars tucked away inside. Brinnin had realised, rightly, that Dylan spent money so quickly that there would have been none left at all if he hadn't played that little trick.

10

The homecoming was happy enough. We had missed each other, as our letters had shown. Aeron and Colm had missed him, too, and his parents were pleased to see him home again in Laugharne, settled back into his quiet routine. They were proud of him, but Dylan could see that his father's health was deteriorating, and that much of the fight had gone from the old man's eyes. Dylan was anxious to tell them, and me, of America; of the forty universities he had visited; of the way poets were treated in the States; of the planes he'd had to catch from town to town as he criss-crossed the continent, and of the kindness shown by the people he had met. Next time, he said, I would have to go with him, and perhaps we would take the children, too, if he was offered a temporary post at one of the universities.

It was so exciting for him – he had broken through. Large audiences wanted to hear his poetry; his work would now be selling better than ever – and next time, yes next time, he would make much more money, because he had learnt from Brinnin's mistakes. This was the first time Brinnin had arranged such a tour, and he had left too little time between readings for travel and rest. Sometimes the travel expenses had been far more than Brinnin had allowed when a reading fee was arranged, and Dylan had been out of pocket. He had expected to come back home with three thousand dollars, but all we had was the eight hundred that Brinnin had left in the handbag. Dylan insisted that it wasn't wholly his fault. Even worse, Brinnin had left him to cope with many of the tour arrangements on his own, buying tickets and catching planes to towns he had never heard of before, in a new country with a strange currency. Some men would have coped with that, but Dylan could not; it was a source of constant confusion, and he had come back exhausted.

Of course, there was some fantasy, too. Dylan was careful, as he always was with me, to make it seem that this had been work work work, with no time for himself. I didn't believe that for a moment, but I didn't suspect him of having an affair there, either; the occasional night of drunken sex, perhaps, but not an affair.

I suppose I must have needed him and loved him very much, in spite of everything that had happened between us: he was my possession, my child; that was one of the things that bound us. I couldn't think of him as a real man like the tall, dark, handsome Caspar – he was my perfect image of a man, who said very little, with his soft, throbbing voice. Dylan was the most imperfect image ever seen, and never stopped talking; just walking along the street with him I felt self-conscious because he looked so comical. That was one of the reasons why, whenever people had talked of his infidelities in the past, I had always said, 'But who would ever go with a comical man like that? It's not possible. These rich women wouldn't want to bother with him, stinking of beer and sweat and stale cigarettes and God knows what.'

And then one morning, when he had gone round to see Ivy at Brown's Hotel and I was pregnant again, I saw these letters sticking out of the pocket of a jacket that he had left over the back of a chair, completely careless as always, making no attempt to hide them. He must have known that I had been through his pockets before, looking for money (although mostly there wasn't much there to get), and there they were – love letters from some woman he had met in America called Pearl. In his book *Dylan Thomas in America*, Brinnin disguises her with the name of 'Sarah', but she signed herself Pearl, and to this day I don't know her surname. When I read them I felt absolute fury – jealousy and fury. It was pretty obvious that they had been to bed together, and I wanted to kill her. When Dylan came back from Brown's and I confronted him, he just shrugged it off and said, 'That's nothing – they're all like that in America. They fling themselves all over every poet that comes along!'

All like that! How many more were there? It was nothing, he said; nothing at all. Wherever he went, women came round to see him after the readings, and some of them wrote to him afterwards; that was all there was to it. Women were like that in America – very forward. It meant nothing to him and he loved only me, forever and forever, as always. And I believed him. Like a fool I believed him, although I wrote a letter to that bloody Pearl and gave her a piece of my mind, telling her what an awful bitch I thought she was and why didn't she find a man of her own. I worked hard at that letter to make sure it really stung.

I knew by then that quite a lot of Dylan's life was an act, and I'd realised (as I think quite a lot of his friends understood in the end) that, beneath all that charm, he was a scoundrel. But I never ceased to love him. There were times when I thought that if only I could manage to leave him, for a short while, he would soon see what life was like without me, and then perhaps he would come back chastened; but I didn't seem able to do that, somehow: I never had the money. One of his problems was that he could never turn a woman down (apart from Margaret Taylor, and he may have weakened in the end even with her because she was so insistent and persevering and had done us so many favours; but I think that would only have been through a sense of duty – she really did get on his nerves).

Dylan was always so loving towards me that I tended to believe what he said. He was never nasty and he never criticised me; he just accepted me as I was. I think he did look upon me as an idealised woman. No matter what he had done, he always told me how much he loved me and that I was the only woman for him. But, of course, sex is quite different from love and there were times when all he needed was a bit of drunken sex, and if I wasn't there he got it from somebody else (and that was all I wanted when he wasn't there as well). I think Dylan always had this need for drunken sex. For one thing, it gave him a bed for the night; it was often as simple as that, because he was very simple in drink. His women would be solely for bed-and-breakfast, and then they would cuddle him and give him warm things to drink, and he *was* very cuddlesome.

In the September of that year Dylan went up to London for a few days, planning to see Brinnin who was passing through, and while I was at the Boat House I received a phone call from Maggs Taylor, who said she had to see me at once; it was urgent, and she was

*Dylan at the White Horse Tavern,
New York, 1952*

Dylan reading in New York

Dylan and Caitlin in Rollie McKenna's studio during Dylan's second trip to America

Taken in 1953, one of the last photos of Dylan and Caitlin, at The Bishop's Palace, St David's, Pembrokeshire

Caitlin returns briefly to Laugharne, 1957. Behind the famous photograph in Brown's, the wallpaper has changed

Caitlin and Aeron with Aeron's son Huw. Maggs Taylor's caravan is still in the back garden of 54 Delancey Street

A simple cross marks Dylan's grave in Laugharne

catching the next train down to Laugharne. She didn't say what it was she had to tell me.

Maggs caught a taxi from Carmarthen station, and when she arrived she put her arms around me, kissed me on the cheek, and followed me down the steps into the kitchen. She sat down at the table while I was standing at the stove, stirring one of my pots of broth, and said, 'Have you heard that Dylan has got this lady friend over from New York and is going all over London with her? She's called Pearl, and he's taking her round the pubs and introducing her to his friends . . .'

What struck me first was that bloody Maggs Taylor was far more worried about losing Dylan herself than she was about me; she sensed that her own interest in Dylan might be eclipsed by this other woman, and that upset her far more than the thought of what this might do to me and the children. I just stood there at the stove, and it really hit me, but I didn't show her what I was feeling because I never do react immediately to joy or sorrow: I register it to myself and my own subconscious and then later fish it out again, and when I did that this time the full impact was very unpleasant. I asked what this other woman was like. I can't remember much of the description except that Maggs said she was dark-haired, with dangling, jingling bracelets. Apparently she was a journalist, and I got the impression that she was very efficient and business-like – one of those blue-stocking women who can do everything. Maggs gave me the idea that this was very serious and that we must get rid of her. Maggs said that this Pearl was going on from London to the south of France, and that she had asked Dylan to join her there.

Had I seen her I would have killed her. She had all the things I hadn't got: I had only my fury, and I just *knew* – without anyone having to tell me – that she had an efficient life, smartness, money and all that odious stuff. With all that rage inside me I was quite capable of knifing her or strangling her. I still think now that she behaved like one hell of a bitch: she knew that I was stuck at home in Laugharne with the children.

Words can't express what I felt for Dylan; I thought he was beneath contempt. I was angry and hurt and I wanted my revenge. I didn't know what to do. Because my pride was hurt, I didn't want to leave the children with Dolly and go chasing after him. That seemed to me a most undignified reaction. I had always tried to act as though I didn't give a damn. The idea now of grovelling in front of Dylan or anyone did not appeal at all. Besides, I thought that one's life should never depend on a man.

What got to me was the fact that she had come all the way from New York to collect Dylan, and then he had started taking her round the pubs just like he used to take me: that was a personal insult – I couldn't accept it. I never forgave him. How could I?

Dylan arrived back from London, penniless as always, not expecting the sort of welcome he got from me. I just came out with it, straight. I told him what Maggs Taylor had said and asked him, 'What's all this about?' He tried to lie his way out of it, as he always did, but he was in deep disgrace, and he could not deny it.

All his friends thought Margaret Taylor had been a bitch to have told me. I thought her motives were suspect, but it didn't seem to me an act of bitchery, more of a kindness; I could see no reason why the wife should always be the last to know. I felt deeply humiliated knowing that Dylan had taken this woman around and introduced her to his friends, and that they had apparently spent a weekend together in Brighton. Whenever I had heard of his infidelities in the past it had hurt me, but this one was obviously far more advanced and more serious. It must have been serious on her part for her to come to London, to write to him care of his club (the Savage), and to go about with him like that. And it must have been serious on his part for him to have been replying to her letters, and to have arranged their meeting. He was, in fact, blatantly encouraging her.

Dylan never told me that he loved her; he would never have said that. He claimed that she was a bloody nuisance, one of these mad American women who kept following him around. There was I, pregnant, and (I have to admit, though I am not proud of it) playing my pregnant belly against the power of this lady because I knew Dylan's soft spot for the babies and his home. I told him, 'You can't possibly leave me in this state' – although that doesn't sound like me. He was hovering, not able to make up his mind whether to leave me or not, and my pregnancy was the only strong weapon I had. I didn't have to make him feel guilty; he was so guilty already; he was torn in two. If I hadn't been pregnant at that time, I'm not sure whether he would have gone off with her or not. One part of me still says he wouldn't, because he never stopped telling me how much he loved me. No matter how black the evidence against him, he always swore that he loved me and that he would never forsake me.

146

There was a big row on the first night he came back to the Boat House. These weren't the first rows we'd had, but this one was probably the most violent to date, and the rows seemed to accumulate after that. Dylan was muted for a bit. We did gradually get back into the old rhythm again, but from that time on there was always this ugly thing between us. It was a very forced peace and I never really forgave him. Most nights something would be said that would trigger a row, and we would end up fighting when we came back from Brown's.

I started taking other lovers, trying to live like him and take my revenge, though now, thinking about it after all these years, I can't much understand my point of view. I suppose a lot of it was just plain jealousy. I had never really trusted him, right from the very beginning, because Dylan was a typical Welshman, a thief and a liar. Taffy was a Welshman, Taffy was a thief – that was a pretty accurate description of Dylan.

We had so many rows after that that I can't pin down what they were about or separate the occasions. They were always late at night after we'd walked back from Brown's, always caused by 'The Affair'. When we had those rows I would throw myself at him, push him to the floor, grab him by the hair and keep banging his head against it, beating the Jesus out of him. He did mildly respond but in no way hurt me. He would struggle for a bit while I was punching and kicking him, although I would never kick him in the balls (I could never do that to a man because they're precious). Sometimes he would pass out and I'd be quite nervous in case I'd banged his head too hard and killed him. Then, after the rows, we would end up in each other's arms; we would get into bed and pass out, and then when we came to we were all over each other, tender and apologetic. The tenderness was always there. How odd it is, that you can be livid with anger, swearing never to touch that person again in your whole life, and then, after a very short time, there you are, with your arms round each other. I have always felt that it was most extraordinary that we could be loving each other again so soon.

One night, after one of those fights, I took the manuscript of a poem that Dylan had shown me earlier that evening and tore it into little pieces; it was his final version of 'In the White Giant's Thigh', which has many sexual allusions, and somehow this got to me. I took the pieces of paper and threw them out of the Boat House window.

147

Our argument ended, as they always did, with us both asleep in bed, but I soon woke up, troubled by the thought of what I had done. I realised, as I lay awake, that I had done something terribly wrong, because his work was sacred to him. Anyone's creative work is sacred, but his was exceptionally so – to me, too, because it was his.

So, in the dark hour of the night, just before dawn, when he was still snoring in bed, I crept down to the mudbanks below the Boat House and retrieved the pieces of paper. I was lucky; the tide was still out, and I was able to scramble through the mud in my nightgown and find every piece, still terribly mad at Dylan for what he had done, but angry with myself, too, for going beyond my own limits. I realised that I must have been very angry with him, to do a thing like that, but I still thought that what I'd done showed real meanness of soul. I left all the pieces on the kitchen table. Dylan didn't say anything next morning as he gathered them up, but a lot later he thanked me for it. I think he realised what it had meant.

After that terrible shock to our marriage, our lives did settle back into some kind of normality, but our relationship was never the same again. I knew that that woman Pearl had meant something to him, that it was more than just a sexual act. It was the first time that I had been aware of such a thing. Secretly, Dylan had been sharing part of his real self with another woman – there was some kind of an intellectual understanding as well – and this was what I couldn't forgive, because *that* had always been mine.

Dammit, he was treating me badly. I had had his children and I loved him, and anything that I said to the contrary was only meant to hurt him in the heat of an argument. I didn't want Dylan to go back to America after that. I thought America had ruined him and that he had lost all his values by going there. Acclaim and success didn't suit him at all; he was too weak to resist the drink or the flattery. Those temptations were enough to break any man – and, incidentally, any woman, and that includes me.

I wanted him to stay with me, in Laugharne, doing his real work. Now, whenever he went away to London for a few days I would think the worst, and probably rightly. Our life at the Boat House had become pretty miserable, and he didn't have much to come home to.

Sometimes in the evenings we would be sitting peacefully,

reading aloud, in perfect harmony for once, when there would be some awful ringing at the telephone and it would turn out to be Marged Howard-Stepney, another lady patroness who had come into our lives. She was very rich, and she came from a family that claimed descent from the Tudors. Marged had inherited huge estates in Carmarthenshire from her father, and lived in a large house near Llanelli. She was a cousin of Richard Hughes' wife, Frances; she had been married twice, and was a year older than Dylan. We got to know her when she invited Dylan to do a reading, and he later described her as his 'best friend in the world', which I thought was pure wishful thinking; we only knew her for a short time.

I think Dylan also saw her in London. She went to some of his readings there, and was certainly doing her best to have an affair with him. She had also been to bed with John Davenport, and I have no doubt that she and Dylan would have gone to bed together – if they ever found the time and the place.

Although she was stinking rich, Marged was a really low alcoholic and used to go around with a kind of keeper-woman. She came down to Laugharne once with this keeper and a little suitcase packed with gin. The keeper was trying to keep a strict eye on her and clearly considered Marged was taking too much drink. Anyway, Marged went to bed in the end with her suitcase under the bed and drank all night long. (I don't know where the keeper had got to.) In the morning, the tide was in and Marged said she was going to have a swim. We tried to warn her that the river was unsafe and the tidal currents dangerous, but after all that gin she wouldn't listen. She was dressed in a pearl necklace and a gold watch, but from her waist down she wore absolutely nothing. When she went into the water she floated away on the tide and we thought we would never see her again – but she came back, and carried on talking as if nothing had happened. Marged was quite good-looking in the perfect-lady style, but she used to drive me crazy because she kept phoning us at all hours of the night. Dylan would say that he had to go and answer, and I would say, 'No, don't. Let it ring. It's only *her* again.' I would hear them in the distance, muttering and whispering, and I would get more irritated.

We had one unfortunate night at her home. There was nobody there except her, Dylan and me. They were at the dinner table, and obviously sealed together. There I was, ignored, and getting more and more mad. Eventually I took a torch from the mantelpiece and banged it down on Dylan's head as hard as I could. He passed out temporarily. 'My God!' she screamed, 'you may have killed him. Don't you realise he's a genius?' When he came round, she gave me one hell of a lecture.

Marged put us in two little beds that night, with electric blankets. We had never seen them before so we didn't turn them off, and in the morning we woke up like fried eggs, with terrible hangovers. Marged gave us lots to drink; she was a real dipsomaniac; much worse than us.

I was still carrying the baby then, and, even though I was dead set against Dylan going back to America for a second tour, I knew that he was determined to go. He said that everything would be all right if I would only go with him; he was very persuasive. He said that I had been mistaken about Pearl, and that if only we went there together I would see the pressures that he was under, and that he could cope with them. In the end that second tour was put off until the following year, but at the time that I was pregnant I knew that I couldn't go in the state that I was in: I was visibly pregnant, nearly six months. So I had to make an awful decision: either to get an abortion and go with Dylan or stay behind (the same kind of decision that I'd had to take over Llewelyn back in 1941). Again I decided to do the wicked thing, to have an abortion, but by then it was late, so I had to have the operation done professionally. Marged knew of a good doctor in London and said she was willing to pay for it (even though it cost a hundred pounds), but she did everything under the sun to stop me having the abortion because she was dying to have a baby herself, and she just couldn't believe that I would want to get rid of one. I said, 'Well, how can we possibly live and keep another one? You know we can't afford the children we've got . . . and I can't go to America otherwise.'

Dylan hardly discussed the abortion with me, though he was much more in favour than not, which meant, I think, that he sincerely thought that his next visit to America would be better with me (when in fact it was much worse). But in any case he was a real escapist. That's why I call him a moral coward; he could never face the ugly side of life. I think I was much stronger than he was. I always had a passion for truth: it seemed to me the only good way to live. I don't know who implanted this passion for truth in me; certainly not my mother, nor my sisters.

These crises in our lives always left me in some ghastly position where I felt steadily trampled on, and had to make every decision alone. It was terrible leaving the abortion to such a late stage in the pregnancy, but for a long time I couldn't make up my mind about it. I was torn between conscience and desire. I thought that I had to go to America with Dylan, that I had to see it once, and at the same time it seemed an awful thing to get rid of a child. I was in a mess, really, with Marged continually trying to persuade me not to do it. But I had been deeply distressed by Dylan's affair with Pearl, and I thought that if I went with him I would be able to deal with all those rampant women. I might have known, if I'd had any sense, that there wasn't much I could do about it, except make a fool of myself. Also, I felt that if I went with him I could see that he worked and lived sensibly and didn't damage his health. This was a rather far-fetched hope, particularly if I had taken into consideration the fact that I was almost as bad as he was. I was very wild, and would have done almost any mad thing, so I was hardly the ideal protector, although I did see myself in that role at the beginning.

And, if I'm honest, I had the abortion because I wanted to give myself a bit of fun and enjoyment. We both thought it would be a marvellous opportunity to go to the States together, and he had insisted that he had missed me so terribly the time before, and that he would be much happier if I went. Although I knew he was fantasising, I wanted to believe him, and I thought that we might be able to make some other plans afterwards, too.

I didn't go through with that abortion to save the marriage. It wasn't as simple as that. If I had been thinking like that, I might have kept the baby, which would have been some inducement for Dylan to remain in Laugharne.

I went to an address in London where there were two doctors and a nurse, running a private clinic. I made all the arrangements myself and handed over the money. (It wasn't difficult arranging an abortion in those days, provided you were discreet and could pay for it.) Naturally, Dylan avoided all the unpleasantness. He had travelled up from Wales with me and came as far as the clinic, but he wouldn't come in; he went to the pub on the opposite side of the road, and I don't know what happened to him after that. He never said, 'Don't do it,' and he never said, 'Do do it,' and I think that was why it was left so late. But I prided myself on *not* being a moral coward, and I looked on it partly as a duty, because we couldn't really afford the children that we had, although that was always a secondary consideration.

The actual aborting business wasn't agonising, but very unpleasant. It was all done professionally. It wasn't a bottle of gin and a hot bath – I had tried all that, as well as falling down stairs, riding and so on. I had none of the traumatic horrors over the abortion that people are said to have, except when it was actually going on. I deliberately drank as much whisky as I could – Dylan plied me with it – but I've always noticed that when you do drink a lot of spirits, the minute the doctor or dentist starts to work on you, all the effects of the alcohol evaporate and you are fully conscious. At six months it was very late: the baby was already well formed, and they chopped it up as they were pulling it out, and then brought it out in chunks. I suppose I was horrified, but by that time I was expecting anything – it was like being in a butcher's shop. They gave me a local anaesthetic. They said they couldn't put me out otherwise they wouldn't have been able to perform the operation. I was fully conscious the whole time. There was a nurse holding me down, holding my head, and two men working down at the bottom, and I was in a most undignified position with my two feet strapped in those clamps they use to keep the legs apart. I kept saying (because I wanted a girl, incidentally), 'Will you just tell me whether it's a girl?' They just didn't answer. They took no notice of me at all. They simply got on with the job, working away at the bottom of the bed, with my feet held high in the air.

When it was over I was put into a private room and I didn't see any more doctors or have any more examinations. I don't know what happened to Dylan; he didn't turn up to collect me the next day and I have no idea where he spent the night – he was never there when I needed him – and when I told him about it afterwards he wasn't very interested. The following day I left early, feeling good. I felt lightened, not only physically but in spirit. Sometimes, after an operation of that kind, you can be pretty sick, but I felt strong and positively gay.

After these events – Pearl, and the abortion – our marriage was very close to breaking, although I wasn't really conscious of it at the time. I didn't know, until Brinnin's book was published four years after Dylan's death, that Dylan himself had thought of leaving me. That thought hadn't crossed my mind; he had never mentioned it, and I still don't know whether it was true. Having rows had become part of the way we lived, but now the tensions ran much deeper.

In January 1951, Dylan went off to Persia (or Iran as it is now called) with Ralph Keene to make a documentary film that had been commissioned by the Anglo-Iranian Oil Company (the film was never made because the Persian Government nationalised the company's assets), and I was angry with him for leaving me alone with the children again in Laugharne, as always without enough money to live on. Though I never thought of divorce, I did think of trying to get away from him and from Laugharne. But where could I go? I thought of going to my mother's, but to go back home an abysmal failure was not a very happy situation. I was captured, and it seemed so unfair.

Dylan sent me letters from Teheran, and most of them were a pack of lies. He was back to trying to woo me with words:

> Caitlin my darling, dear dear Caitlin, oh my love so far away I love you. All these strange lost days I love you, and I am lost indeed without you my dear wife. This is so much further than America, and letters will take so much longer to travel to you and yours to me if you will ever write to me again oh *darling* Cat. And if you do not write to me, and if you do not love me any more, I cannot go on, I cannot go on sleeplessly thinking, 'Caitlin my Cattleanchor, my dear, does not love me, oh God let me die.' I can't live without you; I can't go travelling with this long, wan Bunny through this fearful, strange world unless I am sure that at the end we will be together as we are meant to be together, close and alone except for our cuckoo whom I miss very very very much, more than I could dream of.

The letters went on like that for page after page, with apologies, sandwiched between the professions of love, for not having left me with enough money to live on. The whole point of his being a poet was that he could put all those lies into deceiving poetic language. They are fine letters, some of the better ones that he wrote, but when I received them, I thought, 'Oh, my God! How does he dare?' He would write me these letters with lovely descriptive passages and protestations of undying love, and I would say to myself, 'What, again?' I knew that he was sleeping perfectly well, and that he was just dashing off those letters, like the begging letters he dashed off to Princess Caetani or Margaret Taylor. It didn't seem to me that he'd got to the core of the matter at all; he was just trying to spread a vague romantic counterpane over the tensions between us, and then when he thought I'd taken it all in, he would be off again. I wasn't impressed; I would rather have an old clod of earth and a cow than all that poetic lah-di-dah.

Looking back on it now, I realise that I was his only contact with reality. He called me his cattle-anchor, his sheet-anchor. He knew what he meant, as he always did – I was the only person who wasn't feeding him bullshit. But I could hurt him on a different level to the physical, and *that* he could not take. I don't suppose there was anyone else in his life who had ever used the brutal tactics that I used, saying what I thought of him and beating him up as well; most women are more likely to reduce themselves to tears and pleadings. Dylan never saw me cry. I thought I was too proud to cry, but I did some crying in the end, after he died – then I couldn't stop myself. When he was alive I was never that sentimental, partly because he was, and I didn't want to go along with that. Dylan was full of it. I don't trust sentimentality in men; it goes with tyranny; you can't have one without the other. I never thought I had any sentimentality at all until I had Llewelyn. He couldn't hurt me, but all *men* could. I have always been afraid of being hurt by men, always.

11

It was at this point that I started to retaliate in earnest. There was nothing else I could do, really. I felt that I had lost Dylan because he kept going away without me, and I was no longer able to think about a future for us. It never occurred to me that this must have been a temporary problem that time would resolve; the division had gone too far, and I was now living day by day, doing what I had to do, with Dolly's help, with no life to put in the void. There was no one in Laugharne that I could talk to; no close woman friend I could share my problems with, and it was then that I started going to bed with my Laugharne pick-ups. I did this rather deliberately, out of revenge, although I won't deny that I was attracted to some of them. Of course, it wasn't only revenge: I wanted sex: I didn't want to waste my body waiting for someone who hardly had a body at all, and who was permanently seduced by other females. Mostly, it was done on the spur of the moment, after drinking, and I knew that my escapades meant very little – it was the physical act alone. Sometimes that had been the case with Dylan, but these clever blue-stocking ones were in his mind as well as his body, and I couldn't stand that form of deceit.

It was that damned Pearl that I couldn't get out of my mind; she has haunted me for a long time. There had in fact been a bitterness in me since the war, when I had been aware of his minor flirtations. I now realise that for most of the years we were together, he had been having fleeting affairs with other women, knowing that he could always come home to a loving wife, whether we were at Laugharne in our Sea View days or at Bishopston, Blaen Cwm, Blashford or

South Leigh. Dylan was extremely lucky that I was so ingenuous, and that I had never understood how far these things had gone.

But when I snapped, I snapped. I was furious when he went off to Persia with Bunny Keene. Yes, he was going to make money, but why hadn't he arranged to take me with him? It was unfair. Why was I always left behind?

His letters were packed with endearments, the usual Dylan mix of love, apology, and protestations of undying fidelity, and they made me sick: the bastard, writing to me like that after everything he'd put me through:

Dear Cat Caitlin darling. I love you. There's no meaning to anything without you. There's no meaning without us being together. I love you all the day and night, and I am five thousand miles away. Until I hear from you, Cat, every minute of the day and night's insane. I have to dope myself into nightmare sleep with tablets from Bunny's enormous medicine-chest. I wake up before it is dawn, in this great undersea bedroom under snow mountains, and turn the echoes of your voice over and over in the dark, and look into your blue beautiful undersea eyes five thousand miles away; they're all that is real, the deepnesses of your eyes . . .

and:

Caitlin dear,
I do not know if this letter will reach you at all, or if my other two letters have reached you. I do not know if, whether any of these letters has reached you or will reach you, you will reply to them. I do not know anything, except that I love you. And I do not know if you know me. I love you enough for both of us, but I must know, still, if you are waiting for me, if you want me, if I may come home to you, if there is any cause for me to live. I love you, Caitlin darling dear. Perhaps my letters take very long to travel the miles between us, and so that is why I do not hear from you. Perhaps you have said: 'He is dead to me.' And, if you say that, indeed I will be dead. I love you, love you, love you, always, always, beautiful Cat my love. What I am doing here, without word of you, I just don't know. Yesterday I left Teheran for Abadan, and am stopping here for the night, in an Arabian house, after a twenty-four hour train journey. By plane, the journey would have taken 2½ hours. And so the powerful, tireless Bunny with his immense pharmacopaeia, decided to go by train. It, of course, nearly killed him; and it has done no good to me either. But, if I heard from you, if I knew, for one second, that you are mine, as I am yours, that you might again

love me as I love you forever, I'd travel a thousand hours on the roof of the train. I grope through the nights and days like a blind man; even English around me is an unknown language; I am writing to you, my love, my wife, my darling dear Cat, the one soul and body in the world, as though I didn't know words: stiltedly, awkwardly. I love you. I can at least write that.

Then the letters went on to describe his impressions of Teheran, gliding easily from the protestations of love to anecdotes about old men pissing in gutters, the shortage of alcohol, the clothes of the poor, the smell of incense, food and the weather.

It all seemed so unreal. There was I alone in Laugharne, and there was Dylan, five thousand miles away, talking of the colour of my eyes, the sound of my voice, and a love that would live forever and forever. I just couldn't take any more of that: he had hurt me too much. I wrote to him, saying that it was all over and I was leaving. Sadly, my letter has not survived. He never kept any letters, even mine, and I wish he had kept that one because then I could reassure myself that my memory of events has not altered with the years. I am sure that it hasn't, because Dylan replied:

Caitlin dear,
Your letter, as it was meant to, made me want to die. I did not think that, after reading it so many times till I knew every pain by heart, I could go on with these days and nights, alone with my loneliness – now, as I know too well, for ever – and knowing that, a long way and a lifetime away, you no longer loved or wanted me. (After your cold, disliking letter, you wrote: 'All my love, Caitlin.' You could have spared that irony.) But the bloody animal always does go on. Now I move through these days in a kind of dumb, blind despair, and slowly every day ends. It's the nights I fear most, when the despair breaks down, is dumb and blind no longer, and I am only myself in the dark. I am only alone in an unknown room in a strange town in a benighted country, without any pretences and crying like a fool. Last night I saw you smiling, glad, at me, as you did a thousand years ago; and I howled like the jackals outside. Then, in the morning, it was the same again: walking, in despair, frozen, over a desert. It was even a real desert, the camels aloof, the hyenas laughing. I'm writing this, perhaps last, letter, just before I go to bed. Nobody here, in this writing room, the wireless shouting Persian, can see anything wrong with me. I'm only a little fat foreigner writing a letter: a loving, happy letter to his wife 'waiting at home'. Christ, if they knew. If they knew that the woman I am writing to no longer needs me, has shut her heart and her body against me,

although she is my life. I cannot live without you – you, always – and I have no intention of doing so. I fly back, from Tehran to London, on, I am almost certain, the 14th of February. I shall cable you from Tehran the time of my arrival. You said, before we parted, that you would come up to London to meet me on my return. You will not, I suppose, be doing that now? If you are not, will you please – it is not a great deal to ask – leave a message at the McAlpines. I will not come back to Laugharne until I know that I am wanted: not as an inefficient mispayer of bills, but as myself and for you. If you do not meet me in London, I shall ring the McAlpines. If there is no message there from you, I shall know that everything is over. It is very terrible writing this such a great distance from you. In a few minutes I shall go to my bedroom, climb into bed in my shirt, and think of you. The bedroom knows your name well, as do many bedrooms in this country. 'Caitlin, Caitlin', I will say, and you will come drifting to me, clear & beautiful, until my eyes blur and you are gone. I love you. Oh, darling Cat, I love you.

He did come back, but how he came back I cannot remember. We were unhappy together and unhappy apart, but it wasn't like that all day long: there were brief periods when he settled back into his old Laugharne routine. He was working intermittently on *Under Milk Wood*. During this period he completed one of his finest poems, 'Do Not Go Gentle Into That Good Night', which was prompted by an awareness of his father's approaching death; the poem 'In the White Giant's Thigh', which prompted the incident at the Boat House; the unfinished 'Elegy' (which Vernon Watkins completed after Dylan's death), and scripts for the BBC.

I liked 'Do Not Go Gentle Into That Good Night': the moment he first read it to me I knew it was good. I told him so (I always told him when I liked his work), and I thought of that poem again, a lot, when Dylan himself was dying. He was so conscious of death, but when his own time came he didn't practise what he preached, he slipped very gently into his own good night. I never told him that a poem *wasn't* good enough – I would never have said that – but I did persuade him to economise a lot in his later years. He became very selective, and discarded a great deal, though I still didn't think he discarded enough.

Money was a constant worry now, but it seldom stopped him writing for long (though he would pretend it did when he was begging for money). He was earning more money than ever, enormous fees by most writers' standards, but whenever he had it he gave it away or spent it all on high living. We owed hundreds of pounds to tradesmen in Laugharne, and he would wait until they got really pressing, when Margaret Taylor, or someone like that, would be asked to come to the rescue, and usually did.

As always, Dylan was at his happiest and worried least when he could slip back into the dullest of daily routines. After his morning gossip with Ivy, he would come back to the Boat House for lunch, beer bottles jingling in his bicycle basket, always eating separately from the children in our little dining room. He always read while he ate – novels, poems, comics, even the back of sauce bottles, as long as it was something in print. He loved children's comics and the *New Yorker*, which friends often sent to him; he liked the cartoons and also the work of James Thurber. In the afternoons he would work in the shed until seven before setting off again for Brown's or, sometimes, one of the other dingy Laugharne pubs.

On the surface it seemed that some sort of calm had been restored, but rows could break out again at any time, and did, especially when we'd been drinking, or when he talked of returning to America for another tour. Brinnin had been asking him to go back since the success of the first visit, and in July 1951 he came down to Laugharne with a friend, Bill Read, to discuss the plans in more detail. This was the same Bill Read who later wrote *The Days of Dylan Thomas* (1965), and I liked him because he seemed much more manly than Brinnin. I was mystified by Brinnin; I could never decide whether I liked him or not. He always treated me politely, and I could see that he was attached to Dylan, but he seemed to me to be pretty strange: he had a whole suitcase full of clothes, one for every hour of the day, and a separate suitcase of pills of every variety and colour. Brinnin's visit wasn't a happy occasion; it was every bit as bad as he described it in his book *Dylan Thomas in America* (1956). I wasn't very good at entertaining. I tried to do two special meals for them which turned out terribly wrong. I tried to cook a wild duck that someone had given us. I undercooked it badly and it spurted blood the moment it was touched with a knife. Llewelyn made disgusting noises about the duck; Dylan lost his temper with Llewelyn, and I was upset because nobody liked my duck. I did another meal and got all the rice measures wrong. The whole visit was a disaster. I wanted Brinnin to tell me about Pearl (which he wouldn't), and he was trying to persuade Dylan to go back to America, which upset me, of course, and

159

we ended up fighting in front of him, which didn't go down very well.

The trouble was Pearl; I could never get her out of my mind. I could have easily killed her if I'd met her, but even when things were at their worst between Dylan and me, when the violence was occurring almost nightly, I never thought of killing Dylan. He was sacred. Genius is a terrible thing for other people to live with; it seems to trample all beneath it, but I'd always known that he had it, and I wouldn't have married him otherwise. What I couldn't bear was the thought of his sharing it with another woman.

I tried to have my revenge without killing him – flying at him, knocking him to the ground, sitting across his chest, pummelling him, punching him, grasping his curly hair and banging his head on the floor – but somehow I never wanted to finish him off, and I knew this even while I was punching him, which is something I can't explain. He would whisk himself off into bed, because once he was there he knew that I couldn't hit him again. It was like hide 'n' seek: he was home. Warfare was never carried on in bed; there it was tenderness. After those fights I'd think that I could never go near him again, but within two seconds I'd be in bed with him, and I would be the one who was upset whereas it was Dylan who should have been punished. Immediately he would try to make up to me, unless he passed out with drink.

This agony went on between us for nearly three years, until his death in America, though he never stopped telling me he loved me, forever and forever, and that he could never live without me. He often managed to escape, because he had work to do in London, which made it even worse, because then I was lonely as well.

We kept our misery to ourselves. D.J. may have heard some stories about me carrying on with other men, but he never said so. Granny Thomas appeared not to know; and we were always careful not to let the children see us fighting. They had become so used to their father being away, anyway, and they didn't know that, now, it was different.

There was one night – when an old friend, Elizabeth Lutyens, was staying with us – that Dylan went off to Swansea, saying that he was leaving for good. Then he phoned (I cannot remember whether it was the same night or later) and announced that he was going to commit suicide. We left Colm fast asleep in the Boat House, and Billy Williams drove us to Swansea to pick up Dylan. When we got there we found that he was pretty well drunk, and we had an outrageous row in the pub where he had spent the evening. I didn't care who the hell saw us. He was trying to use Lizzie as a shield, so I bawled him out, and hit him with my fists. I had a fairly good punch in those days, and I was like a tiger when I lost my temper, and had drink in me. I really went for him, shouting, pulling him to the floor, while Dylan grovelled and whined. Lizzie stood well back (I think she was a little anxious lest she got bashed herself). I really did want to kill him that night.

Lizzie Lutyens was used to our goings-on, although she could see that this was a vintage occasion, and she did her best to calm us down and restrain me. She was a good friend of Dylan's and a big drinker, but she was an ugly woman and there was no kind of affair going on. I was getting worried about Colm, alone in the Boat House, but she was quite happy to carry on drinking once peace had been restored. I couldn't get them to move, and in the end I became nearly hysterical. When we eventually got back we found him wandering around the house in his nightclothes. He was less than three years old. I felt very guilty about that.

Eventually, Ivy told him (as I might have guessed she would) that I was 'carrying on' with other men in Laugharne while he was away in London. I wasn't sleeping the night with them: they were just one-hour stands, pick-ups that I took home from Brown's Hotel at the end of an evening. Everyone in Laugharne knew about it: Laugharne is like that (though I must say that Laugharne men were not very accomplished sexually).

When Ivy told him, Dylan would not believe it. He came home to the Boat House and said, 'Ivy tells me you've been carrying on.' I, of course, prevaricated: 'She's exaggerating madly; I don't know what she's talking about.' There was no row; Dylan only mentioned it the once, and when he had heard my denial he said, 'Yes, I knew it was quite absurd. I knew you would never do that.'

No matter what happened between us, Dylan still wanted to keep me on a pedestal. His woman had to be different from the others, rather like the Virgin Mary. Whatever foul thing I did, even if it was right in front of him, he just wouldn't see it. As I fitted him in most other ways, he wasn't going to let some little Laugharne rumour undermine that; he just said he thought they were maligning me (and quite a lot of that happens in Laugharne as well).

12

Dylan did take me with him on the second tour of America, and it was a great mistake. It was my fault as much as his. He kept telling me that I should see the United States for myself, that the people were so much more friendly, and had a respect for poets that the English did not. I should have understood also what that meant, and what kind of life we would lead there – drinking and fighting and no restraints – but I wanted to go. I didn't want to be left out of things again. If Dylan was having a marvellous breakthrough in America, I wanted to share it with him, as we had shared everything in the earlier years.

The fights that we had in America were no worse than the ones we had in Laugharne, but they were on a bigger scale, and much more public. I was very wild and savage when I got going, and it was easy to get going with that beautiful American rye whiskey.

I knew how to drink, but this was a nightmare, chiefly owing to the appalling quantities, and the parties which never seemed to end, or would merge one into another. The drinking never stopped, even on Sundays: when they had those Sunday 'brunches' they would start drinking late in the morning and then continue all day until late at night. Of course neither Dylan nor I could ever say 'No' to a drink; for nearly four months I don't think I ever refused one.

I look back on it now as a frightful waste; we could have had such an enjoyable time if it hadn't been for the drink. I didn't like their pattern of drinking and eating either; after having huge goblets of bourbon on ice, they would go on to have iced water with their food, which seemed very uncivilised to me. They hardly drank wine at all, except in some little foreign restaurants. Dylan just wasn't used to all that bourbon and rye: he was a lifelong beer drinker who rarely touched spirits.

At the beginning we stayed in the Chelsea Hotel, which was pleasant and Bohemian. As Dylan had written the first time, a lot of phoning-up went on. There were old friends like George Reavey, who arranged those terrible Sunday brunches. George liked to do the grand snob act, the big house, the entertaining and so on. God knows where he got the money (Dylan said that he'd never seemed a wealthy man when they'd first met in London, years before). George was always changing his wives and I didn't much like him. Then there was Len Lye, another friend from way back who had gone to America in search of fortune and ended up making abstract films; the sculptor Dave Slivka and his wife Rose (who became a particularly close friend of mine); Oscar Williams and his wife Gene, and the poets Ted Roethke and Ruthven Todd.

Dylan had met Ted Roethke on the previous trip and they liked each other instantly; he was a great hulking man and another drinker. Ruthven Todd had been a friend in London before the war, always borrowing money: once he got to New York he was lucky enough to find a rich wife – it was like striking oil. She must have been another of those women who wanted to marry a poet, although I can't remember much about her. Ruthven was never very prepossessing as a man – quite amusing and funny, but hardly a Don Juan. Dylan was impressed when he heard of Ruthven's good fortune: he thought it was really clever and enviable: 'Lucky bugger,' he said.

Most mornings Dylan would whip out of the Chelsea Hotel very early and into the bar next door to get his usual light ales, and then either return there or go round to the White Horse Tavern, which was the nearest thing to an English pub he had found in New York. I would be left with handfuls of money to go round the shops in Greenwich Village, or into the city, to big stores like Macy's. I was overwhelmed by all those rows and rows of dresses – the embarrassment of choice. When I realised afterwards how much I'd spent I felt extremely guilty (not that it stopped me going back for more the next day).

Most of the money came from Brinnin. He was very kind to us, though at the time I thought he was a snake in the grass. Then I blamed him for distracting Dylan from his real work, although I look back on him more leniently now. When he came round to our hotel he would lend us money and protect us; it wasn't his fault if we spent it. Brinnin was horrified at the speed with which we did spend it. One day we spent four hundred dollars – a lot of money in those days – on clothes and drink. Again, Brinnin saved money for us without telling us; every time he gave money to Dylan he kept some back, and then put it in a bag in the luggage, which was very useful when we got back. My money mostly went on clothes. As the tour progressed, we had forty suitcases following us around. (Dylan had borrowed them from a lady friend, who was getting upset because she wanted them back: we never seemed able to find time to empty them.)

Dylan's money went on drink, but I believe quite a lot was pinched as well – he was always a soft touch. He was always careful, though, not to drink too much before his readings – all he would take were a few light ales – but once they were over he would move on to the shorts and start drinking heavily.

We stayed at the Chelsea for a month. We both liked Greenwich Village, which was a little like Soho with a lot of foreign restaurants – Italian, French, Greek and so on. I found it more human than the rest of New York, with artists and writers somehow living there without much money. We felt at home, and if Dylan wasn't doing a reading we would go down into the Village for a meal in the evenings with friends.

I went to Dylan's reading at Brinnin's Poetry Center. It was the first time I had seen him face such a large audience, and he was good. He was wearing a dapper little suit; I don't know where he got it from. At first he seemed quite shy and awkward, but soon he got into his stride and started booming out. The audience were very impressed, as though they had never seen anything like it before. There were girls in raptures, like young girls these days at a rock concert – I was amazed. It was just like Dylan had told me; they were throwing themselves at him. Standing there on the stage, he seemed so small and, to begin with, insignificant: yet I saw then that he had this ability to appeal to a mass audience; he came across *big*.

I stayed in New York while Dylan travelled around the country to give his readings. Rose Slivka looked after me mostly: she was my best friend there. She stuck by me and let me stay with her. We saw Martha Graham, and a few other shows as well. In fact, my only real moments of enjoyment in the States were spent quietly with her.

We also stayed a couple of nights with the photographer Rollie McKenna. I liked her very much: she was more English than American, and she didn't seem to appreciate men any more than I did. I wasn't exactly anti-men at that time, but I felt I was being pushed into the background, that I didn't belong; everyone made it so obvious – apart from Rose Slivka and Rollie – that I was the secondary wife; I began to feel that I shouldn't be there.

Dylan couldn't pay me much attention because he was always busy, either reading or talking. We hardly saw the sights. I had the abortion so that I could be with him, and now it seemed as though he had cast me off. I don't think he did it deliberately – with so many people surrounding him he couldn't very well stay close to me – but I did feel that he was humiliating me. As well as all the university readings and lectures, he was in demand for radio appearances, and he was always being asked to write something new for someone. He *seemed* able to cope with it, but looking back now I can see that he couldn't, and that it was even worse with me being there. I didn't belong, and I was very vulnerable. I responded by kicking out instead of creeping around like a docile wife; but if I'd done that, it wouldn't have been much fun, either.

I think I was suffering from a certain amount of depression at that time, and although I never linked it with Pearl, and the after-effects of the abortion, it may have been partly that. I suspect, however, that it was due more to the fact that Dylan was now living a life that I couldn't cope with: he wasn't looking after me, with the result that I drank as much as I could to reduce the pain: it never works, of course, but that's what one does it for.

I was very disappointed that nobody bothered to show me New York: when I went away I had no more idea of it than when I arrived: all I knew was the Chelsea Hotel, the Empire State Building, Greenwich Village and a few bars. I never went to see Harlem or Chinatown, and I would have been interested to see how the different people lived. (Dylan was supposed to be doing a book, based on the tour, but it never got written.)

We had one appalling row. I can't remember where we were, or how it started, but we were in a hotel room, and I do remember the room when we left it; everywhere was covered in green toothpaste, the ceiling, the walls, everywhere, and I thought, 'My God, what are they going to do when they see this?' Neither of us could remember what had happened the night before. It was probably something to do with women – most of the rows were. I was appalled at how forward those New York women were, just as Dylan had said.

We were in a taxi one evening with Oscar Williams and two girls who had come along for the evening, and as I got into the front seat, they cuddled up to Dylan in the back. I felt very pushed out, and afterwards I said to Dylan, 'What did you let them do that for?'

Another night we were in the Chelsea Hotel, and a bunch of flowers arrived – not for me, but for Dylan. From a woman! I was disgusted at that: no British woman would ever dream of sending a *man* flowers.

Another awful evening I was with him at the White Horse Tavern when some woman came in, whispered in his ear – and he walked off with her as meekly as a lamb. I was in a quandary. I didn't know what to do. I couldn't go running after him. There was nothing innocent about it (she wasn't a journalist arranging an interview), it stank a mile off, and I went into a sort of decompression after that. I don't know how I got back to the Chelsea Hotel. Someone must have put me in a taxi.

It was always the women who did the pursuing: Dylan was completely passive. That was the thing that particularly irritated me; he never said 'No', and he never thought of the consequences. It was thoroughly irresponsible. Instinct had control of him; he was too weak and too tender, and too much in search of sex to prove his manhood, though, goodness knows, no one in the world ever had as much affection as he did.

I remember losing my temper with a woman who was trying to cure him of drinking; Dylan was going along with it because she was very rich, and he thought he was on to a good thing. I was doing my usual shopping around with Brinnin's mother – a very amiable woman who everybody said was exactly like me (although I couldn't see it) – and we passed this smart restaurant and saw *them* sitting at a corner table, having a quiet, intimate lunch. They weren't actually committing adultery on the table, but Dylan was leaning forward, talking attentively, and I went over to them and told her what I thought of her. I called her a 'bloody bitch!' and told her to 'bugger off!' and said that Dylan didn't need these grand dames slavering all over him and was better off without them, which he was. Dylan didn't say anything, and I just walked off and left them. It must have ruined their lunch. Afterwards, Dylan cursed me and told me that I had ruined a perfectly good friendship, and that she had been on the point of offering us money. If Dylan had had any guts at all, I think he would have risen up from the table and left with me.

I can see the funny side of it now, and the absurdity of a man in his condition offering to go on a vegetarian diet in the hope of conning some woman out of a large sum of money, but I can also remember my rage: I still have some of that rage left, even now.

Mrs Brinnin just stood and watched: she was one of those conciliatory women who agreed with everybody.

One evening I had my revenge. We were staying with Ellen Borden Stevenson, wife of Adlai Stevenson, who was to be the next Democratic Presidential candidate. Everybody thought he was going to win. Dylan was making up to her like mad, playing ridiculous things on the piano: he couldn't play properly – he just dilly-dallied up and down the keys – but he could make some sort of tune out of it. (He could also paint a little, and draw cartoons in an amateurish kind of way; these were talents that he had never bothered to develop, although some of his watercolours were very good.) She was gazing at him as he sat at the piano, and I didn't know what to do. I felt embarrassed watching them, so I wandered off, looking around her home, and I looked through her wardrobe, which contained some very beautiful clothes. There was one beautiful blue Spanish-looking dress, with lots of frills, which I would love to have had, but I didn't dare take it because it was so beautiful. So I took a suit in grey flannel, which was a very humble choice, really. I felt that I had to have something in protest at the way Dylan was behaving, and the way she was lapping it up.

I realise now that sometimes I was jealous for no reason, but Dylan was going on like this to other women all the time, without any discrimination. I couldn't bear being treated like that: I felt humiliated and miserable because he was ignoring me.

Dylan was in his seventh heaven, because all the girls would go backstage after he had given a reading, and he would sit there on a stool holding court. I think his chief appeal to those women was his fame. They clustered around him like they did later with pop stars. And when he started talking – he was a good talker, a better talker than most of them had ever heard before – he was witty and amusing, with his endless repertoire of jokes, stories and limericks that he had told for years in the London pubs, and this had them screaming with laughter. But now it was a female audience; in London, he had always had his own man friends around him. The other thing about these backstage performances was that he was never intellectual. This wasn't T. S. Eliot talking over their heads, but a naturally funny man who knew how to hold an audience in stitches, especially if he had a drink in his hand.

If people did try to persuade him to intellectualise, Dylan would change the subject at once, often so rudely and brusquely that they would never dare try again. There was one occasion when someone asked him to explain his long poem, 'Ballad of the Long-legged Bait', and Dylan just replied, 'It's a description of a gigantic fuck!' And that was the end of that. For him, poetry and performing, writing and reading, were all work, and once he had finished work for the day it was time to play.

As the tour progressed I began to despair. As the girl students gathered around and pestered him, I would say to Dylan, 'When they start doing that, just walk away – who cares?' But he couldn't do that, and I was left alone. I was the only person there who knew him and who could see that Dylan wasn't being his usual human self; no one else could see through the act. To me he seemed to become a different person. With all that flattery and adulation, he seemed to forget about my existence altogether, although he would still *say* that he couldn't live without me.

The only time that I saw him properly was in bed late at night, and by then we would be well primed with drink. We would both pass out, and then have a little chat in the morning before Dylan nipped out to get his light ale recovery-drinks. He would dismiss the events of the night before as though nothing had happened; it was all unimportant, and the people were unimportant. Underneath it all, Dylan was quite hard in that way: his real self had no illusions, but he would get softened up playing his public part of 'The Performer' and he could never resist going back and starting all over again.

In San Francisco we saw quite a lot of Ruth Witt-Diamant, who had been very kind to Dylan on his first tour. Even before I had met her she had sent us parcels of clothes for the children. Dylan had been impressed because she had no blankets on her bed and slept naked in a fur coat. Apart from that, she was intelligent, generous and amusing, although I think she thought I was rather a wild animal because she saw me on the raw. There was one time when I was abusing Dylan for making up to some girl, and she said, 'Well, I had no idea you had such a rich vocabulary!'

Ruth was with us when we had one of the worst rows that we ever had, over Llewelyn and his school fees. Dylan claimed to have made arrangements for the fees to be paid before we left Britain, and then later – after we had received a letter saying that Llewelyn would be thrown out of Magdalen College School if the fees weren't paid – Dylan, who had sufficient money to pay them, said that he had arranged for his agent David Higham to pay them for him. Then we received a telegram saying that Llewelyn had been sent home because the bill had not been paid. I thought this was very tactless and unkind on the part of the school: it was a cruel thing for them to have done to Llewelyn, who had already been hurt so much. I was furious with Dylan because we were earning good sums of money in the States, and the fees should have been no problem.

I flew at him in a terrible rage. 'For God's sake, do something about it,' I told him. 'But I've written to Higham,' protested Dylan. 'What good is that?' I asked. 'Writing to that dolt . . .' (we always called Higham the 'lavatory brush' because his hair stood up on end). Then I really let fly because I could tell that Dylan was lying; I called him a bastard, foul scum, the lowest form of scum, a congenital liar, a craven coward – a whole torrent of abuse. There was no punching or kicking this time; it was a purely verbal occasion. I started to pack my bags and tried to book a ticket on the next plane back to London. I told him that this was it; we were finished; I had had enough. I thought it was disgusting that the prize man in the literary world had had his own son turned out of school for lack of funds when he was being paid huge sums in America, and here we were throwing it around and behaving abominably while Llewelyn was suffering. 'I'm not going on with this bloody stupid life which gives me no pleasure or satisfaction,' I told him. 'I've got to go, and I'm going to leave you.' Empty threats, as usual, because all the works had to be got going before I could catch a plane. Soon after, maybe the next day, the fees were paid and Llewelyn went back to school, but I was very distressed by that

169

because Llewelyn had been through enough, and his humiliation was quite unnecessary.

We wound up the tour with a holiday in Arizona with the painter Max Ernst and Dorothea Tanning. We arrived there broke, having spent all the money that we had made so far, and we spent three days with literally no money at all, getting desperate for drink, because Dylan had scruples about asking Max Ernst for money. We had heard that Ernst could be pretty mean, and that reputation cowed Dylan a bit, and we just had to wait until some more money came through from Brinnin. Those were bleak days, because by that time we could hardly live without drink, but I do remember the barren beauty of the Arizona landscape with the eucalyptus trees and the river.

The night before we left America, I had to tidy up the things in our hotel room and do the packing. Dylan was fast asleep in bed, and I opened this suitcase of papers that he'd carried around with him on the tour. It was packed with unpaid bills and love letters from different women: Dylan had just dropped them into the suitcase, often unopened, and then taken it with him from town to town. I spent the whole night reading through them. I must have had a lot to drink, because the next day I felt completely smashed, and I knew that we had to see two university lecturers before we left. I felt so bad when we got there that I said, 'Do you mind very much if I go and lie down? I feel awful.' One of the lecturers looked rather displeased, and said, 'Well, I've got my bed upstairs, but it's not made or anything.' That didn't worry me; I just lay down. I had a nightmare about the letters that I had read the previous night, and it took me the whole day to recover.

I am thoroughly ashamed of myself over that American visit, because, with all that drinking and fighting, I was quite as bad as Dylan: he at least had the excuse of poet's licence – I had none.

13

As the years go by so much falls into perspective. I can see now that the last years of Dylan's life were his most successful, though it did not feel like that then because of all the stresses within our marriage, our constant worries over money, and the disasters that seemed to befall us as a family.

After we had returned from America Dylan settled down to write *Under Milk Wood*, which he had been turning over in his mind for the past ten years, and during the remaining months of 1952 and early 1953 he continued to work on the script, part of which was published by Princess Caetani in her literary magazine *Botteghe Oscure*, which she produced in Rome. He also prepared his *Collected Poems* for publication, and these were published in Britain in November 1952 and in the United States in March 1953. Another volume of his poems, 'In Country Sleep', was published in America in 1952. He was commissioned to complete his novel *Adventures in the Skin Trade*, which he never found time to finish, and in 1953 his publishers, Dent, published his film treatment based on the Burke and Hare murders, *The Doctor and the Devils*. Dent were also keen to publish a collected volume of his radio scripts, *Quite Early One Morning*, but Dylan died before this could be done, and instead the work was prepared for publication by his old friend Aneirin Talfan Davies, and appeared in 1954, when *Under Milk Wood* was also published.

As well as all this, Dylan was in constant demand from the BBC, who commissioned him to read a four-part selection of his own poems, to narrate David Jones' *The Anathemata*, and to write and read his own scripts giving his impressions of the 1953 International Eisteddfod at Llangollen, and also of Laugharne. The BBC broadcast his earlier scripts *Reminiscences of Childhood* (which Dylan revised) and *Quite Early One Morning*, which was quite similar to *Under Milk Wood* (with a lot of that whimsy which I didn't much like). He took part in seven other BBC radio programmes, and also wrote one of his most successful short stories, 'The Outing', for narration on BBC TV. And then there were frequent requests for press interviews in Laugharne, and for the republication in newspapers and magazines of his earlier work.

Dylan had never been so busy, but it didn't seem to make much difference to our finances. The Inland Revenue had caught up with him at last, and he was now being required to pay back taxes, and also National Insurance contributions, out of current income. We should have realised that the difficulties were only temporary, but we never did: the debts seemed a much bigger worry than they really were, and Dylan would lie in bed at night in the Boat House, tormented by fears of what the morning post might bring, and worried, too, I think, by the tensions between us, and of what might happen to the children if we parted.

No matter how much he earned, Dylan always seemed short of money and was never able to give me enough to manage the home. I know now that his income was very considerable, and that as early as 1947 his earnings had totalled nearly £2,500 a year – and that he was earning much more than that by 1952 and 1953 – but he was so sly and deceitful about money that I never knew then how much was coming in. Dylan would sometimes pay off bits of debts, but he would never pay them all off; he would never make a clean sweep and clear the book. Whenever money came in, I never saw it; he preferred to keep it in *his* pocket, and he bought all the drinks. Whenever I wanted clothes or something special for the children, I would have to buy them on tick in Carmarthen and give Dylan the bill. It wasn't a good system because when the creditors got nasty I got blamed, but it was my only way of getting anything new.

It was largely lack of money that made me have my second abortion. In one of his letters Dylan claimed that he had paid for that abortion with the £250 he received for winning the Foyles Literary Prize for his *Collected Poems*, but that wasn't true; he didn't pay for either of them. The second abortion was a much simpler, cheaper job because it wasn't left so late in the pregnancy. I wasn't even sure that the baby was Dylan's, but, either way, I felt we just couldn't afford to bring up another child. I had already been through that terrible crisis of conscience with the first one so it wasn't as painful this time. I went to a queer little man – a back-street abortionist – whom we all knew around the London pubs; it was well known that he was the person to go to if you wanted to get rid of a baby. I suppose I was taking a bit of a risk, but the first one had been quite straightforward, even though it had been late in the pregnancy, and it never occurred to me that there might be complications, and that he wouldn't have known what to do or had the necessary equipment if anything had gone wrong. I had it done at a friend's house in Hammersmith. The man knocked around inside me with rubber gloves, and it was all over pretty quickly; there was very little to take out. As usual, Dylan was nowhere to be seen.

Dylan had been much more upset by the death of his father. When we returned from America, it had been obvious to Dylan that his father was fading fast. (There had been another time, before the war, when Dylan had expected his father to die. Poor old D.J. had had cancer of the tongue, and had been taken to hospital in London, where he was kept for several months with needles inserted into his tongue. It was terrible, but he'd survived, although he couldn't speak for several months afterwards.) This time, Dylan could see that the end was near. D.J. gradually went blind until, by the end, he had almost totally lost his sight: his memory kept going, too, only to return again, intermittently, and apparently he was in awful pain. The day before he died, D.J. wanted to get out of bed and go to the kitchen, where he thought his own mother was making onion soup. But later that day he came round completely and said his last words, 'It's full circle now,' which shows that he was aware that he was going.

D.J. died at home, at Pelican in Laugharne. Dylan wasn't with him (I don't think he could face that any more than he could face the things that had happened in our life), but Granny Thomas stayed by his bedside until the end. We went round to see her later that day, and I can remember seeing D.J. laid out on the table in that ground-floor front room where Dylan himself was laid out in his coffin less than twelve months later: D.J. looked so small and shrunken, like a cardboard figure.

Dylan was devastated by his father's death, but he didn't show it very much; in fact, I was surprised that he was affected so deeply, because he had never been at all demonstrative towards his father during his lifetime. I can remember him talking to me, very quiet and subdued, saying that all he had ever learnt he had learnt from his father, and saying it with a greater respect and affection than I had ever seen him show before.

There was no funeral service because D.J. was an atheist and had asked to be cremated. There was an appalling scene at the crematorium when someone came up to Dylan afterwards and told him that they had seen his father's body burning through the glass panel in the side of the oven, and that his father's skull had exploded. Dylan was violently sick, and he started drinking more heavily after that. Then, a few months later, Dylan's sister Nancy also died, out in India, where she was living with her second husband, Gordon Summersby.

These deaths affected Dylan deeply, but he wasn't the sort of man to discuss his inner feelings; that was something he reserved for his poetry. His reaction to pain was to go out and drink as much as he possibly could, to try to forget, and hide what he felt; but, of course, that never works for long.

Granny Thomas was most extraordinary: all her family were dying around her and she seemed quite cool about it, though she was normally an emotional woman, who gave vent to her feelings. In the course of little more than ten months her husband died, then her only daughter and, soon after, her only son, and I don't remember her saying anything about any of them. I saw no tears; she must have cried, but I never saw it; she seemed to take it all in her stride. After Dylan died – and I had left Laugharne – she moved into the Boat House, and she seemed to become more serene than she had ever been before, maybe because she had Dolly to help her and she didn't have to spend her life doing domestic tasks. Aeron wrote to her regularly and kept in touch, but I didn't see much of her after leaving Laugharne; we went back once, and that was only for two days.

Dylan was very strong, really. Not many people could have survived the stresses and tensions he was under, and he would be alive now, I believe, if only he had been allowed to be his natural self and had treated himself better, with exercise, good food and sleep, against a normal background. It was the vices, put together, that were the trouble: drinking, smoking and women. He was far stronger than anyone realised, and mentally he was in good shape right to the end. He was very tough, the way he recovered and went on. He managed to keep working, although most people – including FitzGibbon and Ferris – didn't realise how hard he was working because of the public pace that he was setting himself.

Every morning he would cough violently: he had always done that over the years but the coughing got worse with all the drink and the cigarettes. Laugharne may have been the wrong place for someone with his cough: it's so damp there in autumn and winter, especially living where we were, right over the estuary. Dylan hardly ever went to see a doctor; he didn't like them. The family doctor, Dr Hughes, was in St Clears, and I'd call him in when I had to – when the children weren't well (like when I upset a pot of boiling tea all over Colm's front, which peeled the skin from his stomach) or when Dylan had broken one of his bones. Dr Hughes would come and do what had to be done, dressing Colm with penicillin ointment or setting Dylan's arm, but Dylan would never go to a doctor if he could possibly avoid it, probably because he was terrified of being told to cut down on his smoking and drinking. He did suffer from gout. I don't know how bad it was, but he couldn't bear anyone knocking against his leg, and of course the children sometimes did. I think he rather liked walking along the street to Brown's with a limp: it was an affectation that appealed to him. After D.J. died, Dylan started using his father's walking stick – another affectation, but then most things that Dylan did were affectations.

The heavy drinking towards the end of his life, after the death of his father and Nancy, my abortions, his affairs and all the financial worries, were partly a way of blocking everything out, though I don't think it was done deliberately – it was just his way of dealing with the problems. After a few hours' sleep, he would wake up again and start worrying. If he did wake up in the early morning, he wouldn't go downstairs and make himself a cup of tea, or anything sensible like that; he would just lie there, tormenting himself, taking care not to wake me, although he would tell me in the morning that he hadn't been able to sleep.

Having been to America with him on that second trip, I didn't want him to go there again. I had seen all the horrible things that happened and the way the women behaved, and I couldn't face the thought of him going through all that again. I did everything I could to dissuade him. I tried to speak reasonably at first, saying that it would be better for *us* if he didn't go, because any money that he earned there always went down the drain on drink; that this was damaging his health; that he would betray me again, and then return home a wreck. Of course, Dylan protested (he always protested when I talked like that), and insisted that I had it all wrong. We talked about it several times, but I could see that it was a lost cause – he was too keen to go, and I couldn't stop him.

So Dylan went to America, for a third tour, in April 1953. It only lasted six weeks, and coincided with the publication in the United States of his *Collected Poems*. He also performed *Under Milk Wood* on stage for the first time there (the performance, at the Kaufmann Auditorium, was recorded by Caedmon) and, although I didn't know it at the time, he started his second really serious affair, with Liz Reitell, Brinnin's assistant.

He came back to London the day after the Coronation and went to a cricket match at Lord's (where he caught sunstroke, and then complained, with his usual exaggeration, that it had developed into pleurisy). Then we went to a party at Margaret Taylor's house that lasted for two days. (Maggs's parties were never very good because she was too mean and frugal with the drink.)

Poor Dylan – when he got back to Laugharne he was exhausted. I blame myself for that. I made him stay on at the party all that time: he was dying to get home and have a complete rest, but I insisted on staying. I wanted to have some fun: I'd been stuck in Laugharne for so long that I didn't want to see it ever again. Dylan didn't say much, but I could see that he was taking no interest in what was going on. I didn't know how shattered he was; I thought it was just immense fatigue due to bad living, so I wasn't feeling very amiable or sympathetic. I was now nursing such an enormous resentment that, in a way, I wanted to torment him by dancing around and being gay. I don't think he realised the agony that was brewing in me: that came out afterwards, in bits. When we eventually got back to Laugharne, Dylan was almost too shattered to work. He looked miserable, and though he soon slipped back into his old routine, he didn't seem happy to be at home with me and the children. He went round to see his mother in the mornings, and to see Ivy at Brown's, but he didn't really become his old self again, though he still didn't think of going to see a doctor, of course.

I was absolutely furious when I heard that he was planning to go back to New York in October for a fourth tour. Those last few months that we had had together in Laugharne had not been very happy for all kinds of reasons, but I didn't want him to go away again: I was suspicious about his infidelities, and I was sure all that touring was damaging his health. But he had received a huge tax bill – the Inland Revenue were asking for £1,907 – and the National Insurance people were threatening him with a summons. Dylan felt that he was in a corner: he had to go back to America, he said, because that was where he could make the money to pay them off, and there was also the chance that he might work on a major project with Stravinsky, writing a libretto, as Auden had done for *The Rake's Progress*. He may also have been yearning for his lady-love, because I realise now that he was far more serious about Liz Reitell than he had been about anyone else, but I didn't know it at the time, so I didn't know what was upsetting him. When the thought did come to me that there might be a woman in the States, I still thought it was Pearl because no one had told me that that affair was finished. I could see that Dylan was very unhappy: it seemed to me that we had lost all contact, and the marriage wasn't working at all.

We never got to the stage of discussing a divorce. I would never have dreamt of starting divorce proceedings – it didn't enter my mind – but I did think of killing myself. I was close to it at times, but when it came to it, I don't think I could ever have carried it through. I did try to kill myself later, after Dylan's death, but I realise now that they were wilfully feeble attempts: I had become one of those alcoholics who are always making mock-suicide attempts in the sure knowledge that someone will save them. I couldn't imagine, after all we had been through together, that Dylan would leave me for good, but I could see that success had turned him into a kind of playboy, which I hated, and that he had started pushing his real work aside so that he could enjoy the role. Had he been doing an honourable job out in America, like the libretto with Stravinsky, if I had thought it would help his career, I would have swallowed it all for his sake, but I never believed that anything good came of those reading tours.

To my friends and family, our getting married was rather extra-ordinary because, to them, he could have been any little runt that I'd picked up in the pub. It must have seemed like insanity, unless I really believed in him, which I did, right from the very beginning. That was why his later behaviour hurt so much. I could see some God-given quality in him, something special. I think many people could see that magic quality, but he drowned so much of it in drink and exaggeration.

I can see now that after each great crisis in our lives he would go through another period of creativity and calm; it was almost as though I were provoking him. From that point of view, our life together has given me some satisfaction – at least we achieved something – but it was a tragedy that he died when he did because he had so much more to give.

14

Before leaving Laugharne for that fourth and final tour of the United States, Dylan had written and recorded a short radio talk giving his impressions of the town: he had enjoyed writing it because it enabled him to put into words the feelings that he'd had about Laugharne since he first discovered it almost twenty years earlier. Although I haven't included any of his actual writings in this book, other than his letters, I include this because it was one of the last things he wrote, and it proves, conclusively to me, that he was at the peak of his powers as a writer in the last months of his life:

Off and on, up and down, high and dry, man and boy, I've been living now for fifteen years, or centuries, in this timeless, beautiful, barmy (both spellings) town, in this far, forgetful, important place of herons, cormorants (known here as billy duckers), castle, churchyard, gulls, ghosts, geese, feuds, scares, scandals, cherry-trees, mysteries, jackdaws in the chimneys, bats in the belfry, skeletons in the cupboard, pubs, mud, cockles, flatfish, curlews, rain, and human, often all too human, beings; and, though still very much a foreigner, I am hardly ever stoned in the streets any more, and can claim to be able to call several of the inhabitants, and a few of the herons, by their Christian names.

Now, some people live in Laugharne because they were born in Laugharne and saw no good reason to move; others migrated here, for a number of curious reasons, from places as distant and improbable as Tonypandy or even England, and have now been absorbed by the natives; some entered the town in the dark and immediately disappeared, and can sometimes be heard, on hushed black nights, making noises in ruined houses, or perhaps it is the white owls breathing close together, like ghosts in bed; others have almost certainly come here to escape the international police, or their wives; and there are those, too, who still do not know, and will never know, why they are here at all: you can see them, any day of the week, slowly, dopily, wandering up and down the streets like Welsh opium-eaters, half asleep in a heavy, bewildered daze. And some, like myself, just came, one day, for the day, and never left; got off the bus, and forgot to get on again. Whatever the reason, if any, for our being here, in this timeless, mild, beguiling island of a town with its seven public-houses, one chapel in action, one church, one factory, two billiard tables, one St Bernard (without brandy), one policeman, three rivers, a visiting sea, one Rolls-Royce selling fish and chips, one cannon (cast-iron), one chancellor (flesh and blood), one port-reeve, one Danny Raye, and a multitude of mixed birds, here we just are, and there is nowhere like it, anywhere at all.

But when you say, in a nearby village or town, that you come from this unique, this waylaying, old, lost Laugharne, where some people start to retire before they start to work and where longish journeys, of a few hundred yards, are often undertaken only on bicycles, then, oh! the wary edging away, the whispers and whimpers, and nudges, the swift removal of portable objects.

'Let's get away while the going is good,' you hear.

'Laugharne's where they quarrel with boathooks.'

'All the women there's got web feet.'

'Mind out for the Evil Eye!'

'Never go there at the full moon!'

They are only envious. They envy Laugharne its minding of its own strange business; its sane disregard for haste; its generous acceptance of the follies of others, having so many, ripe and piping, of its own; its insular, featherbed air; its philosophy of 'It will all be the same in a hundred years' time.' They deplore its right to be, in their eyes, so wrong, and to enjoy it so much as well. And, through envy and indignation, they label and libel it a legendary lazy little black-magical bedlam by the sea. And is it? Of course not, I hope.

Dylan had written and recorded that talk before he left for America: it was being broadcast from the school hall in Laugharne, with me sitting in the audience, on 5 November 1953 when a telegram was passed to me, with the first news that Dylan was ill in New York. The actual words in the telegram were to the effect that Dylan had been 'hospitalised', which was the first time I had ever heard the expression – it took me a moment or two to realise what the word meant. I think the telegram was from James Laughlin, his

American publisher, and after I had read it I immediately hid it in a pocket, or somewhere, and thought to myself, 'Well, I'm not going to think about that now; I'll keep it until later.' I could feel it gnawing at me though I didn't allow it to upset me there and then, because obviously, if he was 'hospitalised' and I had a telegram, it meant that it must be serious. There were no further details in the telegram.

I waited for a couple of days before joining Dylan in New York; it was preying on me, and yet oddly enough I experienced a strange feeling of relief, a feeling that the struggle was over; that this was it. By then we had been through two years of stress and violence, and I had been longing for it to change. I didn't know what was the matter with Dylan, but I felt quite sure that he would not come out of it. I didn't allow myself to cry or get upset (that evening, after the concert, I seem to remember going to the other hall in Laugharne and dancing). Then, later, there was a distinct feeling of being free and breathing again, yet when I got back to the Boat House everything swamped me and I wanted to vomit – to vomit out all the disgust that I had accumulated over the past two years. Then I had a few drinks – more than a few – and went to bed. That's all I can remember of the first night.

I didn't say anything to anybody at first; I wanted to have a little time to think about it and what I should do next. I mentioned it to Aeron; I just told her that I'd had a telegram saying that Dylan was sick in hospital (I'd always said 'Dylan' when talking to the children, never 'Daddy'). I can't remember quite how she took it, but I tried not to make his illness sound as serious as I realised it probably was. Colm was too young to understand, and Llewelyn was away at school.

I can't remember what made me decide that I must go to New York to see him: I'd heard nothing more from Laughlin or Brinnin and I had no idea whether he was seriously ill or not, and because I never read newspapers or listened to the radio I had no idea what was happening over there. It was the natural thing for me to go, but it took a bit of organising. I can't remember how I got from Laugharne to London – my mind was in a daze. Margaret Taylor may have organised it. I must have arranged for Aeron to stay with Granny Thomas and for Colm to stay with Dolly, but it's all a blank now.

I remember staying the night with Cordelia Locke in London,

and then being taken for a huge send-off meal at Wheeler's, the fish restaurant, with Margaret Taylor and the McAlpines, where we drank a lot of wine. My strange memory of it is that it felt like a celebration lunch. Belatedly, we caught a taxi to the airport, where the plane was held up for me.

I can remember being on the plane (I must have been pushed on it!) and asking if there was a bar. I was told there was a little bar right below; I thought that sounded all right, so I went down there and drank a lot of whiskies, which was a very foolish thing to do. I must have been stinking drunk by the end of it, having had all that wine at Wheeler's first.

Dave and Rose Slivka met me at Idlewild airport, and I was driven into the city with a motor-cycle escort, straight to the hospital. Still nobody had told me precisely what had happened to Dylan. I didn't hear until four years later that Liz Reitell had been with him when he collapsed – I didn't even know her name at the time. Apparently she was at the hospital when I arrived. They kept her away from me, afraid that I would have been violent. They were right.

Brinnin met me at St Vincent's Hospital; I've since read his claim that I greeted him with the words, 'Is the bloody man dead or alive?' although I have no recollection of that at all. When I arrived at the hospital, I remember finding myself in a straggly queue of people. Then somebody bustled me forward, saying, 'Mrs Dylan Thomas . . . this way, please.' Suddenly, it all seemed more urgent; I was pushed in front of everybody, feeling no conscious emotion, just trying to do what I felt I had to do. I was still in a bit of a daze, or a drink haze, probably. The hospital was completely hushed and I could hear my own footsteps as I was led up the stairs to the floor where Dylan was. I came to a corridor, crowded with people – twenty or thirty of them. I didn't know who they were or where they came from, but I realised that they were all looking through a glass partition down the side of the corridor into the room where Dylan lay; it had been turned into a kind of spectacle. There they all were, gawping through the partition, not saying a word. These people had been there for several days and nights, claiming to be his friends, although I knew hardly any of them.

No one had prepared me for this; until that moment I had had no idea how seriously ill he was. Rose Slivka was told that she couldn't go with me as a nurse led me into the room where Dylan lay, and then I saw him, stretched out beneath the bedclothes with what looked like an oxygen tent standing nearby. He was gasping but I couldn't see how he was taking breath. In fact, all I could really see were his hands, resting by his sides. It all seemed deadly final. He looked quite peaceful, but very far away. There was no personal feeling between us because he was as good as dead, and this was the first moment that I had realised it. That was the terrible part, that sudden realisation. I didn't know what to do. I talked to him, but he didn't respond, and I felt so embarrassed with all those people gazing at me through the glass; I felt as though I were on a stage. They were obviously wondering what on earth I was going to do. I sat on the bed and started rolling myself a cigarette, but my hands were shaking, and I couldn't: the stringy tobacco kept falling on the floor, and I thought, 'My God, that isn't the thing to do . . .' I thought I had to make some gesture of affection to Dylan because there they all were, looking at me through that window. I started to try to get closer to him; I wanted to give him a hug, so I sort of rolled on top of him. The nurse came bustling in and pulled me off. 'You'll suffocate him,' she said, and then I saw his little hands again. I took one. It wasn't a dramatic scene in any way because I didn't know how to act, and I was very worried about what my behaviour should have been and wasn't. I didn't know whether they could see how very drunk I was (they probably could). I got on top of him because I just wanted him to feel my body and to warm him up a bit, but it was obviously the wrong thing to do.

Soon after that I left the room. Outside in the passage I saw all those people again, and that was when it suddenly hit me. I started banging my head against the glass partition, as hard as I could, and then they dragged me away, I think. After that I have a very strange impression that I got into one of the wards where there were a lot of steel bars suspended from the ceiling surrounding the beds, and I started hanging on to them, swinging from one to another, travelling around the room. When I went down the stairs I saw this figure of Christ, a big wooden one, about four feet tall, set in the wall and I tore it out of its setting, threw it on the ground and tried to smash it, thinking, 'My God. I have loved Him so much' (I meant Christ, not Dylan) 'and this is what He has done to me.'

Of course, after a bit of that, the little men in white coats came along, and they strapped me into a strait-jacket, terribly tight, in the cruellest manner possible so that I could hardly breathe. Then they took me to the asylum at Belle Vue, where I was left all night, tied up in the strait-jacket, lying on a bed. I was dying of thirst and kept asking for water, just water, some cold liquid after all the drink I had had. They took no notice. I thought I was being punished because I had behaved so badly with the crucifix. Eventually I was released from the strait-jacket, and Rose came round with her husband and pleaded for me to be allowed to leave the asylum, but they wouldn't let me out immediately: I was told that I had to stay there for a couple of days. The next day I was standing there in the ward in my little white asylum shift when a man appeared at the door and said he wanted to see me. He said, 'Dylan has died . . .' At first, I just didn't say a word because I knew that Dylan had been as good as dead when I saw him, and I'd realised then, without anyone telling me, that there was no hope. And now, here was this horrid little man, obviously expecting me to create and have hysterics: I didn't want to give him that satisfaction. So he just went away, and I went back to banging my head on the white-washed walls of the asylum.

By then I really was crying; I couldn't stop. It was the first time I had really let go, and they kept asking me, 'What's the matter with you?' – as if they didn't know.

After a while, Rose came round and she promised that she would look after me and see that I didn't do anything excessive if they would release me from the asylum. I was still wearing the white shift, walking around barefoot, and must have looked very pathetic. Rose got me dressed and we went out together. Dave Slivka was with her, to give more impression of control, but he kept well away from me; he was terrified that I was going to do something awful. On the way back to their place, needless to say, we stopped at a few bars for whiskies. I began to feel a little more human and I kept telling them that I wanted to be taken to see Dylan. But Rose wouldn't let me go; she said he had been taken to a place where they kept the dead for embalming, and that she had seen him, hanging from a hook, just like a piece of butcher's meat – I suppose they were draining the body.

I kept saying to her (it was my passion for the truth coming out), 'I've got to see him; I really must see him.' But Rose would not let me. 'No, it's too ghastly,' she said. 'I don't care, I've got to see him,' I said – but I never did because by that time she had given me so much whisky that I was no longer able to insist. She took me back to her home and put me to bed; she was very kind to me. I had a hot bath in the morning. It was all so unreal, that period: every night we had parties, with people coming in for music and drinking; it was rather a comfort, though I'm not sure how I got through the days.

I can remember, at one point, sitting on a sofa with Brinnin. I could never quite decide whether I liked Brinnin – whether he was kind, or whether he had actually helped to kill Dylan through that punishing work-schedule – but I could see that he was terribly grief-stricken. He didn't say a word to me, and I didn't say anything to him. As for the rest, I had to get rid of all that pent-up emotion, somehow, so I insisted on having very loud Spanish music and doing what I thought was Spanish dancing, making an awful noise, banging my feet and clapping my hands. I just went on dancing until I dropped or passed out.

Later I had to make a lot of fuss in order to be allowed to take Dylan's body back home to Laugharne: they wanted to keep it there in New York. I knew that for Dylan's mother, and his friends, it would make all the difference, so I stubbornly insisted. In the end they gave way and said they would let me take him home.

15

No one ever told me how Dylan had died and I wasn't given his medical records in New York. I didn't ask for them, either, because I thought, 'Well, he's dead. That's it . . .' It was all I needed to know. At the same time I kept hearing stories about his dying, and about the way he spent those last few days before he went into hospital, that somehow didn't seem to fit. Apparently he had been boasting about drinking eighteen whiskies, straight off; he had then got up the following morning, laughing and joking, before going off to the White Horse Tavern for some beers. That didn't sound to me like a man who had gone straight from drinking whisky into a coma. There were also all the stories about drugs. I didn't know what to believe.

I still think that the real truth about his last days in New York has never been told, and I would have been the last to hear it, because Brinnin was keeping everything from me. Looking back now I can see why. Liz Reitell worked for Brinnin, and Dylan had been sleeping at her flat. Years later I discovered that she had been keeping some kind of vigil over Dylan at St Vincent's Hospital before I arrived in New York. There was so much that I wasn't told . . . but I wonder now why I didn't ask more questions, why I kept myself so closed up.

What I couldn't understand then, and still can't, is *why* Dylan had to go into St Vincent's in the first place. If he *had* taken eighteen whiskies – which I doubt – then the thing to have done would have been to make him vomit and then put him to bed (which was what I always did when he came home very drunk). Instead, Liz Reitell called in Dr Feltenstein, who gave him two injections of cortisone (though why I can't think) and some other barbiturates, too, followed by half a grain of morphine, which I am told is nearly three times the normal dose for someone who has had an alcoholic collapse (if, indeed, he had had one). I just cannot understand why the doctor gave him such strong drugs if he really had been drinking that much.

Another problem, of course, was that Dylan would boast about his drinking to people who didn't know him well or whom he was trying to impress. He could easily have said, 'I've had eighteen straight whiskies. I think that's the record,' when he hadn't at all. (It didn't surprise me one bit when I heard later that two of his friends had retraced his steps that night, talking to the barmen where he had been drinking, and had discovered that he had had nothing like that many.)

When Philip Toynbee wrote in the *Observer*, in a review of the *Collected Poems*, that Dylan was 'the greatest living poet', Dylan played it down and said he was talking about somebody else: there was that curious modesty about the things that were important to him, and yet he would tell complete strangers far-fetched stories about his women and his drinking. I think it was partly due to male vanity, and that old idea that a boy isn't a man until he can hold his liquor. Dylan believed all that; he was vain and childish in so many ways. (He was vain about clothes, too, although it's very hard to believe: he always made a fuss about having the right colours and the right tie. Though he didn't have a proper suit until he went to America, these things were still important to him: he might come home in the evenings looking a mess, but he would always have bothered about his appearance before going out.)

When Dylan had money he would buy himself fine shirts and expensive-looking ties, and go to his London club, either the National Liberal Club or the Savage, smoking a fat cigar and looking every bit the successful writer up in town for the day. These superficial vanities were concealing other things: for example, he was very conscious of being short; he wanted to tower over other people and he would buy shoes that were much too big for him, and talk of buying fancy waistcoats and a great big yacht, if ever he made a lot of money. It was all fantasy.

Those people in New York who came to know him briefly towards the end of his life were completely taken in by him: they didn't know the difference between the actor and the man. By the time Dylan reached America he knew just how to make himself the centre of attention, which was what he had always wanted. His charismatic stage presence and beautiful actor's voice, and his gift for talking to people, within minutes of meeting them, as though he had known them all his life, all gave exaggerated effect to his wonderful gift for words. People who were meeting him for the first time would find him quite amazing: they wouldn't realise that he was like this all the time – inventing wonderful stories to encourage people to give him money, making fantastic claims about women and drink, suggesting that his health was going and his talent was drying-up: it was all untrue, and I was the only one who knew it. His new admirers were all charmed because Dylan was so lovable, so human, and so unlike a literary man. All the time, he was keeping his real self carefully concealed, as he had always done.

If Brinnin had taken more care of Dylan in America, I think he might be alive today. His health was basically strong, and with the financial success that he was beginning to achieve I believe he would have sorted himself out and brought his drinking under control, because all the things that made him drink were coming under control as well. But he couldn't do it without a manager. His career was developing so fast and on so many different levels that he needed someone to take care of all the day-to-day administrative and domestic details that he just couldn't cope with.

He was still writing well, right to the end of his life. He had nearly finished *Under Milk Wood* (though he thought he still had some work to do on it, even after the New York stage production), and his radio essays were better than ever. His poems were taking him longer to finish than they had ever done before, but they were far better poems for it. If he hadn't died, I think he would have gone on to write the libretto with Stravinsky. He would probably have gone on to write Hollywood film scripts as well, because he had developed that technique through his work for Donald Taylor and Sidney Box; and his poems would have been improving all the time. His death was a tragic waste.

That view may contradict much of the popular legend that has grown up around Dylan since his death, but so many of those stories were largely untrue. It's a lazy form of popular journalism to portray him as the poet who was determined to die before he was forty, who was perpetually drunk, who was always womanising, and who had burnt himself out: there was a grain of truth in it, as there always is in that kind of legend, but only a grain.

Thinking about it over the years, as I have done night after night, I realise now that there were three aspects of his situation that he would have found it very difficult to cope with, thousands of miles away from his real home: first, his health; second, the fame and all that went with it; and third, he was probably tormenting himself, after all the rows and the violence that we had both gone through, now that he was having an affair with Reitell. I think he was racked with guilt, because he still kept telling me how he loved me and that I was the only woman for him. And so, just as he had always done in a crisis, he went off and got drunk.

Had I been there when he came back to that apartment, saying that he had had eighteen whiskies, I would have made him vomit and then wrapped him up in bed and given him his bread and milk. None of his American friends knew what to do with him. When he died, I had this overpowering feeling that I must get him back home to Laugharne, away from all those people who I thought had killed him.

I have had to face the thought, over the years, that my life might have been worse had he lived. Before Dylan went to New York, it looked as though everything between us was coming to an end. For a long time, I was fairly convinced that he went there to escape (I don't believe that now), because he couldn't cope with his family responsibilities any more: a wife and three children was more than he could bear. This wasn't a wilful irresponsibility (in the way that some people have suggested); it was just that some part of his character was missing, or deficient. Also I have had to face the fact that, had he come out of the coma and lived, he would never have been the same again: that his brain would have been damaged, and his mind gone.

After he had left me in London to go on that fourth trip, I spent days wandering the streets in deep distress, and I wrote to Brinnin telling him that I thought our marriage was over. Brinnin never told Dylan about the letter, but I think the same thoughts were going through Dylan's mind anyway, in New York: he knew, but he didn't know that I knew. It must have been instinct that told me, because I didn't know about the mysterious Reitell, but I think we both knew we could not have survived another shock like Pearl. We had managed to put things back together again, almost, after Pearl and the first abortion, after the agonies of our American trip, and the distress of D.J.'s death and Nancy's. Dylan must have known what finding out about Reitell would do to me, our marriage and the children; he must have known that it would have been the end. That complicated emotional mess is, in my view, as near as anyone will ever get to the truth of his dying, and it is why I found his death such a terrible shock.

So I haven't had memories of love to live with and to support me, but this terrible realisation that Dylan was taken from me right at the very moment when he might have been leaving me, anyway, and I've wondered many times whether his death was an Act of God, one of those strange accidents that happen without any possible earthly explanation. Perhaps his death was something that just couldn't be avoided, for there's something there, in the manner of his dying, that I don't think anyone will ever be able to explain.

Other considerations aside, it was a matter of principle to get Dylan's body back to Laugharne: he belonged to the Welsh, dammit; they couldn't have their great man buried away from Wales. I had to see the British Consul, who was a hypocrite. I said to him, 'If I am going on the ship, whatever happens I must have a private cabin; I'm in a very bad state, and I can't be with anybody else.'

'I'll see to everything,' he replied soothingly. 'You'll be in perfect privacy and in First Class,' and he made it all sound beautiful. But, when I went to my cabin, I found a sort of glamour queen installed, making up at the mirror. It was the very opposite of what I wanted. I was wearing my black funereal dress, which I had bought especially, and I crouched in the corner of my bunk, wondering what I could do to change the situation; categorically I was *not* going to travel with that woman. I went to the purser and asked him if there was anywhere else he could put me, and he said, 'No. It's all full.' In the end I concluded that the only thing to do was to perform my song and dance act.

I went into the bar very early, about five o'clock (it opened officially at six), and I ordered five double whiskies. I said, 'My friends are coming along quite soon,' so they didn't hesitate to put the whiskies on the table, and then I sat back and drank them slowly, knowing that, after a certain amount of time and whisky, I wouldn't have to work anything out because the whisky would do it all for me. When that time came, I rose up and stumbled forward, caught hold of the table and swished everything off it. I then pulled the table up by the roots (it was screwed to the floor), and fell beneath it. I got up again and began a mad dance of destruction. Anything that came near me I flung away or broke.

There was glass everywhere. I was as strong as a lion, and if anybody had come near me then I might possibly have killed them. Then I started doing the splits, walk-overs forwards and backwards, cartwheels, and high kicks, all in a total frenzy.

Eventually the Captain came along and looked on for a bit. He started to smile and gave me a big juicy wink, and I thought, 'I'll be able to use him . . .' He said to somebody, 'Give her a bunk in the hold.' They took me down into the bottom of the hold and gave me a seaman's bunk, right next to Dylan's coffin, and I thought, 'My God, this is exactly where I wanted to be . . .'

I was quite happy with that little bunk in the hold, as happy as I could be, and it was even better because there were a bunch of sailors down there, playing cards on Dylan's coffin, and I thought, 'Dylan would have liked that.' So that was the beginning of my journey, and I felt more relaxed now that I was with Dylan. The seamen came and went without saying very much, and I could be alone with my grief. I felt closer to Dylan when I saw the men's beer bottles and playing cards laid out on the coffin. I don't think they knew who I was, or that the box was a coffin.

After a time, I began to get bored and I wrote a little letter to the Captain beseeching him to let me out, vowing on my honour that I would behave myself impeccably. He said, 'If you would like to come and sit next to me at the Captain's Table, I shall allow you just two double drinks, and we'll see how you get on.' So I got myself all dressed up. A huge hamper of clothes had been sent aboard for me by some very kind coloured actor friends in New York; they had collected them for me round the stores, and as I always lusted after clothes I couldn't help being delighted. At dinner time I sat down next to the Captain, and was on my very best behaviour, sipping daintily at the whisky. One thing that gave me a lot of pleasure was seeing the glamour queen from my cabin looking up at me in amazement, seeing that I had 'arrived'.

That night I went back to my bunk to sleep, because I liked it there. I can't recall what happened during the rest of the voyage, although I do remember that the Captain made a pass at me, which was rather awkward. He asked me to his cabin. He was quite presentable in his uniform, but looked pretty revolting in his underpants. When I saw that, I said, 'Oh, no – it's impossible!' I tried to do it tactfully: I didn't want to insult him because he had done me a lot of favours, so I blamed it on how unwell I had been.

When we arrived back in Southampton, there was a bevy of journalists: they were all very friendly and nice. I was in my black dress again, and we ended up laughing and cheerful together, which I am sure was all wrong. I hadn't fully taken everything in yet: one moment I was hilarious, the next I was at the bottom of the well, and most of the time I was full of whisky.

There was a car waiting for me. Billy Williams had driven over from Laugharne to collect me and take Dylan's coffin home. I can't remember how we managed it, but we took a wrong turning at one stage and ended up in either Somerset, Devon or Cornwall, having stopped at quite a few pubs on the way with Dylan's coffin left parked outside.

The first time I saw Dylan's body was when he was laid out in his coffin in the downstairs front room at Pelican, almost opposite Brown's Hotel. I was horrified to see that his whole face had been made up with coloured make-up. He looked quite ludicrous, not like Dylan at all, more like some Grand Guignol figure, dressed up in a suit and a bow tie. His friends came in to see him and I think his mother was glad that I had brought him home. I didn't stay long looking at him; I just touched his hands; they couldn't do much to them.

Granny Thomas continued to surprise me: though she was devoted to Dylan, she took it all in her stride. At the end, she was the only one who seemed quite unmoved. She was very hospitable on the day of the funeral. There was a big service at Pelican with some priest orating in the background, and people standing all around the coffin and in the passageway. By that time I was down on my knees, howling like a wolf. I had about a hundred handkerchiefs and kept bringing them out, blowing my nose, and starting all over again.

All the old friends came down for the funeral. Dan Jones took on the job of 'chief protector' because he considered himself Dylan's best friend: he looked after me as they carried the coffin in procession down the town's main street to St Martin's Church. I don't remember the service in the Church at all, only my thoughts: that here we were burying Dylan in the church where we had christened our children, and Dylan saying 'Do not go gentle . . .'; and his mother putting aside half-a-crown a week to be buried 'tidy', and here we were, doing it; and standing at the edge of the grave with the Williams brothers, who had carried the coffin, with Dan holding on to me very tightly, because he must have known I was ready to do something crazy, like flinging myself on top of the coffin; and then it was 'Ashes to ashes, dust to dust . . .', and people started to fade away from the churchyard, including us. There was a kind of wake going on, all over town, in all the pubs and at Pelican, where Dylan's childhood friends were visiting Granny Thomas. The Welsh are like the Irish and all primitive peoples: they make a big thing out of death. It was a fairly wild funeral: people were fighting and getting drunk all over town, and some of Dylan's papers were stolen from his shed.

Nicolette had come down to be with me before and over the funeral, and Richard Hughes had invited us to spend the night at Castle House. I told Nicolette that I wanted to go for a walk along the cliff, but she knew what I meant – that I was thinking of throwing myself over – so she did everything she could to stop me, and we went to Brown's Hotel instead, where I'm afraid I knocked a tray of drinks clean out of Fred Janes' hands. Then someone offered me a box of chocolates, and I thought, 'Dear God – they ought to have a little more tact than to offer me chocolates!' and I took the chocolates and flung them against the ceiling. That wasn't very popular, either. The whole thing got out of hand; there was much too much emotion around.

In the weeks that followed the funeral I felt desolate. Dan Jones was kinder to me than he had ever been before, and he came over from Swansea several times to see how I was. He became one of the original trustees of the Trust that was set up to administer Dylan's estate.

I could never settle down again in Laugharne – there was too much of a gap. I felt moments of acute despair: when I saw the empty bed I had to climb into it, and then the despair seemed to come in waves. I tried to keep going, but those were the moments when it hit me, and the only cure that I have for grief is to keep moving all the time. I went quite wild at first: fighting, drinking and taking men to bed was my form of escape, but I realised I couldn't go on like that. All the time I was planning to get away as soon as I could. Within a few weeks, I had gone . . .

Postscript

Over thirty years have passed, and still there's a terrible rage inside me: it is permanently there, not consciously, but there, and depression pushes it to the surface.

I still can't get over the fact that Dylan died at the very moment when we had both reached the point of thinking our marriage was over. He must have known (because he always *knew*) that I had written to Brinnin in New York telling him what I thought. My letter was more sad than angry because I was miserable and lonely as hell. It was a two-page letter, and I don't know whether it has survived or not. Brinnin told me he was going to destroy it.

We were both truly desperate by the end. It had all become too much for him and I don't think he could have faced me again after Liz Reitell.

In the years that followed I made several futile attempts to commit suicide, and was treated in clinics and asylums in London, Rome and Catania. For twenty years I suffered from alcoholism until I decided, ten years ago, to join Alcoholics Anonymous in Rome. They saved my life.

I was not the type for suicide, I had too much vitality and curiosity about life and people; and how could I possibly have left my beloved children in the lurch? When we were staying in the little island of Porcida, I once went to its farthest-away point and slid into the sea with the intention of swimming out as far as I could and never coming back again. But the sea was so delicious I could not resist playing around in it and at last swimming slowly back to the shore in the twilight. It was the most romantic bathe I had ever had.

I still feel that Dylan is with me. No matter what happened to us, right to the end he always said that he loved me, and I think he did. I felt he was right for me from the very beginning, and if you think someone is meant for you, you can accept a lot. There was always that sense of belonging together which never left us. Our love was pretty simple, really. But I have never been able to rationalise the manner of his dying.

His death was very painful for me, but I don't think I was as aware of the pain then as I am now. I was at times, obviously, but at such moments you don't have time to think. I certainly thought afterwards, but much of my last thirty years has been an emotional blank: I haven't felt the same intensity of emotions since Dylan died. I feel as though I am out of this world; I just keep going, that's all, and I am very attached to my children.

I am aware of Dylan constantly. I think of his head and his hands; that's the image that I keep, day after day. Whenever I am at all down, I have it more. His small, narrow hands were white and long-fingered, as artists' hands are supposed to be, while mine, in contrast, were square, red clodhoppers coming directly from my father. His were white, useless things that had never done a stroke of work except hold a pen. That was the last thing that hit me when he died. When I saw him at the hospital in New York, those two little fish's fins stuck out from the cover of his bed. His face was covered in tubes from the oxygen machine, and all I could see were those two little hands. When I brought him back to Laugharne and saw him for the last time in his coffin at Pelican, there they were again. Those two little hands. That's the thing that gets under my skin most. They seemed so utterly useless, and yet they said so much.

Chronology

1913
December 8   Caitlin Macnamara born in Hammersmith, London

1914
October 27   Dylan Marlais Thomas born at 5 Cwmdonkin Drive, Uplands, Swansea

1929
     Caitlin's romance with Caspar John

1931
     Caitlin and Vivien John go to London and Caitlin begins a two-year dancing course
July   Dylan leaves Swansea Grammar School to become a junior reporter on the *South Wales Daily Post*

1932
     Dylan joins Swansea Little Theatre
December   Dylan leaves *South Wales Daily Post*

1933
     Caitlin goes to Dublin and then Paris with Vera Gribben; stays a year in Paris and has an affair with Russian painter Segall
May 18   'And Death Shall Have No Dominion' published in *New English Weekly* (Dylan's first poem to be published outside Wales)

August	Dylan first visits London, staying with his sister Nancy and visiting editors of literary magazines
September	'That Sanity Be Kept' published in the *Sunday Referee*; this is seen by Pamela Hansford Johnson, who writes to Dylan; their correspondence begins

1934

February 23	Dylan's second visit to London; he stays with Pamela Hansford Johnson and her mother in Battersea
November	Dylan takes first lodgings in London, with Fred Janes and Mervyn Levy, at 5 Redcliffe Street, Earls Court
December 4	Dylan's first appearance in book form: his poem 'Light Breaks Where No Sun Shines' in *The Year's Poetry*
December 18	Dylan's first book, *18 Poems*, published jointly by the *Sunday Referee* and Parton Bookshop

1935

May	Dylan stays for a month with Alan and Margaret Taylor at Higher Disley in the Peak District

1936

February 21	Second impression of *18 Poems* published
April 12	Dylan and Caitlin meet at the Wheatsheaf and then spend a week together at the Eiffel Tower Hotel
April/May	Dylan in Cornwall
June	International Surrealist Exhibition at the New Burlington Galleries, London
July 15	Dylan and Caitlin meet again at Richard Hughes' home in Laugharne; Dylan's fight with Augustus John
September 10	Publication of *Twenty-five Poems* by J. M. Dent & Sons Ltd, the fifteenth volume in their New Poetry series

1937

April 21	Dylan's first radio broadcast, 'Life And the Modern Poet' (BBC Welsh Service)
June/August	Dylan and Caitlin in Cornwall
July 11	Dylan and Caitlin marry at the Penzance Register Office
September	Stay with Dylan's parents at Bishopston, Swansea; Caitlin's first meeting with his family
October/April	Stay with Caitlin's mother at Blashford near Ringwood

1938
April   Stay at Bishopston; then with Richard and Frances Hughes at Castle House, Laugharne

May   Move to fisherman's cottage, Eros, in Gosport Street, Laugharne

August   Move to Sea View, Laugharne

October 18   Dylan takes part in 'The Modern Muse' radio broadcast with Louis MacNeice, W. H. Auden, Kathleen Raine and Stephen Spender (BBC Home Service)

November/April   Dylan and Caitlin stay at Blashford awaiting the birth of their first baby

1939
January 30   Llewelyn Edouard Thomas born

August 24   Publication of *The Map of Love* by J. M. Dent & Sons Ltd

December 20   *The World I Breathe* published in the United States (collection of poems and short stories)

December/February   Stay at Blashford

1940
March/April   Move back to Sea View

April 4   *Portrait of the Artist as a Young Dog* published by J. M. Dent & Sons Ltd

May   Dylan fails Army medical at Llandeilo

May   Dylan and Caitlin 'sneak away' from Sea View to Bishopston, returning after friends have paid their debts

June/August   Stay with John Davenport at The Malting House, Marshfield, in a house-party of musicians and artists

September   Dylan begins working for Strand Films (details of the sixteen projects on which he worked are given in Appendix 2 of *The Life of Dylan Thomas*, by Constantine FitzGibbon); his work for Strand continued through the war to 1945

September 24   *Portrait of the Artist as a Young Dog* published in the United States

December/April   Dylan and Caitlin stay at Bishopston

1941
May/July   Dylan and Caitlin stay at Castle House in Laugharne with Frances Hughes

August   Dylan and Caitlin move back to London, leaving Llewelyn at Ringwood

1942	
July	Fortune Press publish second edition of *18 Poems*
	Dylan and Caitlin rent one-room studio at Wentworth Studios, Manresa Road, London SW3, which remains their London base for several years
	During 1942–44, Caitlin stays periodically at Laugharne and at Talsarn, Cardiganshire, while Dylan divides his time between there and London

1943	
February	*New Poems* published in the United States by New Directions
March 3	Aeronwy Bryn Thomas born in London

1944	
April/June	Dylan and Caitlin stay at Far End, Old Bosham, to avoid the London air raids, and then move to Hedgerley Dean, near Beaconsfield, to stay with Donald Taylor
July/August	Stay with Dylan's parents, who have now moved to Blaen Cwm, Llangain
September	Move to Majoda, New Quay, where Dylan writes several major poems and *Twenty Years A'Growing*
October 2	Dylan fails to attend Vernon Watkins' wedding

1945	
August/ September	Stay at Blaen Cwm
December/ March 1947	Dylan and Caitlin spend Christmas with Alan and Margaret Taylor at Holywell Ford, Oxford, and then move into their summerhouse
	Between December 1945 and May 1949 Dylan either wrote, narrated or took part in over a hundred BBC radio programmes. These are detailed in an Appendix to *The Life of Dylan Thomas*, by Constantine FitzGibbon

1946	
February 7	*Deaths and Entrances* published by J. M. Dent & Sons Ltd
August	Dylan and Caitlin spend four days at Puck Fair at Cahirciveen, County Kerry, with Bill and Helen McAlpine

| August | Stay at Blaen Cwm |
| November 8 | *Selected Writings of Dylan Thomas* published in the United States by New Directions |

1947

January	Llewelyn rejoins the family at Oxford
March 26	Society of Authors awards Dylan a £150 Travelling Scholarship with a recommendation that he should visit Italy
April/August	Dylan and Caitlin and her sister Brigid take the family to stay first at Rapallo, then Florence and Elba. In Florence, Dylan writes 'In Country Sleep'
June 15	BBC broadcasts his programme on the Swansea of his youth, 'Return Journey'
June	Margaret Taylor buys the Manor House at South Leigh, Oxfordshire, for the Thomas family
September	Dylan and Caitlin move to South Leigh on returning from Elba

1948

March/April	Dylan visits his parents at Blaen Cwm and goes to Laugharne, hoping to find somewhere there for the family
April	D.J. and Florence Thomas arrive in South Leigh
Summer	Dylan begins work on his three film scripts for Gainsborough Films – *Me and My Bike*, *Rebecca's Daughters*, and *The Beach at Falesa* – but the company goes into liquidation before any of the films are made
October	Margaret Taylor visits Laugharne to see if she can find a house there for the Thomas family; she tries to lease Castle House and then later buys the Boat House

1949

March	Guild Books publish paperback edition of *Portrait of the Artist as a Young Dog*
March 4	Dylan flies to Prague as a guest of the Czechoslovak Writers' Union
May	Dylan and family move to the Boat House in Laugharne; his parents move to Pelican
July 24	Colm Garan Hart Thomas born

1950

| January | *Twenty-six Poems* published by J. M. Dent & Sons Ltd in a limited signed edition of 150 copies |

February 20	Dylan flies to New York to begin his first tour of the United States
February 23	Dylan's first reading at the Kaufmann Auditorium
June 1	Dylan returns to Britain on board the *Queen Elizabeth*
September	Pearl visits London; Margaret Taylor goes down to Laugharne to tell Caitlin that he has a mistress and that she has arrived in London; this provokes the first great crisis in the marriage

1951

January/February	Dylan visits Persia to write a film script for the Anglo-Iranian Oil Company; Caitlin writes to him suggesting that the marriage is over
February	They are reconciled
July	John Malcolm Brinnin stays with Dylan and Caitlin in Laugharne
Summer/Autumn	Dylan writes 'Lament', 'Poem on His Birthday', 'Do Not Go Gentle Into That Good Night', Author's Prologue and half *Under Milk Wood* in Laugharne
	Dylan threatens suicide in Swansea; Caitlin goes to retrieve him with Elizabeth Lutyens
	Margaret Taylor acquires 54 Delancey Street, Camden Town, so that the Thomases will have a London home as well as their home in Laugharne
	Caitlin's first abortion

1952

January 20	Dylan and Caitlin depart for the United States on board the *Queen Mary* (this second US tour lasts until 16 May)
February 22	Dylan records his poems for Caedmon
February 28	'In Country Sleep' published in the United States in a limited signed edition of 100 copies followed by a trade edition
November 10	*Collected Poems* published in Britain by J. M. Dent & Sons Ltd. Limited signed edition of 65 copies and also trade edition
December 16	D. J. Thomas dies aged 76

1953

January	Caitlin's second abortion
March 31	*Collected Poems* published in the United States by New Directions

April 16	Dylan's sister Nancy dies in Bombay
April 21	Dylan leaves for New York to begin his third American tour, and during this tour begins his affair with Liz Reitell
May 14	*The Doctor and the Devils* published by J. M. Dent & Sons Ltd
May 14	First stage performance of *Under Milk Wood* in New York with Dylan narrating (recorded by Caedmon)
June 2	Dylan records again for Caedmon
June 3	Dylan returns to London
August 10	Dylan makes his first and only TV appearance for the BBC reading his story 'The Outing'
October 19	Dylan leaves for New York to begin his fourth American tour
October 29	Dylan's last public engagement – a lunchtime reading at the City College of New York
November 5	Dylan collapses at the Chelsea Hotel
November 9	Dylan dies at St Vincent's Hospital
	Caitlin brings his body back to Laugharne, and then a few weeks after the funeral leaves Laugharne for Elba

Select Bibliography

Dylan Thomas
- *18 Poems* (Sunday Referee and Parton Bookshop, 1934)
- *Twenty-five Poems* (Dent, 1936)
- *The Map of Love* (Dent, 1939)
- *Portrait of the Artist as a Young Dog* (Dent, 1940)
- *Deaths and Entrances* (Dent, 1946)
- *Twenty-six Poems* (Dent, limited edition, 1950)
- *Collected Poems* (Dent, 1952; there was also a limited edition, bound in leather with each copy signed)
- *The Doctor and the Devils* (Dent, 1953)
- *Under Milk Wood* (Dent, 1954)
- *Quite Early One Morning* (Dent, 1954)
- *Adventures in the Skin Trade* (Putnam, 1955)
- *A Prospect of the Sea* (Dent, 1955)
- *Letters to Vernon Watkins* (Dent and Faber, 1957)
- *The Beach at Falesa* (Cape, 1964)
- *Twenty Years A'Growing* (Dent, 1964)
- *Rebecca's Daughters* (Triton, 1965)
- *Me and My Bike* (Triton, 1965)
- *Selected Letters*, edited by Constantine FitzGibbon (Dent, 1966)
- *Poet in the Making: The Dylan Thomas Notebooks* (Dent, 1968)
- *Dylan Thomas: The Poems*, edited by Daniel Jones (Dent, 1971)
- *Dylan Thomas: Early Prose Writings*, edited by Walford Davies (Dent, 1971)
- *The Death of the King's Canary*, with John Davenport (Hutchison, 1976)

– *Dylan Thomas: The Collected Stories,* edited by Leslie Norris (Dent, 1983)
– *The Collected Letters of Dylan Thomas,* edited by Paul Ferris (Dent, 1985)

Caitlin Thomas
– *Leftover Life to Kill* (Putnam, 1957)
– *Not Quite Posthumous Letters to My Daughter* (Putnam, 1963)

Ackerman, John, *Dylan Thomas: His Life and Work* (OUP, 1964)
Brinnin, John Malcolm, *Dylan Thomas in America* (Dent, 1956)
Cleverdon, Douglas, *The Growth of Milk Wood* (Dent, 1969)
Davies, Aneirin Talfan, *Dylan: Druid of the Broken Body* (Dent, 1964)
Devas, Nicolette, *Two Flamboyant Fathers* (Collins, 1966)
Ferris, Paul, *Dylan Thomas* (Hodder and Stoughton, 1977)
FitzGibbon, Constantine, *The Life of Dylan Thomas* (Dent, 1965)
Heppenstall, Rayner, *Four Absentees* (Barrie and Rockcliff, 1960)
Jones, Glyn, *The Dragon Has Two Tongues* (Dent, 1968)
Lewis, Min, *Laugharne and Dylan Thomas* (Dennis Dobson, 1967)
Read, Bill, *The Days of Dylan Thomas* (Weidenfeld, 1964)
Sinclair, Andrew, *Dylan Thomas*
Treece, Henry, *Dylan Thomas: Dog Among the Fairies* (Lindsay Drummond, 1949)

This is an abbreviated bibliography. There have been a great many books and pamphlets published in many languages about Dylan Thomas in the past thirty years, and the two principal bibliographies are already out of date. Both are essential reference works – *Dylan Thomas: A Bibliography* by J. Alexander Rolph (Dent, 1956) and *Dylan Thomas in Print* by Ralph Maud (Dent, 1971)

Index

CT stands for Caitlin Thomas, DT for Dylan Thomas.